CCNP

Routing and Switching v2.0 Exam Practice Pack

Denise Donohue, CCIE No. 9566

Brent Stewart

Cisco Press

800 East 96th Street

Indianapolis, Indiana 46240 USA

CCNP Routing and Switching v2.0 Exam Practice Pack

Denise Donohue, Brent Stewart

Published by:
Cisco Press
800 East 96th Street
Indianapolis, IN 46240 USA

Printed in the United States of America

First Printing November 2014

Library of Congress Control Number: 2014952876

ISBN-13: 978-1-58714-431-8

ISBN-10: 1-58714-431-x

Publisher	Paul Boger
Associate Publisher	Dave Dusthimer
Business Operation Manager, Cisco Press	Jan Cornelssen
Executive Editor	Brett Bartow
Managing Editor	Sandra Schroeder
Development Editor	Marianne Bartow
Senior Project Editor	Tonya Simpson
Copy Editor	Paula Lowell
Technical Editor	Sean Wilkins
Editorial Assistant	Vanessa Evans
Cover Designer	Mark Shirar
Composition	Studio Galou
Indexer	Brad Herriman
Proofreader	Megan Wade-Taxter

Warning and Disclaimer

Trademark Acknowledgments

Special Sales

For information about buying this title in bulk quantities, or for special sales opportunities (which may include electronic versions; custom cover designs; and content particular to your business, training goals, marketing focus, or branding interests), please contact our corporate sales department at corpsales@pearsoned.com or (800) 382-3419.

For government sales inquiries, please contact governmentsales@pearsoned.com.

For questions about sales outside the U.S., please contact international@pearsoned.com.

Feedback Information

At Cisco Press, our goal is to create in-depth technical books of the highest quality and value. Each book is crafted with care and precision, undergoing rigorous development that involves the unique expertise of members from the professional technical community.

Readers' feedback is a natural continuation of this process. If you have any comments regarding how we could improve the quality of this book, or otherwise alter it to better suit your needs, you can contact us through email at feedback@ciscopress.com. Please make sure to include the book title and ISBN in your message.

We greatly appreciate your assistance.

Americas Headquarters
Cisco Systems, Inc.
170 West Tasman Drive
San Jose, CA 95134-1706
USA
www.cisco.com
Tel: 408 526-4000
800 553-NETS (6387)
Fax: 408 527-0883

Asia Pacific Headquarters
Cisco Systems, Inc.
168 Robinson Road
#28-01 Capital Tower
Singapore 068912
www.cisco.com
Tel: +65 6317 7777
Fax: +65 6317 7799

Europe Headquarters
Cisco Systems International BV
Haarlerbergpark
Haarlerbergweg 13-19
1101 CH Amsterdam
The Netherlands
www-europe.cisco.com
Tel: +31 0 800 020 0791
Fax: +31 0 20 357 1100

Cisco has more than 200 offices worldwide. Addresses, phone numbers, and fax numbers are listed on the Cisco Website at **www.cisco.com/go/offices.**

©2007 Cisco Systems, Inc. All rights reserved. CCVP, the Cisco logo, and the Cisco Square Bridge logo are trademarks of Cisco Systems, Inc.; Changing the Way We Work, Live, Play, and Learn is a service mark of Cisco Systems, Inc.; and Access Registrar, Aironet, BPX, Catalyst, CCDA, CCDP, CCIE, CCIP, CCNA, CCNP, CCSP, Cisco, the Cisco Certified Internetwork Expert logo, Cisco IOS, Cisco Press, Cisco Systems, Cisco Systems Capital, the Cisco Systems logo, Cisco Unity, Enterprise/Solver, EtherChannel, EtherFast, EtherSwitch, Fast Step, Follow Me Browsing, FormShare, GigaDrive, GigaStack, HomeLink, Internet Quotient, IOS, IP/TV, iQ Expertise, the iQ logo, iQ Net Readiness Scorecard, iQuick Study, LightStream, Linksys, MeetingPlace, MGX, Networking Academy, Network Registrar, Packet, PIX, ProConnect, RateMUX, ScriptShare, SlideCast, SMARTnet, StackWise, The Fastest Way to Increase Your Internet Quotient, and TransPath are registered trademarks of Cisco Systems, Inc. and/or its affiliates in the United States and certain other countries.

All other trademarks mentioned in this document or Website are the property of their respective owners. The use of the word partner does not imply a partnership relationship between Cisco and any other company. (0609R)

About the Author(s)

Denise Donohue, CCIE No. 9566, is a senior solutions architect with Chesapeake NetCraftsmen. She has worked in IT since the mid-1990s. Focusing on network design since 2004, she has consulted on a wide range of networks, private and public, of all sizes, across most industries. She is author or co-author of numerous Cisco Press networking, voice, and design books. Denise lives in Maryland with her wonderfully patient and supportive husband, Kevin, and their two much less patient dogs.

Brent Stewart, CCNP, CCDP, CCSI, MCSE, is the vice president of Managed Services at Stalwart Systems (stalwartsystems.com), an innovative IT engineering firm focused on secure IT architectures. His experience includes designing and managing a large-scale worldwide voice, video, and data network. He was a course director for Global Knowledge and participated in the development of BSCI with Cisco and has written and taught extensively on CCNA and CCNP. Brent lives in Hickory, North Carolina, with his beautiful wife, Karen, and their mischievous children Benjamin, Kaitlyn, Madelyn, and William.

About the Technical Reviewer

Sean Wilkins is an accomplished networking consultant for SR-W Consulting and has been in the field of IT since the mid-1990s, working with companies such as Cisco, Lucent, Verizon, and AT&T, as well as several other private companies. Sean currently holds certifications with Cisco (CCNP/CCDP), Microsoft (MCSE), and CompTIA (A+ and Network+). He also has a Master of Science in information technology with a focus in network architecture and design, a Master of Science in organizational management, a Master's Certificate in network security, a Bachelor of Science in computer networking, and Associates of Applied Science in computer information systems. In addition to working as a consultant, Sean spends most of his time as a technical writer and editor for various companies; check out his work at his author website: www.infodispersion.com.

Acknowledgments

From Denise: Brent and I have been working on this book, in one form or another, for ten years! The first iteration was a book of flash cards covering the BSCI, BCMSN, BCRAN, and CIT exams in 2004, with Tim Sammut. In 2008, the exams were BSCI, BCMSN, ISCW, and ONT, and Jay Swan worked with us. Because there were only three exams in the 2010 version of CCNP, Brent and I tackled the book by ourselves, as we have done with this edition. Hopefully, the version you are reading—the fourth iteration—is the best yet. It contains a distillation of the knowledge we've gained from the previous ones, as well as working in networking all this time. Thank you, Tim and Jay, and especially to Brent, for inviting me to join you in writing the original book! Thank you also to the Cisco Press team, who are great to work with and really care about producing high-quality material. Sean Wilkins is one of the best technical editors I've worked with. This book is better because of his efforts, and we very much appreciate it.

From Brent: Denise and I have been friends and partners on various projects for a long time. I have always been better for having worked with her. I would also like to express my appreciation for our executive editor, Brett Bartow, and the folks at Cisco Press who have been extremely supportive. To our readers: Thank you—I hope this reference is a valuable tool in your success!

This book is dedicated, as am I, to Karen.

Contents at a Glance

Contents

Command Syntax Conventions

The conventions used to present command syntax in this book are the same conventions used in the IOS Command Reference. The Command Reference describes these conventions as follows:

- **Boldface** indicates commands and keywords that are entered literally as shown. In actual configuration examples and output (not general command syntax), boldface indicates commands that are manually input by the user (such as a **show** command).

- *Italic* indicates arguments for which you supply actual values.

- Vertical bars (I) separate alternative, mutually exclusive elements.

- Square brackets ([ ]) indicate an optional element.

- Braces ({ }) indicate a required choice.

- Braces within brackets ([{ }]) indicate a required choice within an optional element.

Introduction

The Cisco Certified Network Professional (CCNP) Routing and Switching certification validates knowledge and skills required to install, configure, and troubleshoot converged local and wide area networks. With a CCNP Routing and Switching certification, a network professional demonstrates the knowledge and skills required to configure, manage, and troubleshoot the routers and switches that form the network core, LAN, and WAN.

The *CCNP Routing and Switching v2.0 Exam Practice Pack* was written to help you prepare for the three exams in the CCNP Routing and Switching certification. Some readers tell us that they use this book before beginning their exam preparation to find which areas they are weak in. This helps target their studying. Others use it after studying or taking the course as a concise learning resource during their final preparation for the exam.

This book can also help after your exams are over, when you need a quick answer about a technology or a reminder about configuration steps.

Who Should Read This Book?

Current and aspiring network engineers will find this book useful in two ways. First, those preparing for the CCNP Routing and Switching certification will appreciate the targeted review of exam topics. It will help them understand the technologies, not just memorize questions. This will lead to success on the exam and improved on-the-job performance. Second, the book serves as a reference for those not pursuing the certification. Its short descriptions and many examples come in handy when you need a fast answer to a question, or to configure something quickly. It deserves a place on every network engineer's bookshelf.

How This Book Is Organized

The book is organized by exam. ROUTE is first, followed by SWITCH, and then TSHOOT. The topics within each exam section correspond with those on the exam blueprint. This edition includes more emphasis on working with IPv6, newer ways to configure routing protocols and network technologies such as DHCP, network management, and security. Additionally, RIP is back. The following is a description for each section.

Part I: ROUTE

- **Chapter 1, "Networking Overview":** This chapter provides a review of basic IP, TCP, and UDP operations, such as fragmentation and windowing. It also reviews routing fundamentals including AD, types of protocols, packet forwarding, and loop prevention.

- **Chapter 2, "IPv6 Overview":** This chapter provides an overview of IPv6 addressing, routing, and route summarization. This rather in-depth introduction to IPv6 covers the IPv6 address format, ways for hosts to acquire their addresses, and IPv6 routing. It also includes strategies for integrating IPv4 and IPv6, such as in various types of tunnels. More detailed applications of IPv6 are covered in the chapters for each routing protocol and for the various technologies.

- **Chapter 3, "RIP":** Configuring and verifying RIPv2 and RIPng for IPv6 are described in this chapter.

- **Chapter 4, "EIGRP":** This chapter contains an in-depth description of EIGRP for IPv4 and IPv6 operation and configuration, including neighbor establishment and route exchange. It covers using EIGRP with Frame Relay, Ethernet over MPLS (EoMPLS), and Layer 3 MPLS VPNs. It also includes EIGRP named mode, ways to optimize EIGRP, and securing EIGRP through authentication.

- **Chapter 5, "OSPF":** Chapter 5 describes OSPF's structure and operation. It covers OSPF design requirements, neighbor establishment, and LSA information for both OSPFv2 and OSPFv3. The configuration portion provides OSPF configuration for LAN and WAN networks. The chapter additionally covers optimizing and securing OSPF.

- **Chapter 6, "Advanced Routing Techniques":** This chapter examines various methods of controlling routing updates, such as route maps, prefix lists, and distribute lists. It describes how to configure route maps and how to use them for policy-based routing, controlling route redistribution, and tagging routes. Additionally, techniques such as IP SLA and VRF Lite are covered.

- **Chapter 7, "BGP and Internet Connectivity":** This chapter gives an overview of BGP operation and basic configuration. BGP path selection is covered, along with ways to influence the path selection and filter routes. Additionally, methods to verify BGP operation are shown. Multi-protocol BGP, using BGP with IPv6 routing, is covered.

- **Chapter 8, "Infrastructure Security":** This chapter examines ways to secure the routing infrastructure and the routers themselves, as well as the data transmitted. It looks at IPv4 and IPv6 ACLs, device access control, and various types of traffic tunneling techniques.

- **Chapter 9, "Infrastructure Services":** This chapter describes useful network management services, such as SNMP, logging, debugging, and NetFlow. It covers DHCP for both IPv4 and IPv6, NAT for both IPv4 and IPv6, and NAT virtual interface.

Part II: SWITCH

- **Chapter 1, "LAN Switching Basics":** Chapter 1 reviews the basics of LAN switching and Layer 2 protocols such as CDP and LLDP. It includes traffic monitoring with SPAN and RSPAN and the use of SDM templates.

- **Chapter 2, "VLANs":** This chapter gives an overview of VLANs, along with port and VLAN roles. It covers 802.1Q trunking and VTP, including best practices, configuration, and troubleshooting.

- **Chapter 3, "EtherChannels":** The design, configuration, and troubleshooting of EtherChannels are covered in this chapter. This includes both Layer 2 and Layer 3 EtherChannels, load balancing, and features such as EtherChannel Misconfiguration Guard.

- **Chapter 4, "Spanning Tree Protocol":** Chapter 4 goes into detail on Spanning Tree, Rapid Spanning Tree, and Multiple Spanning Tree. It covers spanning-tree tuning mechanisms such as UDLD, Loop Guard, BackboneFast, and BPDU Guard. It also includes troubleshooting Spanning Tree and Spanning-Tree best practices.

- **Chapter 5, "First Hop Redundancy Protocols":** Chapter 5 looks at HSRP, VRRP, and GLBP. It describes their operation, the differences between them, and how to configure and tune them. It also includes using the three FHRPs with IPv6.

- **Chapter 6, "InterVLAN Routing":** Routing between VLANs using a router and a multilayer switch are covered in Chapter 6. Uses of SVIs and routed ports are discussed. This chapter additionally describes Layer 2 and Layer 3 switch forwarding processes and CEF operation and verification.

- **Chapter 7, "Switch Security Features":** This chapter is concerned with ways in which the LAN might be attacked and its security compromised. It covers four types of attacks: MAC address attacks, VLAN-based attacks, spoofing attacks, and attacks against the switch itself. Prevention techniques are shown for each type of attack. The chapter additionally discusses using AAA.

- **Chapter 8, "Campus Network Design":** Chapter 8 covers design considerations for small, medium, and large campuses. It describes the benefits of high availability and how to achieve network resiliency through thoughtful network design. It also examines the role of features such as SSO, NSF, ISSU, VSS, and Stackwise in creating a stable, reliable network.

Part III: TSHOOT

- **Chapter 1, "Tools and Methodologies of Troubleshooting":** This chapter focuses on minimizing time-to-repair. It examines the techniques that can be applied to decrease downtime. The scientific method is suggested as a model for troubleshooting. Descriptions of tasks commonly used to maintain performance and prepare for problems, such as documentation and scheduled preventative maintenance, are provided. Finally, it covers IOS tools, such as archiving, logging, and configuration rollback, that are valuable in the troubleshooting process.

- **Chapter 2, "Troubleshooting Switching Technologies":** Ethernet is ubiquitous in campus networks and data centers. More and more services are traveling on Ethernet, such as storage, virtualization, and telephony. This chapter describes troubleshooting the critical pieces: Spanning Tree, VLANs, InterVLAN routing, and gateway redundancy.

- **Chapter 3, "Troubleshooting IP Networking":** This chapter describes issues around IP services and starts with a discussion of IP addressing. It also discusses services such as NTP, syslog, and SNMP.

- **Chapter 4, "Troubleshooting Routing Technologies":** This chapter covers troubleshooting link layer connectivity, OSPF, EIGRP, and BGP routing protocols and router performance.

CHAPTER 1

Networking Overview

IP, TCP, and UDP Operations

This book assumes that the reader is already familiar with basic IP, TCP, and UCP operations; their header structures; and IPv4 addressing. This section briefly discusses some additional points about these protocols.

IP Operations

Packet fragmentation is handled differently in IPv4 and IPv6. Each link has a maximum transmission unit (MTU) size associated with it. If the IPv4 packet is larger than the interface MTU, it is fragmented (unless the Don't Fragment bit is set in the IP header, in which case it will be dropped). Fragments of the same original packets are marked identically in the Identifier field of the IP header, so that the receiving router knows they belong together. The Fragment Offset field gives that fragment's place in the original packet, so that it can be reassembled correctly.

IPv6 uses Path MTU Discovery to determine the minimum MTU along the path and so does not fragment packets by default. When a too-large packet is sent, ICMPv6 returns a packet-too-big message. TCP reduces its packet size accordingly, but UDP cannot do that so the source host must fragment the packet. If fragmentation is required, the fields needed to reassemble the packet are placed in an Extension header between the IPv6 header and the TCP/UDP header. IPv4 can also use Path MTU Discovery to ensure that all packets fit the minimum path size and thus will not be fragmented.

The Internet Control Message Protocol (ICMP) has many types of messages and numerous uses in an IP network. Its "TTL Exceeded" message can be used along with the Time to Live (TTL) field in an IP header for performing trace routes. Its "Redirect" message notifies a host to use an alternate default gateway, saving an unneeded hop. Probably ICMP's most common uses are the "Echo Request" and "Echo Reply" messages used, along with the "Destination Unreachable" messages, by PING.

TCP Operations

TCP, as a connection-oriented protocol, uses fields in its header to negotiate various settings with its peers. Window size is one of these settings. Rather than sending one segment at a time and waiting for an acknowledgement, TCP groups multiple segments and sends them. The size of this group is called its *window*. The Window Size field in the TCP header tells how many bytes of data the host can accept at a time, in one window. The sending router adjusts the amount of data it sends to fit its peer's window size.

The default maximum window size is 65,535 bytes. You might want to increase that size to get greater throughput from TCP applications. For instance, on any given link the greatest throughput you can get is expressed by the window size divided by link latency. Increasing window size is generally much easier than decreasing link latency! A larger window size is especially useful on links with a high Bandwidth Delay Product (BDP) to be able to send a large amount of data before having to wait for an acknowledgement. Bandwidth Delay Product is equal to the link bandwidth multiplied by end-to-end delay; slower links have higher BDPs.

The TCP header also contains an Options field, and a most commonly used option is maximum segment size (MSS). This option helps avoid fragmentation at the IP layer. Hosts check the link MTU, subtract 40 bytes to account for the IP and TCP headers, make sure that value does not overrun the interface buffer, and then send that value to their peer as the MSS value. The peer must then set its "Send MSS" to that value.

You should be aware of one other issue with TCP—that of global synchronization. When a TCP segment is dropped, it reduces its send rate and then gradually ramps back up. If a sudden event caused all the TCP traffic on an interface to be dropped, then every flow would back off at the same time, and ramp back up at the same time. At some point, the interface would become congested and the flows would all drop again, repeating the cycle. Thus every flow's sending pattern becomes synchronized, which results in inefficient link utilization. Some QoS tools such as Weighted Random Early Detection (WRED) can help prevent global synchronization.

UDP Operations

UDP does not behave in the same way as TCP when its traffic is dropped. It continues sending at the same rate because, being connectionless, it does not know whether or not anything was dropped. On an interface with both TCP and UDP flows, UDP uses the bandwidth whereas TCP backs off and then ramps back up. In fact, TCP's operation might allow even more UDP flows, which can result in *TCP starvation*. Output queues fill with UDP traffic, and the TCP traffic continues getting dropped.

Latency is another concern with UDP traffic. Most applications that use UDP send small packets of interactive traffic such as voice. The quality of the application performance depends on few packet drops and low, predictable delay. However, large packets such as an FTP file transfer could hold up the transmission of a small UDP traffic, causing higher latency. Variable latency, or *jitter*, is a common problem with UDP traffic and one that can be addressed with QoS.

Routing Fundamentals

Routers must know how to reach remote networks to forward packets toward them. They can learn this either by manual configuration (*static route*) or by using a routing protocol to exchange information about network reachability. To configure a static route, use the global command:

```
(IPv4) ip route [destination_network] [subnet_mask] [next_hop_IP]
(IPv6) ipv6 route [destination_network]/prefix-length [next_hop_
    IP]
```

Another special type of route is a *default route*, designated in IPv4 by 0.0.0.0 with a subnet mask of 0.0.0.0 and in IPv6 by ::/0. Default routes are used when no other route exists to the destination network.

Cisco routers support multiple routing protocols, but the ROUTE exam covers only Routing Information Protocol (RIP), Enhanced Interior Gateway Routing Protocol (EIGRP), Open Shortest Path First (OSPF), and Border Gateway Protocol (BGP). This section gives an overview of routing protocols and some key differences between them.

The Routing Table

Routers maintain a database of the routes they will use to forward a packet. To build this routing table, the router rules out invalid routes, and then considers the remaining options. The procedure is defined in the following steps:

1. For each route received, verify the next hop. If invalid, discard the route.

2. If multiple identical, valid routes are received by a routing protocol, choose the lowest metric. Routes are identical if they advertise the same prefix and mask, so 192.168.0.0/16 and 192.168.0.0/24 are separate paths and may each be placed into the routing table.

3. If the same valid route is advertised by different routing protocols, choose the path with the lowest AD.

Part I: ROUTE

After the routing table is built, routers choose which route to use for a specific packet by looking for a match to the destination IP address. Rarely will a route match the destination IP address exactly, so the router looks for the longest match. For instance, suppose a packet is bound for the IP address 10.1.1.1. The routing table has a route for 10.1.0.0/16, one for 10.1.1.0/24, and a default route of 0.0.0.0. The default route matches 0 bits of the destination address, the 10.1.0.0 route matches 16 bits of the destination address, and the 10.1.1.0 route matches 24 bits of the destination address. The 10.1.1.0 route is the longest match, so it will be used to forward the packet.

To view the routes in the routing table, and verify any static or default routes, use the command **show ip route**.

Administrative Distance

Cisco routers are capable of supporting several IP routing protocols concurrently. When identical prefixes are learned from two or more separate sources, Administrative Distance (AD) is used to discriminate between the paths. Cisco routers assign an AD value to each routing protocol; in some cases different AD values are assigned to routes learned natively by the protocol versus those redistributed into the protocol. All other things being equal, routers choose paths advertised by the protocol with the lowest AD. AD can be manually adjusted.

Table 1-1 lists the default values for various routing protocols.

Table 1-1   Routing Protocols and Their Default Administrative Distance

Information Source	AD
Connected	0
Static	1
External BGP	20
Internal EIGRP	90
OSPF	110
IS-IS	115
RIP	120
External EIGRP	170
Internal BGP	200
Unknown	255

Choosing a Routing Protocol

A group of network devices (routers, switches, and so on) under one common administration is termed an *autonomous system*, or AS. This is typically a company or organization, or perhaps one division of an organization. Routing protocols that are used inside an AS are called *Interior Gateway Protocols*, or IGPs, and those used to exchange routes between AS's are termed *Exterior Gateway Protocols*, or EGPs. IGPs need to respond quickly to changes, converging rapidly. They should be fairly easy to figure and optimize. They might need to scale to manage very large networks, but not as large as EGPs can handle. An EGP can operate in very large networks and are used on the Internet. The only EGP in use today is Border Gateway Protocol (BGP). An AS might want to tightly control what routes it advertises outside its borders, what routes it accepts, and the metrics of those routes. EGPs do not need to converge as quickly as IGPs but they must be very stable, extremely scalable, and support customizable policies.

Classify routing protocols based on the method they use to calculate the best paths. Three types of protocols are discussed in this section.

Distance Vector Protocols

Distance vector protocols have only two pieces of information about a network: the distance (or metric) to reach it, and the next-hop neighbor on the path (or vector) to that network. RIP and EIGRP are distance vector protocols. "Distance" for RIP is hop count, whereas for EIGRP it is a more complex metric. Distance vector protocols in general can be slow to converge because they have to query their neighbors for an alternate route when there is a topology change, but EIGRP compensates for this by proactively selecting an alternate route when possible.

Link State Protocols

Link state protocols pass along information about individual links connected to the routers in their portion of the network. Each link-state router then builds a map of the logical topology and chooses the best path using the Shortest Path First (SPF) algorithm. In a topology change, link state routers do not need to query their neighbors; they can choose an alternate path from their topology database. OSPF and IS-IS are link state protocols.

Path Vector Protocols

Path vector protocols are similar to distance vector protocols in that they do not maintain a complete picture of the network, only the next-hop router address. However, they do exchange information about the path to the

Part I: ROUTE

destination network as part of their updates, using it as part of the metric and as a loop prevention mechanism. An example of this is the AS-path part of BGP updates. BGP is the only path vector protocol in common use today.

Table 1-2 compares routing protocols.

Table 1-2   Comparison of Routing Protocols

Property	RIP v2	EIGRP	OSPF	BGP
Method	Distance vector	Distance vector	Link state	Path vector
Summarization	Auto/ Manual	Auto/Manual	Manual	Auto/Manual
Metric	Hop count	Bandwidth + sum of path delays	Sum of link costs	Complex metric
Timers: Update (hello/dead)	Every 30 sec and Triggered	Triggered (LAN 5/15, WAN 60/180)	Triggered, but LSA refreshes every 30 minutes (NBMA 30/120, LAN 10/40)	Triggered (60/180)
Network Size	Small	Large	Large	Very large

Packet Forwarding

Routing a packet essentially involves two functions: deciding the best path for the packet, and then forwarding it out the exit interface. The exchange of routing information and building of the route table are handled by the control plane. Forwarding the packet and placing the correct Layer 2 header on is handled by the data plane.

Three methods of forwarding packets are process switching, fast switching, and Cisco Express Forwarding.

Process switching is performed completely in software, so it is the most CPU intensive and thus the slowest method. For each frame, the router strips off the incoming Layer 2 header, sends it to the CPU for the Layer 3 next hop, outgoing interface, and Layer 2 header.

Fast switching is accomplished partially in hardware, so it is faster than process switching. The router builds a fast-switching cache. When a frame comes in, the destination is checked against this cache. If an entry is present, then the Layer 2 header is added and the frame is sent to the outgoing interface. If no entry is present, the packet is sent to the router and processed as with process switching. An entry is added to the fast-switching cache and subsequent packets are fast switched.

Cisco Express Forwarding (CEF) is the default switching mode for modern platforms. It is also the fastest mode. The router proactively determines the outgoing interface, next-hop adjacency, and Layer 2 information for every route in the routing table. Packets are then forwarded completely in hardware, without the need for CPU intervention. CEF caches routing information in the forwarding information base (FIB) and next-hop Layer 2 information in an adjacency table.

Not all types of traffic can be handled by CEF. Some forms that are *punted* (sent to the processor for handling) are

- Packets with IP header options

- Tunneled traffic

- Unsupported encapsulation types

- Packets with an expiring TTL

- Packets that exceed the MTU and must be fragmented

Configuring and Troubleshooting CEF

By default, CEF is enabled for IPv4 and disabled for IPv6. Enabling IPv6 routing automatically enables CEF for IPv6. The default load sharing type is per destination. To disable CEF on a per-interface basis, use the interface-level command **no ip route-cache cef**. To disable CEF for the entire router, use the global command **no ip cef**.

Verify that CEF is enabled or disabled on an interface with the following command:

```
# show ip interface [interface]
```

You should see output that says either "IP CEF switching is enabled" or "IP CEF switching is disabled."

View the FIB with the following command:

```
# show [ip | ipv6] cef {interface} {detail}
```

View or troubleshoot CEF adjacencies with the following command:

```
# show adjacency
```

Part I: ROUTE

Loop Prevention Mechanisms

Incorrect routing information can result in traffic looping throughout the network, being sent back and forth between the same routers. The traffic might be dropped or blackholed. Looping is especially prevalent in distance vector protocols. Route advertisements can cause this problem in two ways:

- A router can hear about a network from its neighbor, and then advertise that network back to the same neighbor.

- A router can keep sending traffic to a network that is down.

Two techniques to prevent this type of looping are split horizon and route poisoning.

Split Horizon

Enabling *split horizon* causes the router to never advertise a route out of the interface where it learned that route. Some protocol implementations add a poison reverse to that, by advertising the route back to its neighbor with a metric of "unreachable," thus ensuring the neighbor does not consider it a viable path to the network. Split horizon is useful on point-to-point links but can cause problems on multipoint links such as Frame Relay. It is enabled by default, so it must be manually disabled on a multipoint link.

Route Poisoning

To speed up convergence and prevent traffic from being blackholed, distance vector protocols implement route poisoning. As soon as a router learns that a network is down, it advertises that network out all of its interfaces, including the one where it received the route advertisement, with an "unreachable" metric. The logic behind this breaking of the split horizon rule is a multi-access network (such as Ethernet) with several routers on it. If one router did not receive the initial update for some reason, this provides another chance for it to be processed.

CHAPTER 2

IPv6 Overview

This chapter assumes the reader is very familiar with IPv4 addressing and operation. IPv6 is an extension of IP addressing with several advanced features:

- Larger address space.

- Simpler header for increased router efficiency.

- No more broadcasts.

- Stateless autoconfiguration.

- Built-in support for Mobile IP.

- Built-in support for IPsec security.

- Rich transition features.

- Easy IP address renumbering.

- Support for multiple addresses per interface.

- Routers create link-local addresses for use by Interior Gateway Protocols (IGPs).

- As with IPv4, the addresses can be obtained from an Internet service provider (ISP) or can be provider independent.

The primary adoption of IPv6 is driven by the need for more addresses. Given the growth in Internet use and the emergence of large groups of Internet users worldwide, this is a significant requirement. Another reason to use IPv6 is growth in the size of the current Internet routing table. IPv4 addresses are not summarized enough to keep the size down, increasing the load on Internet routers. Additionally, although the use of Network Address Translation (NAT) has postponed the need for IPv6, it breaks TCP/IP's end-to-end networking model.

IPv6 is not enabled by default on Cisco routers. To enable IPv6 routing, the command is **ipv6 unicast-routing** at the global configuration mode.

IPv6 Addressing

IPv4 addresses are 32 bits long and written in dotted decimal, whereas IPv6 addresses are 128 bits and written in hexadecimal. IPv6 addresses are written in groups of four numbers, separated by colons. Each number represents 4 bits and thus has a value of 0–F. Addresses are typically divided into a 64-bit network portion and a 64-bit host portion. An IPv6 address might look something like 2001:db80:aabb:1111:2222:3333:4444:ffff/64. There is no equivalent of the IPv4 dotted decimal subnet mask—the prefix length (network portion of the address) is written in CIDR notation. Having host addresses that end in 0 or F is legal.

The first 48 bits of the network portion are considered *global address space*. These bits consist of the following elements:

- The first three bits (/3) of a unicast address are always 001.

- The next 13 bits (/16) identify the top-level aggregator (TLA), the upstream ISP or address authority.

- The subsequent 24 bits (/40) identify the next-level aggregator, a regional ISP or address authority.

The next 16 bits are available for creating subnetworks within the enterprise. The host interface portion of the address is the last 64 bits. Because IPv6 does not use broadcasts and separates the interface address portion from the network portion, interface addresses of all zeroes and all ones are legal. Figure 2-1 shows the address components.

Figure 2-1   IPv6 Address Structure

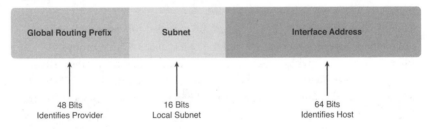

Simplifying an IPv6 Address

There are two ways to shorten the representation of an IPv6 address. Take the example address 2001:0000:0001:0002:0000:0000:0000:ABCD.

- Leading zeros can be omitted, which reduces the preceding address to 2001:0:1:2:0:0:0:ABCD.

- Sequential zeros can be shown as double colons. *This is allowed only once per address.* This simplifies the aforementioned address even further, to 2001:0:1:2::ABCD.

Be sure that you can distinguish between correct and incorrect IPv6 addresses. For instance, the address 2001::1:2::ABCD is incorrect because it uses double colons twice.

Special Addresses

IPv6 does not support broadcasts but replaces them with multicasts. IPv6 also uses *anycast*, which involves using the same address on multiple devices. Anycast is used to implement redundancy and has been backported to IPv4.

Each IPv6 system must recognize the following addresses:

- Its unicast addresses.

- Link local address (begins with FE80/10).

- Loopback (::1/128).

- All-nodes multicast (FF00::1).

- Site-local multicast (FF02::2).

- Solicited-nodes multicast (FF02::1:FF00/104).

- Default route (::/0).

- Routers must support subnet-router anycast (all zeros EUI-64).

- Routers must support local all-routers multicast (FF01::2), link-local (FF02::2), and site-local (FF05:2).

- Routers must support routing protocol multicast groups.

Additionally, some systems also use the following addresses:

- IPv4-compatible address (::/96 | 32-bit, IPv4 address)

- Second unicast address shared with another system (anycast)

- Additional multicast groups

IPv6 Host Addressing

IPv6 uses one special type of address called a *link-local address*. In IPv6, this is composed of the network prefix FE80:: and the host or interface MAC address. This address is valid only on the local network segment. To make sure that the address is not already being used, a host sends a neighbor solicitation message to that address to make sure no other device answers. Even if you assign a routable, global address to the interface, it still has its link-local address. IGP routing protocols use the link-local address to form neighbor relationships. The link-local address is also the next-hop address that is installed in the routing table by IGPs. You can see an example of a link-local address later in Example 2-2.

An IPv6 host can obtain a routable IP address by manual assignment; physically designating the network part of the address only using Stateless Address Autoconfiguration (SLAAC) or by using DHCPv6. DHCPv6 is covered in Chapter 9, "Infrastructure Services."

To ping any IPv6 address, including link-local addresses, use the command **ping** [**ipv6**] *destination-address* [**source** *exit-interface*]. Note that the source interface is required when pinging a link-local address.

Neighbor Discovery Protocol

Neighbor Discovery Protocol uses ICMPv6 and assists in IPv6 addressing in several ways:

- **Duplicate address discovery (DAD):** The host uses neighbor solicitation (NS) to send a message to its own address. No response means that the address is unique. This is used when a host creates its link-local address.

- **Neighbor discovery:** Similarly to ARP, the host discovers the link-local address of neighbors using an NS message. This is ICMP type 135. Neighbors respond with an ICMP type 136 message.

- **Router discovery:** IPv6 routers periodically send router advertisements (RAs) listing the network prefix. When a host comes online, it immediately sends a router solicitation (RS) message asking for prefix information rather than waiting for the RA. This is sent to the all-routers multicast address.

Manual IP Address Assignment

To manually assign an IPv6 address to a router interface, use the command **ipv6** *address* ipv6-address/prefix-length. Example 2-1 shows two router interfaces configured with IPv6 addresses. In the first address, note that leading zeroes are omitted in two of the quartets. In the second address, note the use of the double colons.

Example 2-1   IPv6 Address Configuration

```
Router(config)# ipv6 unicast-routing
!
Router(config)# interface gigabitethernet0/0
Router(config-if)# ipv6 address 2001:db8:aabb:1:2222:3333:4444:f
 fff/64
!
Router(config)# interface gigabitethernet0/1
Router(config-if)# ipv6 address 2001:db8:aabb:2::1 /64
```

Manual Network Assignment

Although statically assigning IP addresses to router interfaces is a best practice, routers can create their own IPv6 address when they know the network prefix. Assuming the end system has a 48-bit MAC address, the router or host flips the global/local bit (the seventh bit) and inserts 0xFFEE into the middle of the MAC address. The resulting 64-bit number is called the *EUI-64 address*. The prefix and EUI-64 address are concatenated to form the host IPv6 address. The command is **ipv6 address** *ipv6-prefix::/prefix-length* **eui-64**.

Example 2-2 shows this command and the resulting link-local and global unicast address. Note the interface MAC address and how it relates to the IPv6 addresses.

Example 2-2   Configuring an EUI-64 Address

```
Router(config)# interface ethernet0/0
Router(config-if)# ipv6 address 2001:db8:1234:aabb::/64 eui-64
!
Router# show int e0/0
Ethernet0/0 is up, line protocol is up
 Hardware is AMDP2, address is 001d.a188.33c1 (bia 001d.a188.33c1)
<output omitted>
!
Router# show ipv6 int e0/0
Ethernet0/0 is up, line protocol is up
 IPv6 is enabled, link-local address is FE80::21D:A1FF:FE88:33C1
 No Virtual link-local address(es):
```

Part I: ROUTE

Example 2-2   Continued

```
Global unicast address(es):
  2001:DB8:1234:AABB:21D:A1FF:FE88:33C1,subnet is
  2001:DB8:1234:AABB::/64[EUI]
Joined group address(es):
  FF02::1
  FF02::2
  FF02::1:FF00:1A00
<output omitted>
```

Stateless Address Autoconfiguration

One big benefit of IPv6 is the capability of a host to automatically acquire an IP address without DHCP, called *Stateless Address Autoconfiguration* or *SLAAC*. To enable stateless autoconfiguration, use the interface command **ipv6 address autoconfig**. Acquiring an address involves the following steps:

Step 1.   The host creates a link-local address.

Step 2.   It sends an NS message to its link-local address out the interface.

Step 3.   If there is no reply, DAD declares the address unique.

Step 4.   If the host doesn't receive an RA, it sends an RS.

Step 5.   A router on the subnet sends an RA, listing its interface prefix.

Step 6.   The host uses that prefix and the interface MAC address to create its IPv6 address.

Use the command **show ipv6 interface** to verify your configuration. Example 2-3 shows this command and the resulting IPv6 address.

Example 2-3   IPv6 Autoconfiguration

```
Router(config)# int e0/0
Router(config-if)# ipv6 address autoconfig
!
Router# show ipv6 int e0/0
Ethernet0/0 is up, line protocol is up
  IPv6 is enabled, link-local address is FE80::21D:A1FF:FE6C:D238
  No Virtual link-local address(es):
  Global unicast address(es):
    2001:DB8::21D:A1FF:FE6C:D238, subnet is 2001:DB8::/64 [EUI/CAL/
  PRE]
      valid lifetime 2591828 preferred lifetime 604628
<output omitted>
```

Securing NDP

NDP is an essential part of IPv6, enabling SLAAC and allowing MAC addresses to be learned and hosts to be redirected to better routes. But because it starts operating when IPv6 unicast routing is enabled, it can expose the router to problems such as man-in-the-middle attacks and black-holing of traffic.

If there is no need for router advertisement messages on a link, disable them with the command **ipv6 nd suppress-ra**.

Another option is to use Secure Neighbor Discovery (SeND). SeND is an extension to NDP that provides some additional security, such as

- Proof of address ownership to prevent address hijacking

- Message integrity and replay protection

- Router authorization for specific prefixes only

SeND requires a pair of public and private keys for all IPv6 nodes. Its deployment can become complex and its use can be CPU intensive.

DHCPv6

DHCP can also be used to assign IP addresses on an IPv6 network. DHCP for IPv6 is covered in Part I in the "DHCP" section of Chapter 9.

Renumbering

IPv6 supports easy network renumbering. Note in Example 2-3 that lifetimes are listed for the subnet address. When it is time to change the subnet, simply configure the router to advertise the old prefix with a short lifetime and the new prefix with a longer one. You can even configure the router to expire a prefix at a certain date and time. The router sends out an RA with both prefixes and their lifetimes. Hosts then update their addresses. Anyone who has had to renumber a large range of IPv4 addresses can testify to how useful this feature is!

IPv6 Routing

Routing with IPv6 will seem familiar to you. The same IGPs—RIP, EIGRP, and OSPF—are used as in IPv4; they have been adapted to carry IPv6 routes. BGP extensions enable it to perform IPv6 routing. The same rules for metric and administrative distance apply. The commands are similar, too. The main difference in commands is that you must specify that the command

pertains to IPv6 because IPv4 is the default. One big configuration difference is that IGPs no longer use the **network** command to initiate routing; it
is enabled at each interface instead. BGP still uses the network command to
designate which networks to advertise.

The specific commands and examples are given in the chapters for each
routing protocol. The following is some general information that applies to
all protocols.

Static Routing

Static routing with IPv6 works exactly like it does with version 4. Aside
from understanding the address format, there are no differences. The syntax
for the IPv6 static route command is

```
Router(config)# ipv6 route ipv6-prefix/prefix-length {ipv6-
  address | interface-type
interface-number [ipv6-address]} [administrative-distance]
[administrative-multicast-distance | unicast | multicast] [tag
  tag]
```

The following configuration shows the command in context as it might
be applied. The first line shows a static route that lists a next-hop address.
The second line shows a directly connected static default route that lists an
outbound interface. The third line shows a fully specified static route, which
lists both the next-hop address and the outbound interface:

```
Router(config)# ipv6 route 2001:db8:1:2::/64 2001:db8:1:1::1
!
Router(config)# ipv6 route ::/0 serial1/0/0
!
Router(config)# ipv6 route 2001:db8:1:2::/64 serial1/0/1
  2001:db8:1:1::1
```

Verify your configuration with the **show ipv6 route** command.

IPv6 Route Summarization

You must summarize IPv6 routes for the same reasons as you summarize
IPv4 routes. There might even be a greater need because you can have so
many more IPv6 routes! Originally, the idea was to use the 16-bit local
subnet portion of the address for local routes, but you can use part of the
64 bits allocated for host addresses for subnetting, too. As in IPv4, this just
gives you fewer possible hosts. After you understand the concept, you can
apply it to any portion of the IPv6 address you need.

Recall that each number in an IPv6 address is 4 bits, which gives you 16 possible values: 0–F. Each of the quartets separated by colons is thus 16 bits. For instance, consider the following set of networks. How would you summarize them?

- 2001:db8:1:0::/64

- 2001:db8:1:1::/64

- 2001:db8:1:2::/64

- 2001:db8:1:3::/64

The fourth quartet is the one we are interested in. The binary equivalents for the fourth quartet of the preceding networks are

- 0000 0000 0000 0000

- 0000 0000 0000 0001

- 0000 0000 0000 0010

- 0000 0000 0000 0011

You can see that the last two bits are the ones you can summarize. It doesn't matter whether their value is 0 or 1. You need only to focus on the value of the first 14 bits in this quartet. The bit mask for the summary breaks down this way:

    2001:   db8:   1:   0::

    16 bits + 16 bits + 16 bits + 14 bits = 62 bits

Thus, the summarized address is 2001:db8:1:0::/62.

Integrating IPv4 and IPv6

Several strategies exist for migrating from IPv4 to IPv6. Each strategy must be considered when organizations decide to make the move to IPv6 because each has positive points to aiding a smooth migration. It should also be said that there does not have to be a global decision on strategy—your organization might choose to run dual-stack in the United States, convert completely to IPv6 in Japan, and use tunneling in Europe. The transition mechanisms include

- **Dual stack:** Running IPv6 and IPv4 concurrently on the same interface.

Part I: ROUTE

- **Tunneling:** Routers that straddle the IPv4 and IPv6 worlds encapsulate IPv6 traffic inside IPv4 packets.

- **Translation:** Using an extension of NAT, NAT64, to translate between IPv4 and IPv6 addresses. This is covered in Chapter 9.

Tunneling IPv6 over IPv4

A tunnel serves as a virtual point-to-point link between IPv6 domains. It doesn't matter what the underlying IPv4 structure is if there is IP reachability between the tunnel endpoints.

There are several ways to tunnel IPv6 over IPv4:

- Manual tunnels

- GRE tunnels

- 6to4 tunnels

- Intra-Site Automatic Tunnel Addressing Protocol (ISATAP)

Manual Tunnels

When you manually create the tunnel, the source and destination IP addresses are IPv4 addresses because IPv4 is the transport protocol. Use loopback addresses for increased stability. IPv6 addresses go on the tunnel interfaces because IPv6 is the passenger protocol. Because IPv6 considers the tunnel a point-to-point link, the address of each end of the tunnel is in the same subnet. Include the command **tunnel mode ipv6ip** in tunnel configuration mode to enable IPv6 over IP encapsulation.

To verify your configuration use the commands **debug tunnel** or **show interface tunnel** *int-number*.

GRE Tunnels

GRE is the default tunnel mode for Cisco routers. It provides more flexibility because it is protocol-agnostic. It can carry multiple protocols, including IPv6 and routing protocols.

Configuring an IPv4 GRE tunnel to carry IPv6 traffic is the same as configuring a manual tunnel except you do not have to specify the tunnel mode because GRE is the default. You can allow a routing protocol on the tunnel interface, too. The process is the same as enabling it on a physical interface.

To configure a completely IPv6 GRE tunnel, use IPv6 interface addresses as the tunnel source and destination. Give the tunnel endpoints IPv6 addresses, too. You need a command to identify that the transport protocol is IPv6. That command, given in tunnel configuration mode, is **tunnel mode gre ipv6**.

6to4 Tunnels

This technique dynamically creates tunnels that IPv6 considers point-to-multipoint interfaces. Use the reserved prefix 2002::/16 in your IPv6 domain, and then add the IPv4 address of the dual-stack router on the other side of the IPv4 domain as the next 32 bits of the network address. This means you must translate that IP address into hexadecimal.

When IPv6 traffic arrives at an edge dual-stack router with a destination IPv6 prefix of 2002::/16, the router examines the first 48 bits, derives the embedded IPv4 address from them, and uses it to determine the packet destination. The router then encapsulates the IPv6 packet in an IPv4 packet with the extracted IPv4 address as the packet destination.

Configure a tunnel as before, using IPv4 addresses as the source, but do not manually specify a destination. Give the tunnel an IPv6 address as previously described, with the tunnel destination embedded in its prefix. The tunnel mode command is **tunnel mode ipv6ip 6to4**.

Each router needs a route to its peer on the other side of the IPv4 network. The only current options for this are static routes and BGP.

ISATAP Tunnels

ISATAP tunnels are similar to the other two tunnel techniques in that an IPv4 address is encoded into the IPv6 address. It is meant to be used within a site, between hosts and routers, although it can be used between sites.

The tunnel source address is an IPv4 address. Do not specify a tunnel destination. The IPv6 address of the tunnel itself combines the network prefix, 0000:5EFE, and the 32-bit IPv4 tunnel source address. The IPv4 address is encoded into the least significant 32 bits of the address. Use any network prefix. The tunnel interface link-local address still starts with FE80 and then uses 0000:5EFE plus the encoded IPv4 address.

For instance, the link-local address of a tunnel that uses 10.8.8.8 as its source is

FE80::5EFE:A08:808

Part I: ROUTE

The unicast IPv6 address of that same tunnel interface, assuming that prefix 2001:db8:1:3/64 was assigned to the interface, is

> 2001:db8:1:3:0:5EFE:A08:808

ISATAP tunnels do not support multicast. A route is needed to the tunnel destination if it is in a different subnet; this can be either a static route or a BGP route.

IPv6 Link Types

IPv6 recognizes three types of links:

- Point-to-point
- Point-to-multipoint
- Multiaccess

Point-to-Point Links

Recall that an IPv6 interface uses its MAC address to create its link-local address. A serial link has no MAC address associated with it, so it uses one from an Ethernet interface. You can manually configure the link-local address to make it more recognizable. Be sure to begin the IPv6 address with the link-local prefix FE80.

Point-to-point links do not necessarily need global unicast addresses. The routers can communicate with only link-local addresses, but you could not reach those interfaces from off the network because the link-local is not a routable address.

Point-to-Multipoint Links

For point-to-multipoint links, such as Frame Relay, you must map the destination IPv6 address to the correct DLCI, just as with IPv4. The difference is that with IPv6 you must also map the link-local address to the DLCI because it is used as the next hop for routing. So for each DLCI, you must have at least two mappings: the remote router's IPv6 global unicast address and the remote router's link-local address. The map command is

```
frame relay map ipv6 destination-address out dlci dlci-number
  broadcast
```

In a hub-and-spoke topology, the hub must be configured for IPv6 unicast routing for the spokes to communicate with each other.

Multiaccess Links

Devices on multiaccess links, such as Ethernet, build a table mapping destination Layer 3 addresses to Layer 2 addresses, whether you use IPv4 or IPv6. IPv4 uses a separate protocol, ARP, to accomplish this. In IPv6, the process is built in to the IPv6 protocol and uses the Neighbor Discovery Protocol. An IPv6 device sends a neighbor solicitation (NS) multicast with a prefix of FE02. The neighbor responds with a neighbor advertisement (NA) message listing its MAC address. As with ARP, these mappings have a set lifetime called the *reachable time*, so an NS can also be sent periodically to verify that a neighbor is still reachable.

To add a static entry to the Neighbor Discovery table, use the command **ipv6 neighbor** *ipv6-address interface-type interface-number hardware-address*. A static address does not age out of the table.

Display the mappings with the **show ipv6 neighbors** command.

CHAPTER 3

RIP

RIP Version 2

Routing Information Protocol (RIP) has been in existence since 1988. It is a basic distance vector protocol that uses hop count as its metric, and thus does not pick up any differences in bandwidth between different routes. RIPv2 is a classless protocol—it carries subnet mask information in its updates, enabling you to use various subnet masks in the network. Some other characteristics of RIPv2 include the following:

- Uses UDP port 520.

- All routes advertised every 30 seconds, along with triggered updates due to topology change.

- Administrative distance is 120.

- Updates sent as multicasts to IPv4 address 224.0.0.9.

- Maximum metric (hop count) is 15. A hop count of 16 is considered infinity, poisoning the route.

- Supports plain text and MD5 authentication.

- No neighbor relationship formation process exists—all interfaces participating in RIP send route updates whether or not another RIP router is out of that interface.

- Route summarization is performed at each interface.

- Supports variable-length subnet masks but does auto-summary by default.

- Load balances across up to four equal metric paths by default.

RIP implements *split horizon* to help prevent routing loops. This does not allow a router to advertise out an interface a route learned via that interface. Split horizon typically comes into play on multiaccess interfaces where advertisements from multiple neighbors are learned via the same interface.

RIPv2 Configuration

To configure RIP, enter the RIP routing process in global configuration mode, and specify the interfaces that will run RIP by using the **network** command. The router then multicasts its routing table out all interfaces with IP addresses within the networks specified by that command. The **passive-interface** *interface* command stops RIP from sending updates out an interface. Use the **neighbor** *ip-address* command to inform RIP to send updates as unicasts to the specified neighbor.

Example 3-1 shows the configuration that enables RIP on all interfaces with IP addresses in the 10.0.0.0 range. The version of RIP is set to version 2, interface e0/1 is passive for RIP, and neighbor 10.1.1.2 is on a nonbroadcast network, thus updates are sent as unicast.

Example 3-1 RIPv2 Configuration

```
Router(config)# router rip
Router(config-router)# version 2
Router(config-router)# no auto-summary
Router(config-router)# network 10.0.0.0
Router(config-router)# passive-interface e0/1
Router(config-router)# neighbor 10.1.1.2
```

RIPng for IPv6

RIP next generation (RIPng) is the IPv6 version of RIP and is defined in RFC 2080. Like RIPv2 for IPv4, RIPng is a distance vector routing protocol that uses a hop count for its metric and has a maximum hop count of 15. It uses UDP but on port 521 instead of 520, and still has an administrative distance of 120. RIPng also sends periodic multicast updates—every 30 seconds—to advertise routes. The multicast address is FF02::9. The source address of RIPng updates is the link-local address of the outbound interface.

Two important differences exist between the old RIP and the next-generation RIP. One is that RIPng supports multiple concurrent processes, each identified by a process name. Another is that RIPng is initialized in global configuration mode and then enabled on specific interfaces. There is no **network** command in RIPng.

Part I: ROUTE

RIPng Configuration

Example 3-2 shows the syntax used to apply RIPng to a configuration. Notice that the syntax is similar to traditional RIP. You must first enable IPv6 routing. The global command to enable RIPng is optional; the router creates it automatically when the first interface is enabled for RIPng. You might need the command for additional configuration, such as originating a default route, as shown in Example 3-2.

Example 3-2   RIPng Configuration

```
Router(config)# ipv6 router rip process-name
!
Router(config)# interface type number
Router(config-if)# ipv6 rip process enable
Router(config-if)# ipv6 rip process default-information originate
```

Like RIP for IPv4, troubleshoot RIPng by looking at the routing table (**show ipv6 route** [**rip**]), by reviewing the routing protocols (**show ipv6 protocols**), and by watching routing updates propagated between routers (**debug ipv6 rip**).

Part I: ROUTE

CHAPTER 4

EIGRP

EIGRP Overview

Enhanced Interior Gateway Routing Protocol (EIGRP) is a Cisco proprietary, advanced distance vector, classless routing protocol that uses a composite metric based on multiple factors. The following are some features of EIGRP:

- Fast convergence.

- Partial updates conserve network bandwidth.

- Runs directly over IP, using protocol number 88.

- Support for all Layer 2 (data link layer) protocols and topologies.

- Sophisticated metric that supports load-balancing across unequal-cost paths.

- Use of multicast (and unicast where appropriate) instead of broadcasts.

- Support for authentication.

- Manual summarization at any interface.

- Uses multicast address 224.0.0.10 for EIGRPv4 and FF02::A for EIGRPv6.

EIGRP's function is controlled by three key technologies:

- **Neighbor discovery and maintenance:** Periodic hello messages

- **The Reliable Transport Protocol (RTP):** Controls sending, tracking, and acknowledging EIGRP messages

- **Diffusing Update Algorithm (DUAL):** Determines the best loop-free route

EIGRP uses three tables:

- The **Neighbor table** is built from EIGRP hellos and is used for reliable delivery.

- The **Topology table** contains EIGRP routing information for best paths and loop-free alternatives.

- EIGRP places best routes from its topology table into the common **Routing table**.

EIGRP Neighbor Establishment

EIGRP uses various message types to initiate and maintain neighbor relationships and to maintain an accurate routing table. It is designed to conserve bandwidth and router resources by sending messages only when necessary and only to those neighbors that need to receive them.

Packet Types

EIGRP uses five packet types:

- **Hello:** Identifies neighbors and serves as a keepalive mechanism

- **Update:** Reliably sends route information

- **Query:** Reliably requests specific route information

- **Reply:** Reliably responds to a query

- **ACK:** Acknowledgment

EIGRP is reliable, but hellos and ACKs are not acknowledged. The acknowledgment to a query is a reply.

If a reliable packet is not acknowledged, EIGRP periodically retransmits the packet to the nonresponding neighbor as a unicast. EIGRP has a window size of one, so no other traffic is sent to this neighbor until it responds. After 16 unacknowledged retransmissions, the neighbor is removed from the neighbor table.

Neighbor Discovery and Route Exchange

When EIGRP first starts on an interface, it goes through a process of neighbor discovery and route exchange as shown in the following steps:

Step 1.   Router A sends out a hello.

Step 2.   Router B sends back a hello and an update containing routing information. EIGRP AS number and K values must match to form a neighbor relationship. Timers do not have to match.

Step 3. Router A acknowledges the update.

Step 4. Router A sends its update.

Step 5. Router B acknowledges.

When two routers are EIGRP neighbors, they use periodic hellos between them as keepalives. Additional route information is sent only if a route is lost or a new route is discovered. A neighbor is considered lost if no hello is received within three hello periods (called the *Hold time*). The default Hello/Hold timers are as follows:

- 5 seconds/15 seconds for multipoint circuits with bandwidth greater than T1 and for point-to-point media

- 60 seconds/180 seconds for multipoint circuits with bandwidth less than or equal to T1

Unicast Neighbors

EIGRP neighbors can also be statically defined using the command **neighbor** {*ipv4-address | ipv6 address*} *interface-type interface-number.* Messages to statically defined neighbors are sent as unicasts rather than multicasts. The neighbor IP address must be in the same subnet as one of the router's own interfaces.

Troubleshooting and Verifying EIGRP Neighbors

You can view the neighbor exchange process using **debug ip eigrp packets** and see the update process in real time using **debug ip eigrp**. You can see the neighbor table with the command **show ip eigrp neighbors** for IPv4 and **show ipv6 eigrp neighbors** for IPv6.

EIGRP Route Selection

EIGRP, as an *advanced* distance vector protocol, has a metric and route selection process that is more complex than other IGPs. The metric has the ability to reflect the actual usability of links within the network and can scale to accommodate today's faster bandwidths. EIGRP can use multiple paths, even if they do not have an equal metric.

EIGRP Metric

The traditional EIGRP metric is composed of

- **Bandwidth:** Minimum path bandwidth, in kb per second

- **Delay:** Cumulative path delay, in 10s of microseconds

- **Load:** Range from 1–255, with 255 being fully loaded

- **Reliability:** Range from 1–255, with 255 being most reliable

These values are associated with each interface and can be seen with the **show interface** command.

MTU and hop count are passed along but not used in the metric calculation.

The EIGRP metric is a 32-bit number calculated using the formula shown in Figure 4-1.

Figure 4-1   EIGRP Traditional Metric Formula

$$metric = 256(k1 \times \frac{10^7}{BW_{min}} + \frac{k2 \times BW_{min}}{256 - load} + k3 \times \sum delays)(\frac{k5}{reliability + k4})$$

The k values are constants with default values of k1 = 1, k2 = 0, k3 = 1, k4 = 0, and k5 = 0. If k5 = 0, the final part of the equation (k5 / [reliability + k4]) is ignored.

If default k values are used, this works out to be 256 * (BW + cumulative delay).

Bandwidth is the largest contributor to the metric. The delay value enables you to choose a more direct path when bandwidth is equivalent.

Wide Metrics

Traditional EIGRP metrics are scaled in a way that does not pick up bandwidth differences in links over 10G and delay differences in links over 1G. (Specifically, the bandwidth value used is actually 10^7/Interface-BW and the delay value actually used is Delay/10.) To address this, EIGRP release 8.0 and later supports *wide metrics*. Wide metrics use the actual, unscaled interface bandwidth reported in kb/sec. Delay is converted to picoseconds and is termed *latency*. Two additional metric values are included: jitter and energy. *Jitter* is variable delay, and *energy* is a measure of battery life for mobile networks. These are controlled via a new constant, k6, which is typically zeroed out. The resulting metric formula is shown in Figure 4-2 and still defaults to bandwidth + delay.

Figure 4-2   EIGRP Wide Metric Formula

$$\left[\left(K_1 \cdot Throughput + \left\{\frac{K_2 \cdot Throughput}{256 - Load}\right\}\right) + (K_3 \cdot Latency) + (K_6 \cdot Ext\ Attrib)\right] \cdot \frac{K_5}{K_4 + Reliability}$$

EIGRP neighbors exchange capability information, and EIGRP has mechanisms to allow both traditional and wide metrics to function in the same network. A mixed network could cause some suboptimal routing and may require some adjustment with redistribution. For details, see the Cisco website for datasheets on wide metrics.

Diffusing Update Algorithm

Diffusing update algorithm (DUAL) is the algorithm used by EIGRP to choose the best loop-free paths. An EIGRP router receives advertisements from each neighbor listing its own metric to a network, plus the path delay and minimum bandwidth. This is the *reported distance*, or RD. The EIGRP router then compares its interface bandwidth and adds its interface delay to calculate its own metric. This is called the *feasible distance*, or FD.

Note

The reported distance (RD) is sometimes called the advertised distance (AD).

The path with the lowest feasible distance is called the *successor* and is submitted to the routing table. Nonsuccessor paths with a lower RD than the FD of the successor path are guaranteed loop-free and called *feasible successors*. They are included in the topology table as backup paths. If the successor path is lost, the router can use a feasible successor immediately without recalculating or risk of loops.

After the router has chosen a path to a network, it is passive for that route. If a successor path is lost and no feasible successor is identified, the router goes active for that route. It sends out queries on all interfaces in an attempt to identify an alternative path. No successor can be chosen until the router receives a reply to all queries. If a neighbor does not reply within 3 minutes, the router becomes stuck in active (SIA). In that case, it resets the neighbor relationship with the neighbor that did not reply.

Three common causes for SIA routes are as follows:

- CPU or memory usage is so high on the neighbor that it cannot process the query or reply.

- The link between the routers drops packets. Enough packets get through to maintain the neighbor relationship, but some queries or replies are dropped.

- Unidirectional link, so the router never receives packets from its neighbor.

Part I: ROUTE

Newer versions of EIGRP use SIA-Queries and SIA-Replies to prevent the loss of a neighbor unnecessarily during SIA conditions. A router sends its neighbor an SIA-Query after no reply to a normal query. If the neighbor responds with an SIA-Reply, the router does not terminate the neighbor relationship after 3 minutes because it knows the neighbor is available, just not able to answer the query.

You can see the active or passive state of a route, its successors, and feasible successors with the command **show ip eigrp topology** or **show ipv6 eigrp topology**.

EIGRP for IPv4

This section examines configuration for EIGRP for IPv4, along with some advanced options and ways to optimize EIGRP.

Basic Configuration

EIGRP for IPv4, commonly called *EIGRPv4*, is configured by entering router configuration mode and using the **network** command to identify the interfaces on which it will run. By default, EIGRP looks for neighbors out any interface with an IP address falling within the networks specified by that command. When setting up EIGRP, an autonomous system number must be used (7 is used in the example). Autonomous system numbers must agree for two routers to form a neighbor relationship and to exchange routes.

```
Router(config)# router eigrp 7
Router(config-router)# network 192.168.1.0
```

The wildcard mask option can be used with the **network** command to more precisely identify EIGRP interfaces. For example, suppose a router has two interfaces—e0/0 (192.168.1.1) and e0/1 (192.168.1.33)—but needs to run EIGRP only on e0/0. Using a **network** command of 192.168.1.0 enables EIGRP on both interfaces, an undesired result. In this case, the following command can be used:

```
Router(config-router)# network 192.168.1.0 0.0.0.1
```

In this instance, a wildcard mask of 0.0.0.1 matches only two IP addresses in network 192.168.1.0–192.168.1.0 and 192.168.1.1. Therefore, only interface e0/0 is included in EIGRP routing.

To include all interfaces into EIGRP routing use **network 0.0.0.0**, which matches all IP addresses.

To ensure that the correct metric is calculated, or to influence the metric, you might want to configure the bandwidth on the interface. Use the **interface** command:

```
R1(config)# interface s0/0/0
R1(config-if)# bandwidth kbps
```

Optimizing the EIGRP Configuration

EIGRP provides some ways to customize its operation, such as passive interface, unicast neighbors, route summarization, unequal-metric load balancing, and authentication. This section describes how to configure these.

Passive Interface

The **passive-interface** command prevents either routing updates or hello messages from being sent out an interface, depending on the protocol. RIP does not send updates when it is enabled; EIGRP and OSPF do not send hellos, and thus they don't discover neighbors or form an adjacency out that interface. To disable the protocol on one interface, use the routing protocol configuration command **passive-interface** *interface*. To turn off the protocol on all interfaces, use **passive-interface default**. Then use **no passive-interface** *interface* for the ones that should run the protocol, as shown here:

```
Router(config)# router eigrp 7
Router(config-router)# passive-interface default
Router(config-router)# no passive-interface e0/0
```

Advertising a Default Route

EIGRP is typically configured to advertise a default route in the following ways:

- Create a static default route and redistribute it into EIGRP.

- Summarize route advertisements to 0.0.0.0 at an interface. Only neighbors out the interface receive the default route advertisement. This is shown in Example 4-1 in the next section.

Summarization

Route summaries are configured manually on an interface. When a summary is produced, a matching route to null0 is automatically placed in the routing table as a loop prevention mechanism. Configure a summary route out a particular interface using the **ip summary-address eigrp** *autonomous_system* command. Example 4-1 advertises a default route out

Part I: ROUTE

GigabitEthernet0/1 and the summary route 172.16.104.0/22 out Serial0/0/0 for EIGRP AS 7.

Example 4-1   Configuring EIGRP Summary Routes

```
Router(config)# int gi0/1
Router(config-if)# ip summary-address eigrp 7 0.0.0.0 0.0.0.0
!
Router(config)# int s0/0/0
Router(config-if)# ip summary-address eigrp 7 172.16.104.0
 255.255.252.0
```

Load Balancing

Like most IP routing protocols, EIGRP automatically load balances over equal metric paths. What makes EIGRP unique is that you can configure it to proportionally load balance over *un*equal metric paths. The **variance** command is used to configure load balancing over up to six loop-free paths that have a metric lower than the product of the variance and the best metric. Figure 4-3 shows routers advertising a path to the network connected to R1.

Figure 4-3   EIGRP Unequal-Cost Load Balancing

FD: 14,869,333
AD: 14,357,333

256k

R4   R5

192k   128k

All links have a
delay of 20000us.

FD: 21,024,000
AD: 2,170,031

R2   192k   R3

576k   1544k

R1

Destination Network

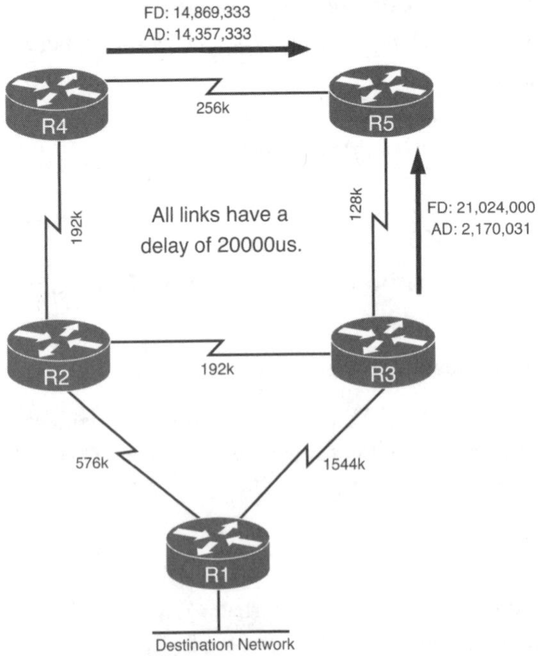

By default, R5 uses the path through R4 because it offers the lowest metric (14,869,333). To set up unequal cost load balancing, assign a variance of 2 under the EIGRP process on R5, which multiplies the best metric of 14,869,333 by 2 to get 29,738,666. R5 then uses all loop-free paths with a metric less than 29,738,666, which includes the path through R3. R5 then sends traffic along each path in proportion to its metric.

```
R5(config)# router eigrp 7
R5(config-router)# variance 2
```

EIGRP Authentication

By default, no authentication is used for any routing protocol. Some protocols, such as RIPv2, IS-IS, and OSPF, can be configured to do simple password authentication between neighboring routers. In this type of authentication, a clear-text password is used. EIGRP does not support simple authentication. However, it can be configured to authenticate each packet exchanged using an MD5 hash created from a preconfigured, shared password. This is more secure than clear text because only the message digest is exchanged, not the password. The password is called the *key*.

EIGRP authenticates each of its packets and verifies the source of each routing update by including the hash in each one. If the hash value does not match, the packet is silently dropped.

To configure the router for EIGRP authentication, follow these steps:

Step 1. Configure a key chain to group the keys.

Step 2. Configure one or more keys within that key chain. The router checks all inbound packets against the list of keys and uses the first valid one it finds.

Step 3. Configure the password or authentication string for that key. Repeat Steps 2 and 3 to add more keys if desired.

Step 4. Optionally configure a lifetime for the keys within that key chain. If you do this, be sure that the time is synchronized between the two routers.

Step 5. Enable authentication and assign a key chain to an interface.

Step 6. Designate MD5 as the type of authentication.

Example 4-2 shows a router configured with EIGRP authentication. It shows configuring a lifetime for packets sent using key 1 that starts at 10:15 and lasts for 300 seconds. It also shows configuring a lifetime for packets received using key 1 that starts at 10:00 and lasts until 10:05. Router clocks must be synchronized when using lifetimes, so use an NTP server.

Part I: ROUTE

Example 4-2   Configuring EIGRP Authentication

```
Router(config)# key chain RTR_Auth
Router(config-keychain)# key 1
Router(config-keychain-key)# key-string Password
Router(config-keychain-key)# send-lifetime 10:15:00 300
Router(config-keychain-key)# accept-lifetime 10:00:00 10:05:00
!
Router(config)# interface e0/0
Router(config-if)# ip authentication mode eigrp 10 md5
Router(config-if)# ip authentication key-chain eigrp 10 RTR_Auth
```

Verify your configuration with the **show key chain** command. **show ip eigrp neighbors** is also useful because no neighbor relationship is formed if authentication fails. Using the **debug eigrp packets** command shows packets containing authentication information sent and received, and it enables you to troubleshoot configuration issues. The debug output lists an authentication mismatch message if authentication does not succeed.

EIGRP Stub Routing

A stub router is connected to no more than two neighbors and should never be a transit router. Stub routing is one way to limit queries. When a router is configured as an EIGRP stub, it notifies its neighbors. The neighbors then do not query that router for a lost route. An EIGRP stub router still receives all routes from its neighbors—turning on stub routing does not cause its neighbor to advertise only a default route. You must manually configure that.

Under router configuration mode, use the command **eigrp stub [receive-only|connected|static|summary|redistributed]**. If you use only the command **eigrp stub**, then the router advertises only connected and summary routes. To change this, use one or more of the options listed in Table 4-1.

Table 4-1   eigrp stub Command Options

Command Option	Effect
receive-only	Prevents the router from advertising any networks, including its own. Cannot be combined with any other option. BE CAREFUL with this option—it will prevent other routers from learning the local routes.
Connected	Enables the router to advertise connected routes. These must either be included in a network statement or redistributed into EIGRP. Enabled by default.

Command Option	Effect
Static	Enables the router to advertise static routes. They must be redistributed into EIGRP before they will be advertised.
Summary	Enables the router to advertise summary routes, both those created manually and automatically. Enabled by default.
Redistributed	Enables the router to advertise routes redistributed into EIGRP from another protocol or AS.

Verify a neighbor router's stub status with the **show ip eigrp neighbor detail** or **show ipv6 eigrp neighbor detail** command.

EIGRP for IPv6

EIGRP has been expanded to support IPv6, although you must verify that your specific version of IOS is capable of doing this. EIGRP for IPv6 is based on the IPv4 version, and the two can run in tandem on the same router and on the same interfaces. EIGRPv6 is still an advanced distance vector routing protocol that uses a complex metric, has a reliable update mechanism, and uses DUAL to retain fallback paths. Like EIGRPv4, it sends multicast hellos every 5 seconds, but the multicast address is now FF02::A. Messages are exchanged using the interface link-local address as the source address.

The router ID must still be in the form of an IPv4 address. If there are no active IPv4 addresses on the router, you must statically assign an ID; it does not need to be a routable address. Like RIPng, there is no **network** command; EIGRP routing is enabled at each interface. After this is accomplished, the router looks for neighbors out that interface and advertises the interface networks by default. Example 4-3 shows how to enable basic IPv6 EIGRP.

Example 4-3   Basic EIGRP IPv6 Commands

```
Router(config)# ipv6 unicast-routing
!
Router(config)# ipv6 router eigrp AS
Router(config-rtr)# router-id ipv4-address
!
Router(config)# interface type number
Router(config-if)# ipv6 eigrp AS
```

IPv6 EIGRP can summarize routes at the interface, and the stub feature is also available, just as with the IPv4 version. Example 4-4 shows a sample

Part I: ROUTE

configuration for IPv6 EIGRP, with both summarization and stub routing enabled. Notice that the routing protocol is enabled under each interface.

Example 4-4   Configuring EIGRP for IPv6

```
Router(config)# ipv6 router eigrp 1
Router(config-rtr)# eigrp router-id 10.255.255.1
Router(config-rtr)# eigrp stub connected summary
!
Router(config)# interface gigbitethernet0/0
Router(config-if)# description Local LAN
Router(config-if)# ipv6 address 2001:DB8:0:10::1/64
Router(config-if)# ipv6 eigrp 1
!
Router(config-if)# interface serial 1/0/1
Router(config-if)# description point-to-point link to Internet
Router(config-if)# ipv6 address 2001:DB8:0:11::2/64
Router(config-if)# ipv6 eigrp 1
Router(config-if)# ipv6 summary address eigrp 1 2001:DB8:0:10::/63
```

Verifying and Troubleshooting EIGRP

The commands for verifying EIGRP differ slightly between IPv4 and IPv6 versions. In the following commands, the first one listed is the IPv4 command and the second one is the IPv6 command:

- **show ip route/show ipv6 route** displays the routing table.

- **show ip route eigrp/show ipv6 route eigrp** filters the routing table and displays only the routes learned from EIGRP.

- **show ip protocols/show ipv6 protocols** verifies autonomous system, timer values, identified networks, and EIGRP neighbors (routing information sources).

- **show ip eigrp topology/show ipv6 topology** shows the EIGRP topology table and identifies successors and feasible successors.

- **show ip eigrp neighbors/show ipv6 neighbors** verifies that the correct routers are neighbors.

- **show ip eigrp traffic/show ipv6 traffic** shows the amount and types of EIGRP messages.

- **show ip eigrp interfaces/show ipv6 eigrp interfaces** lists the interfaces participating in EIGRP and any neighbors located out those interfaces, along with some other statistics.

Like EIGRP for IPv4, troubleshoot EIGRPv6 by looking at the routing table (**show ipv6 route**), by reviewing the routing protocols (**show ipv6 protocols**), and by monitoring neighbors (**show ipv6 eigrp neighbors**).

EIGRP Named Mode

Basic EIGRP separates IPv4 and IPv6 configuration in different places. Group the configuration by using EIGRP in *named* mode. To accomplish this, create a named EIGRP instance, and then all other configuration is given under either an IPv4 or IPv6 address family. You can configure actions such as summary addresses, stub routing, variance, and redistribution. There are three general configuration modes:

- **Address-family:** Configures general settings such as router ID, stub, and network (for IPv4)

- **Address-family Interface:** Configures interface specific settings such as authentication, timers, passive interface, and summary address

- **Address-family Topology:** Configures settings that impact the topology table such as variance, redistribution, and metrics

Example 4-5 shows how named mode can be used to configure EIGRP for both IPv4 and IPv6.

Example 4-5   Configuring EIGRP Named Mode

```
Router(config)# router eigrp CCNP
Router(config-router)# address-family ipv4 autonomous-system 2
Router(config-router-af)# network 0.0.0.0
!
Router(config-router-af)# af-interface default
Router(config-router-af-interface)# passive-interface
!
Router(config-router-af)# af-interface e0/0
Router(config-router-af-interface)# summary-address 172.16.1.0/24
Router(config-router-af-interface)# no passive-interface
!
Router(config-router-af-interface)# topology base
Router(config-router-af-topology)# variance 2
!
Router(config-router)# address-family ipv6 unicast autonomous-
  system 2
Router(config-router-af)# eigrp router-id 1.1.1.1
Router(config-router-af)# eigrp stub
!
```

Example 4-5   Continued

```
Router(config-router-af)# af-interface e0/0
Router(config-router-af-interface)# summary-address
 2001:db8:0:100::/62
!
Router(config-router-af)# topology base
Router(config-router-af-topology)# variance 2
```

EIGRP Over WAN Links

EIGRP can be used across many types of WAN links. This section examines how it operates over some of them.

Layer 3 MPLS WAN

MPLS provides either a Layer 2 or a Layer 3 connection. In MPLS terminology, your WAN edge routers are called *CE* (customer edge) routers, and the ISP's WAN edge routers are called *PE* (provider edge) routers. Within the ISP's network are *P* (provider) routers, but they are not visible to the CE.

PE routers are involved in routing when using EIGRP over Layer 3 MPLS VPNs. Connected PE and CE routers form an EIGRP neighbor relationship. The PE router is just another neighbor to the CE router; it is not aware of the MPLS network or the ISP's P routers.

In Figure 4-4, CE1 creates an EIGRP neighbor relationship with PE1. CE1 sends routing updates about its networks to PE1, which installs the routes in the correct Virtual Routing and Forwarding (VRF) table and then transmits them across the WAN as MPLS packets to PE2. PE2 is an EIGRP neighbor to CE2, so it forwards the route advertisements as normal EIGRP updates.

Figure 4-4   Using EIGRP with Layer 3 MPLS WAN

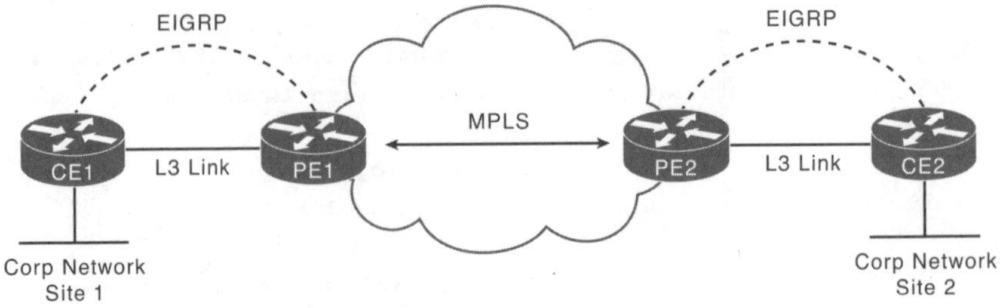

Part I: ROUTE

When using EIGRP over MPLS, the customer and the provider need to use the same basic EIGRP configuration such as AS number and authentication.

Layer 2 WAN

When you use a Layer 2 WAN such as Metro Ethernet or Layer 2 MPLS, each router forms a neighbor relationship with all other CE routers on the WAN link. In reality, each CE router has an Ethernet connection to its local PE router, but the WAN acts as a Layer 2 switch to the CE routers.

Figure 4-5 shows how this works. The PE1 router receives Ethernet frames from CE1; encapsulates them into an MPLS packet (in this case the WAN is MPLS); and then forwards them across the WAN to PE2, which is the local router connected to CE2. PE2 deencapsulates the packet, rebuilds the Ethernet frame, and sends it to the CE2.

Figure 4-5   Using EIGRP with Layer 2 WAN

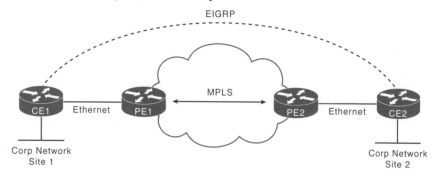

It is important to understand that CE1 and CE2 build an EIGRP neighbor relationship with each other. The ISP routers are not involved in routing with the CE routers. Additionally, the PE routers do not learn any MAC addresses or participate in Spanning Tree.

Frame Relay

An issue with using EIGRP over Frame Relay is that one physical interface can support multiple logical connections, each identified by a Data Link Connection Identifier (DLCI). These are Layer 2 connections and must be mapped to a Layer 3 neighbor IP address. This mapping can be done either dynamically or statically. Multipoint interfaces are used in partial and full mesh topologies.

Part I: ROUTE

Dynamic mapping uses Inverse ARP. Routers form EIGRP neighbor adjacencies only with routers to which they connect via a Frame Relay virtual circuit (VC). Static mapping requires manual configuration under each interface but enables routers without VC connections to become neighbors. The static mapping command is given under interface configuration mode:

```
frame-relay map ip remote-ip-address local-dlci broadcast
```

The **broadcast** keyword is required because Frame Relay is, by default, a nonbroadcast medium. Static mapping can be used with both physical multipoint interfaces and subinterfaces. Note that a multipoint interface stays up if one DLCI is active, so a neighbor loss might not be detected until the Hold timer expires.

Frame Relay can emulate physical point-to-point links by using point-to-point subinterfaces, used in a hub-and-spoke topology. Neighbor loss is detected much more quickly on point-to-point links for two reasons:

- The default timers are shorter: 5 second Hold timer and 15 second Dead timer.

- The subinterface goes down when its associated DLCI goes down.

By default, EIGRP limits itself to bursting to half the link bandwidth. This limit is configurable per interface using the **ip bandwidth-percent** command. The following configuration assumes EIGRP AS 7 and limits EIGRP to one-quarter of the link bandwidth:

```
Router(config)# int s0/0/0
Router(config-if)# ip bandwidth-percent eigrp 7 25
```

The real issue with WAN links is that the router assumes that each link has 1544 kbps bandwidth. If interface Serial0/0/0 is attached to a 128 k fractional T1, EIGRP assumes it can burst to 768 k and could overwhelm the line. This is rectified by correctly identifying link bandwidth:

```
Router(config)# int serial 0/0/0
Router(config-if)# bandwidth 128
```

Figure 4-6 shows a situation in which these techniques can be combined: Frame Relay.

Figure 4-6   EIGRP with Frame Relay

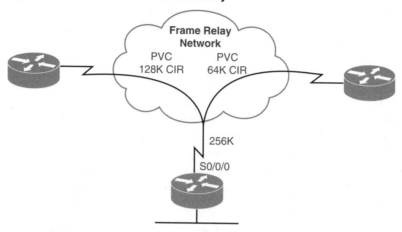

In Figure 4-6, the hub router has a 256 kbps connection to the Frame Relay network and two permanent virtual circuits (PVC) with committed infor-mation rates (CIR) of 128 Kpbs and 64 Kbps. EIGRP divides the interface bandwidth evenly between the neighbors on that interface. What value should be used for the interface bandwidth in this case? The usual sugges-tion is to use the CIR, but the two PVCs have different CIRs. You can use the **bandwidth-percent** command to allow SNMP reporting of the true bandwidth value, while adjusting the interface burst rate to 25 percent, or 64 kbps.

```
Router(config)# int serial 0/0/0
Router(config-if)# bandwidth 256
Router(config-if)# ip bandwidth-percent eigrp 7 25
```

A better solution is to use point-to-point subinterfaces and identify band-width separately. In Example 4-6, s0/0/0.1 bursts to 64 k, and s0/0/0.2 bursts to 32 k, using EIGRP's default value of half the bandwidth.

Example 4-6   Configuring Frame Relay Subinterfaces

```
Router(config)# int serial 0/0/0.1 point-to-point
Router(config-if)# bandwidth 128
Router(config-if)# frame-relay interface-dlci 100
!
Router(config)# int serial 0/0/0.2 point-to-point
Router(config-if)# bandwidth 64
Router(config-if)# frame-relay interface-dlci 101
```

Part I: ROUTE

In cases where the hub interface bandwidth is oversubscribed, it might be necessary to set bandwidth for each subinterface arbitrarily low and then specify an EIGRP bandwidth percent value over 100 to allow EIGRP to use half the PVC bandwidth.

EIGRP Over the Top

EIGRP Over the Top (OTP) is a technique to run EIGRP across a WAN that is transparent to the WAN provider. It does not require route redistribution between BGP and EIGRP on customer edge routers and can be used over any type of WAN link. Location ID Separation Protocol (LISP) encapsulates and routes the EIGRP traffic over the WAN. This feature was introduced in IOS version 15.4(1)T.

Basically, you configure unicast EIGRP neighbors on each CE router, but you must also specify LISP encapsulation for them.

```
Router(config) # router eigrp CCNP
Router(config-router) # address-family ipv4 autonomous-system 2
Router(config-router-af) # neighbor 172.16.1.2 e0/0 lisp-encap 1
```

In large networks with many CE routers, you might want to use EIGRP route reflectors to cut down on the number of EIGRP neighbor relationships that must be maintained. For more information on this, see the documentation at Cisco.com.

CHAPTER 5

OSPF

OSPF Overview

Open Shortest Path First (OSPF) is an open-standard link-state routing protocol that uses the Shortest Path First (SPF) algorithm to determine its best path to each network. OSPFv2 supports IPv4 routing and OSPFv3 supports both IPv4 and IPv6 routing.

Link-state routers create a database that reflects the structure of their area in the network. Link-state routing protocols learn more information on the structure of the network than other routing protocols and thus can make more informed routing decisions.

OSPF routers exchange hellos with each neighbor, learning router ID (RID) and cost. Neighbor information is kept in the Adjacency database. The router then constructs the appropriate link-state advertisements (LSA), which include information such as the RIDs of, and cost to, each neighbor. Each router keeps the complete set of LSAs in the link-state database (LSDB).

Each router runs the SPF algorithm to compute best paths. It then submits these paths for inclusion in the routing table or forwarding database.

OSPF Network Structure

OSPF routing domains are broken up into areas. An OSPF network must contain an Area 0 and might contain other areas. The SPF algorithm runs within an area, and interarea routes are passed between areas. OSPF has a two-level hierarchy: Area 0 is designed as a transit area, and other areas should be attached directly to Area 0 and only to Area 0. The link-state database must be identical for each router in an area. OSPF areas typically contain a maximum of 50 routers to 100 routers, depending on network volatility.

Figure 5-1 shows a network of five routers that has been divided into three areas: Area 0, Area 1, and Area 2.

Figure 5-1   OSPF Areas

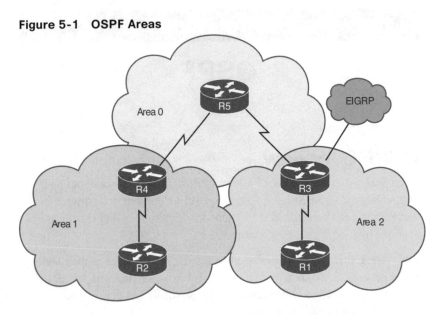

Dividing an OSPF network into areas accomplishes the following:

- Minimizes the number of routing table entries

- Contains LSA flooding to a reasonable area

- Minimizes the impact of a topology change

- Enforces the concept of a hierarchical network design

The following are several types of areas:

- **Backbone area:** Area 0, which is attached to every other area.

- **Regular area:** Nonbackbone area; its database contains both internal and external routes.

- **Stub area:** Its database contains only internal routes, summary routes, and a default route.

- **Totally Stubby Area:** Cisco proprietary area designation. Its database contains routes only for its own area and a default route.

- **Not-so-stubby area (NSSA):** Its database contains internal routes, summary routes, routes redistributed from a connected routing process, and optionally a default route.

- **Totally NSSA:** Cisco proprietary area designation. Its database contains only routes for its own area, routes redistributed from a connected routing process, and a default route.

OSPF defines router roles as well. One router can have multiple roles, such as the following:

- An internal router has all interfaces in one area. In Figure 5-1, Routers R1, R2, and R5 are all internal area routers. They maintain a link-state database for their own area only.

- Backbone routers have at least one interface assigned to Area 0. R3, R4, and R5 are backbone routers.

- An area border router (ABR) has interfaces in two or more areas. In Figure 5-1, R3 and R4 are ABRs. ABRs separate LSA flooding areas, can summarize area routes, and can source default routes. They maintain a link-state database for each area to which they are connected.

- An autonomous system boundary router (ASBR) has interfaces inside and outside the OSPF routing domain. In Figure 5-1, R3 functions as an ASBR because it has an interface in an EIGRP routing domain.

OSPF Metric

OSPF uses a cost value as its metric; in Cisco routers, the cost is based on the interface bandwidth. Routers assign a cost to each interface that is equal to 100 Mbps divided by the interface bandwidth. The cost for each link is then accrued as the route advertisement about that link traverses the network.

This default formula results in a cost of 1 for interfaces with speeds of 100 Mbps and faster. It assigns the same cost to a Fast Ethernet interface and a 10Gigabit Ethernet interface, for example. The cost formula can be adjusted using the **auto-cost** command under the OSPF routing process. Values for bandwidth (in kbps) up to 4,294,967 are permitted (1 Gbps is shown in the following line):

```
Router(config-router)# auto-cost reference-bandwidth 1000
```

The cost can also be manually assigned under the interface configuration mode. The cost is a 16-bit number, so it can be any value from 1 to 65,535.

```
Router(config-if)# ip ospf cost 27
```

Link-State Advertisements

Each router maintains a database, called the *link-state database (LSDB)*, containing the latest received LSAs. A separate LSDB is maintained for each area connected to the router.

Part I: ROUTE

LSA Operation

Each LSA is assigned a sequence number, and a timer is run to age out old LSAs. The default timer is 30 minutes.

When a LSA is received, it's compared to the LSDB. If it is new, it is added to the database and the SPF algorithm is run. If it is from a router ID that is already in the database, the sequence number is compared and older LSAs are discarded. If it is a new LSA, it is incorporated in the database and the SPF algorithm is run. If it is an older LSA, the newer LSA in memory is sent back to whomever sent the old one.

OSPF sequence numbers are 32 bits. The first legal sequence number is 0x80000001. Larger numbers are more recent. The sequence number changes only under two conditions:

- The LSA changes because a route is added or deleted.

- The LSA ages out. (LSA updates are flooded within the area every half hour, even if nothing changes.)

The command **show ip ospf database** shows the age (in seconds) and sequence number for each router.

LSA Types

OSPF uses different types of LSAs to advertise different types of routes, such as internal area or external routing domain. Many of these are represented in the routing table with a distinctive prefix. OSPFv3, for IPv6, has added some LSA types and renamed some others. OSPFv3 LSA types are covered later in the section "OSPF for IPv6."

Table 5-1 describes the LSA types for OSPFv2.

Table 5-1   OSPF LSA Types

Type	Description	Routing Table Symbol
1	Router LSA. Advertises intra-area routes. Generated by each OSPF router. Flooded only within the area.	O
2	Network LSA. Advertises routers on a multi-access link. Generated by a Designated Router (DR). Flooded only within the area.	O
3	Summary LSA. Advertises interarea routes. Generated by an ABR. Flooded to adjacent areas.	O IA

Type	Description	Routing Table Symbol
4	ASBR summary LSA. Advertises the route to an ASBR. Generated by an ABR. Flooded to adjacent areas.	O IA
5	External LSA. Advertises routes in another routing domain. Generated by an ASBR. Flooded to adjacent areas. E1—Metric increased by each router E2—Metric does not increase (the default)	O E1 O E2
6	Group membership LSA. Used in multicast OSPF operations. Not supported by Cisco.	
7	Not-so-stubby area (NSSA) LSA. Advertises routes in another routing domain. Generated by an ASBR within a not-so-stubby area. Flooded only within the NSSA. N1—Metric increased by each router N2—Metric does not increase (the default)	O N1 O N2
8	External attributes LSA. Used in OSPF and BGP interworking.	

OSPF Operation

OSPF uses several different message types to establish and maintain its neighbor relationships and to maintain correct routing information.

OSPF Packets

OSPF uses five packet types. It does not use UDP or TCP for transmitting its packets. Instead, it runs directly over IP (IP protocol 89) using an OSPF header. One field in this header identifies the type of packet being carried. The five OSPF packet types are as follows:

- **Hello:** Identifies neighbors and serves as a keepalive.

- **Link-state request (LSR):** Request for a link-state update (LSU). Contains the type of LSU requested and the ID of the router requesting it.

- **Database description (DBD):** A summary of the LSDB, including the RID and sequence number of each LSA in the LSDB.

Part I: ROUTE

- **Link-state update (LSU):** Contains a full LSA entry. An LSA includes topology information; for example, the RID of this router and the RID and cost to each neighbor. One LSU can contain multiple LSAs.

- **Link-state acknowledgment (LSAck):** Acknowledges all other OSPF packets (except hellos).

OSPF for IPv4 traffic is multicast to either of two addresses: 224.0.0.5 for all OSPF routers or 224.0.0.6 for all OSPF DRs. OSPF for IPv6 routing uses the multicast addresses FF02::5 for all OSPF routers and FF02::6 for all OSPF DRs.

OSPF Neighbor Relationships

OSPF routers send out periodic multicast packets to introduce themselves to other routers on a link. They become neighbors when they see their own router ID included in the Neighbor field of the hello from another router. This signals to each router that they have bidirectional communication. In addition, two routers must be on a common subnet for a neighbor relationship to be formed. (Virtual links are sometimes an exception to this rule.)

Certain parameters within the OSPF hellos must also match for two routers to become neighbors. They include

- Hello/dead timers

- Area ID

- Authentication type and password

- Stub area flag

DBD packets also contain the interface MTU information. This must match on both sides of the link or the neighbor relationship will be stuck in Exstart state.

OSPF routers can be neighbors without being adjacent. However, only adjacent neighbors exchange routing updates and synchronize their databases. On a point-to-point link, an adjacency is established between the two routers when they can communicate. On a multiaccess link, each router establishes an adjacency only with the DR and the backup DR (BDR).

Hellos also serve as keepalives. A neighbor is considered lost if no hello is received within four hello periods (called the dead time). The default hello/dead timers are as follows:

- 10 seconds/40 seconds for LAN and point-to-point interfaces

- 30 seconds/120 seconds for nonbroadcast multiaccess (NBMA) interfaces

These steps show the process of neighbor establishment and route exchange between two OSPF routers:

Step 1. **DOWN state:** OSPF process not yet started, so no hellos sent.

Step 2. **INIT state:** Router sends hello packets out all OSPF interfaces.

Step 3. **Two-way state:** Router receives a hello from another router that contains its own router ID in the neighbor list. All other required elements match, so routers can become neighbors.

Step 4. **Exstart state:** If routers become adjacent (exchange routes), they determine which one starts the exchange process.

Step 5. **Exchange state:** Routers exchange DBDs listing the LSAs in their LSD by RID and sequence number.

Step 6. **Loading state:** Each router compares the DBD received to the contents of its LS database. It then sends an LSR for missing or outdated LSAs. Each router responds to its neighbor's LSR with a link-state update. Each LSU is acknowledged.

Step 7. **Full state:** The LSDB has been synchronized with the adjacent neighbor.

Basic OSPFv2 Configuration

OSPF is configured by entering router configuration mode and identifying the range of interface addresses on which it should run and the areas they are in. When setting up OSPF, a process ID must be used (8 is used in the example), but the process ID does not need to agree on different OSPF devices for them to exchange information. The **network** statement uses a wildcard mask and can specify any range from a single address to all addresses. Unlike EIGRP, the wildcard mask is not optional. The following example shows a router configured as an ABR. Interfaces falling within the 192.168.1.0/24 network are placed in area 0, and interfaces falling within the 172.16.1.0/24 network are placed in area 1.

```
Router(config)# router ospf 8
Router(config-router)# network 192.168.1.0 0.0.0.255 area 0
Router(config-router)# network 172.16.1.0 0.0.0.255 area 1
```

Part I: ROUTE

Alternatively, you can enable OSPF directly on an interface rather than use a **network** statement. This is especially helpful on unnumbered interfaces and enables very granular control over which interfaces run OSPF.

```
Router(config)# int s0/0/0
Router(config-if)# ip ospf 8 area 0
```

The **ip ospf area** interface command takes precedence over a **network** command.

Router ID

The SPF algorithm maps the shortest path between a series of nodes. This causes an issue with IP because an IP router is not identified by a single IP address; its interfaces are. For this reason, a single IP address is designated as the "name" of the router: the router ID (RID).

By default, the RID is the highest loopback IP address. If no loopback addresses are configured, the RID is the highest IP address on an active interface when the OSPF process is started. The RID is selected when OSPF starts and—to maintain network stability—is not changed until the OSPF process restarts. The OSPF process can be restarted by rebooting the router or by using the command **clear ip ospf process**. Either choice affects routing in your network for a period of time and should be used only with caution.

A loopback interface is a virtual interface, so it is more stable than a physical interface for RID use. The loopback address does not need to be included in the OSPF routing process, but if you advertise it, you can ping or trace to it. This is helpful in troubleshooting.

A way to override the default RID selection is to statically assign it using the **ospf router-id** command. Router ID is typically statically assigned for predictability if a process is forced to unexpectedly restart. It does not have to be an actual IP address used by the router, but best practice is to use a loopback interface address.

```
Router(config)# router ospf 8
Router(config-router)# router-id 10.0.0.1
```

Verifying and Troubleshooting OSPF

You can view the neighbor initialization process using the **debug ip ospf adj** command. You can see the neighbor table with **show ip ospf neighbors**, which also identifies adjacency status and reveals the designated router and backup designated router. Use the **debug ip ospf packet** command to view all OSPF packets in real time.

Often, the first place you notice OSPF issues is when inspecting the routing table: **show ip route**. To filter the routing table and show only the routes learned from OSPF, use **show ip route ospf**.

The command **show ip protocols** offers a wealth of information for any routing protocol issue. Use this command to verify parameters, timer values, identified networks, and OSPF neighbors (routing information sources).

Use **show ip ospf** to verify the RID, timers, and counters. Because wildcard masks sometimes incorrectly group interfaces to areas, another good place to check is **show ip ospf interface**. This shows the interfaces on which OSPF runs and their current correct assigned area.

OSPF Network Types

The SPF algorithm builds a directed graph—paths made up of a series of points connected by direct links. One of the consequences of this directed-graph approach is that the algorithm has no way to handle a multiaccess network, such as an Ethernet segment. The solution used by OSPF is to elect one router, called the *designated router* (DR), to represent the entire segment. Point-to-point links fit the SPF model perfectly and don't need any special modeling method. On a point-to-point link, no DR is elected and all traffic is multicast to 224.0.0.5.

OSPF supports five network types:

- **NBMA:** Default for multipoint serial interfaces and physical frame relay interfaces. RFC-compliant mode that uses DRs and requires manual neighbor configuration.

- **Point-to-multipoint (P2MP):** Doesn't use DRs so adjacencies increase logarithmically with routers. Resilient RFC-compliant mode that automatically discovers neighbors.

- **Point-to-multipoint nonbroadcast (P2MNB):** Proprietary mode that is used on Layer 2 facilities where dynamic neighbor discovery is not supported. Requires manual neighbor configuration.

- **Broadcast:** Default mode for LANs. Uses DRs and automatic neighbor discovery. Proprietary when used on WAN interface.

- **Point-to-point (P2P):** Proprietary mode that discovers neighbors and doesn't require a DR.

If the default interface type is unsatisfactory, you can statically configure it with the command **ip ospf network** under interface configuration mode:

```
Router(config-if)# ip ospf network network-type
```

When using the NBMA or P2MP nonbroadcast mode, neighbors must be manually defined under the routing process:

```
Router(config-router)# neighbor 172.16.0.1
```

The command **show ip ospf interface** displays the network type for each link.

Designated Routers

On a multiaccess link, one of the routers is elected as a DR and another as a backup DR (BDR). All other routers on that link become adjacent only to the DR and BDR, not to each other. (They stop at the two-way state.) The DR is responsible for creating and flooding a network LSA (type 2) advertising the multiaccess link. NonDR (DROTHER) routers communicate with DRs using the IP address 224.0.0.6. The DRs use IP address 224.0.0.5 to pass information to other routers.

The DR and BDR are elected as shown in the following steps:

Step 1. A router starting the OSPF process listens for OSPF hellos. If none are heard within the dead time, it declares itself the DR.

Step 2. If hellos from any other routers are heard, the router with the highest OSPF priority is elected DR and the election process starts again for BDR. A priority of zero removes a router from the election.

Step 3. If two or more routers have the same OSPF priority, the router with the highest RID is elected DR and the election process starts again for BDR.

After a DR is elected, elections do not take place again unless the DR or BDR are lost. Because of this, the DR is sometimes the first device that comes online with a nonzero priority.

The best way to control DR election is to set OSPF priority for the DR and BDR for other routers. The default priority is 1. A priority of 0 means that a router cannot act as DR or BDR; it can be a DROTHER only. Priority can be set with the **ip ospf priority** command in interface configuration mode.

```
Router(config)# int gi0/1
Router(config-if)# ip ospf priority 2
```

Verify the DR and BDR election with the **show ip ospf neighbor** command as shown in Example 5-1.

Example 5-1   The show ip ospf neighbor Command

```
Router# show ip ospf neighbor
Neighbor ID   Pri   State      Dead Time   Interface ID   Interface
4.4.4.4       1     FULL/DR    00:00:38    3              Ethernet0/0
3.3.3.3       1     FULL/BDR   00:00:36    4              Ethernet0/1
```

Nonbroadcast Multiaccess Networks

Routing protocols assume that multiaccess links support broadcast and have full-mesh connectivity from any device to any device. In terms of OSPF, this means the following:

- Frame Relay map statements should include the broadcast attribute.

- The DR and BDR should have full virtual circuit connectivity to all other devices.

- Hub-and-spoke environments should either configure the DR as the hub or use point-to-point subinterfaces, which require no DR. Use OSPF priority 0 to prevent spokes from becoming DR.

- Partial-mesh environments should be configured using point-to-point subinterfaces, especially when no single device has full connectivity to all other devices. If there is a subset of the topology with full connectivity, that subset can use a multipoint subinterface.

- Full-mesh environments can be configured using the physical interface, but often logical interfaces are used to take advantage of the other benefits of subinterfaces.

- Statically identifying neighbor IP addresses might be necessary.

OSPF over Layer 2 and Layer 3 MPLS

A Layer 2 Multiprotocol Label Switching (MPLS) connection provides logical mesh connectivity at Layer 2 and OSPF operates just as it would on an Ethernet network. It forms a neighbor relationship with the customer edge (CE) router across the WAN, and they elect a DR and BDR. The OSPF network type is multiaccess broadcast.

A Layer 3 MPLS virtual private network (VPN) requires that the CE routers form an OSPF neighbor relationship with their connected provider edge (PE) router. The PE router appears to the enterprise as just another router within their network. The OSPF network type is determined by the type of link between the CE and PE. Carefully consider your area design when using this type of WAN.

Advanced OSPF Configuration

OSPF provides many different ways to customize its operation to fit your network needs. This section discusses route summarization, passive interfaces, default routes, stub areas, and virtual links.

OSPF Summarization

Summarization helps all routing protocols scale to larger networks, but OSPF especially benefits because its processes tax the router memory and CPU resources. OSPF's multiple databases use more memory the larger they are. Summarization decreases the number of routes exchanged, and thus the size of the databases. Summarization localizes the impact of a topology change. It prevents topology changes from being passed outside an area and thus saves routers in other areas from having to run the SPF algorithm. One disadvantage is that summarization hides information, and any time you hide data you decrease the router's capability to make informed routing decisions.

Unlike EIGRP, OSPF can only summarize routes on specific routers—ABRs and ASBRs. There are two types of summarizations:

- Inter-area (LSA type 3) route summarizations are created on the ABR under the OSPF routing process using the **area range** command. A summary route is advertised as long as at least one subnet within the summary is active in the area. The summary route's metric is the lowest cost route within the summary range. The router automatically creates a static route for the summary, pointing to Null0.

  The following command advertises 172.16.0.0/12 from Area 1:

  ```
  Router(config-router)# area 1 range 172.16.0.0 255.240.0.0
  ```

- External (LSA type 5) route summarization is done on an ASBR using the **summary-address** command under the OSPF routing process. It can also be done on the ABR of a NSSA to summarize type 7 routes before advertising them as type 5. The router automatically creates a static route for the summary, pointing to Null0. The following configuration summarizes a range of external routes to 192.168.0.0/16 and injects a single type 5 route into OSPF:

```
Router(config-router)#summary-address 192.168.0.0 255.255.0.0
```

Passive Interface

The **passive-interface** command prevents OSPF from sending hello messages out an interface. Thus, an OSPF router does not discover neighbors or form an adjacency out that interface. To disable the protocol on one interface, use the routing protocol configuration command **passive-interface** *interface*. To turn off the protocol on all interfaces, use **passive-interface default**. Then use **no passive-interface** *interface* for the ones that should run the protocol.

OSPF Default Routes

Default routes are a special type of summarization; they include all networks in one route announcement. By reducing routing information to a minimum, a default route provides such benefits as the following:

- Routers have a smaller routing table.

- Less use of router resources to advertise multiple routes.

- Routers do not need to keep information on external routes.

A default route is injected into OSPF as a *type 5 route*. There are several ways to use the router IOS to place a default route into OSPF. The best-known way is to use the **default-information** command under the OSPF routing process. This command, without the keyword **always**, advertises a default route learned from another source (such as a static route) into OSPF. If the **always** keyword is present, OSPF advertises a default even if that route does not already exist in the routing table. The **metric** keyword sets the starting metric for this route.

```
Router(config-router)# default-information originate [always]
  [metric metric]
```

Alternatively, a default summary route can also be produced using the **summary-address** command or the **area range** command. These commands can cause the router to advertise a default route pointing to itself.

Stub and Not-So-Stubby Areas

Another way to reduce the route information advertised is to create a *stub* area. Configuring a stub area forces its ABR to drop all external (type 5) routes and replaces them with a default route. To limit routing information even more, an area can be made *Totally Stubby* using the **no-summary** keyword on the ABR only. In that case, all interarea and external routes are dropped by the ABR and replaced by a default route. The default route starts with a cost of 1; to change it, use the **area default-cost** command. The example that follows shows Area 2 configured as a Totally Stubby Area, and the default route injected with a cost of 5:

```
Router(config-router)# area 2 stub no-summary
Router(config-router)# area 2 default-cost 5
```

Stub areas are attractive because of their low overhead. They do have some limitations, including the following:

- Stub areas can't include a virtual link.

- Stub areas can't include an ASBR.

- Stubbiness must be configured on all routers in the area.

- Area 0 cannot be a stub area.

Another kind of stub area is a *not-so-stubby area (NSSA)*. NSSA is like a stub or totally stub area but enables an ASBR within the area. External routes are advertised as type 7 routes by the ASBR. The ABR converts them to type 5 external routes when it advertises them into adjacent areas. NSSA is configured with the **area nssa** command under the OSPF routing process. The **no-summary** keyword on the ABR configures the area as *Totally NSSA*; this is a Cisco proprietary feature. By default, the ABR does not inject a default route back into an NSSA area. Use the **default-information-originate** keyword on the ABR or ASBR to create this route:

```
Router(config-router)# area 7 nssa [no-summary]
  [default-information-originate]
```

Virtual Links

OSPF requires that all areas be connected to Area 0 and that Area 0 must be contiguous. When this is not possible, you can use a virtual link to bridge across an intermediate area. Virtual links provide the following:

- Connect areas that do not have a physical link to Area 0. (This should be a temporary solution.)

- Connect a discontiguous Area 0—when merging two company networks, for instance. (This should also be a temporary solution.)

Figure 5-2 shows a virtual link connecting two portions of the backbone Area 0.

Figure 5-2   OSPF Virtual Link

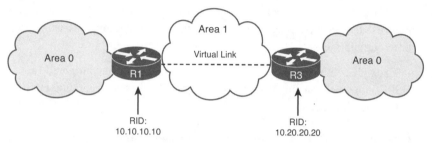

Area 1 is the transit area for the virtual link. Configure each end of a virtual link on the ABRs of the transit area with the command **area** *area-number* **virtual-link** *router-id*. Each end of the link is identified by its RID, *not* its interface IP address. The area listed in the command is the transit area, *not* the area being joined by the link. The configuration for router R1 is

```
R1(config)# router ospf 1
R1(config-router)# area 1 virtual-link 10.20.20.20
```

The configuration for router R3 is

```
R3(config)# router ospf 1
R3(config-router)# area 1 virtual-link 10.10.10.10
```

Verify whether the virtual link is up with the **show ip ospf virtual-links** command. Additionally, virtual interfaces are treated as actual interfaces by the OSPF process, and thus, their status can be verified with the **show ip ospf interface** *interface-id* command.

OSPF Authentication

By default, the router does no routing protocol authentication. For security purposes, you can configure OSPF to authenticate every OSPF packet and the source of every OSPF routing update. OSPF supports two types of authentication:

- Simple (plain text) authentication

- MD5 authentication

Example 5-2 shows a router configured for simple password authentication in OSPF Area 0, using a password (or *key*) of "simple." Note that authentication commands are configurable under the OSPF process and the interface configuration. Use the OSPF process configuration mode to enable authentication for all interfaces within an area. You must still configure a password at the interface mode when you use this command. Use the interface configuration mode to enable authentication on a specific interface only. All OSPF neighbors reachable through an interface configured for authentication must use the same password. You can, however, use different passwords for different interfaces.

In Example 5-2, interface gi0/1, which is in Area 2, is also configured for OSPF authentication and a password of "simple." This configuration is given at the interface mode.

Example 5-2   OSPF Simple Password Authentication

```
Router(config-if)# router ospf 1
Router(config-router)# area 0 authentication
!
Router(config)# int gi0/0
Router(config-if)# ip ospf authentication-key simple
!
Router(config)# int gi0/1
Router(config-if)# ip ospf authentication-key simple
Router(config-if)# ip ospf authentication
```

Example 5-3 shows the same router configured for OSPF MD5 authentication for Area 0, using a password of "secure." Note that the commands are slightly different. The optional keyword **message-digest** is required in two of the commands, and a key number must be specified. Any neighbors reachable through the Gi0/0 interface must also be configured with the same key.

Interface gi0/1, which is in Area 2, is also configured for OSPF authentication and a password of "secure." This configuration is given at the interface mode.

Example 5-3   OSPF MD5 Authentication

```
Router(config-if)# router ospf 1
Router(config-router)# area 0 authentication message-digest
!
Router(config-router)# int gi0/0
Router(config-if)# ip ospf message-digest-key 2 md5 secure
!
Router(config-router)# int gi0/1
```

```
Router(config-if)# ip ospf message-digest-key 2 md5 secure
Router(config-if)# ip ospf authentication message-digest
```

Use the following commands to verify and troubleshoot OSPF authentication:

- **debug ip ospf adj:** The debug shows an error message if there is a key mismatch.

- **show ip ospf neighbor:** If a neighbor relationship has been established, you can assume the authentication worked properly.

- **show ip route:** Verify whether route information is being exchanged between the two authenticating routers.

OSPF for IPv6

OSPFv3, which supports IPv6 routing, is a link-state routing protocol that uses the Dijkstra algorithm to select paths just like OSPFv2. Whereas OSPFv2 uses IPv4 as its transport, OSPFv3 uses IPv6. Neighbors peer using their link-local addresses.

OSPFv3 routers have the following characteristics:

- Use the same packet types as OSPFv2

- Form neighbors in the same way

- Flood and age LSAs identically

- Support the same topologies and techniques, such as NSSA and on-demand circuits

OSPFv3 differs from its predecessors principally in its new address format. OSPFv3 advertises using multicast addresses FF02::5 and FF02::6 but uses its link-local address as the source address of its advertisements. This means that OSPF can form adjacencies with neighbor routers that are not on the same global subnet. Multiple instances of OSPFv3 can run on each link. Authentication relies on the underlying IPsec capabilities of IPv6 but still requires configuration.

OSPFv3 configuration is similar to RIPng and EIGRP. The routing process is created and routing properties are assigned to it. As with EIGRP, the router ID must be in 32-bit dotted-decimal format, like an IPv4 address. If you do not manually set a router ID, then OSPF chooses one from IPv4 addresses currently active on the router. If there are no IPv4 addresses,

Part I: ROUTE

OSPF fails. Interfaces are associated with the OSPF process under interface configuration mode.

Interarea route summarizations still use the **area range** command. External route summarizations employ the command **summary-prefix**, a small change from OSPFv2.

OSPFv3 LSAs

OSPFv3 has renamed two of the LSAs and added two. Network Summary LSAs are now called *Interarea Prefix LSAs*. ASBR Summary LSAs are now called *Interarea Router LSAs*. A Link LSA and an Intra-area Prefix LSA have been added.

LSA type codes are now written in hexadecimal and include flooding scope information. If the first bit is 0, the LSA is only flooded on the local link—this is used by the new Link LSA. If it is 2, then it is flooded within an area—this is used by the majority of LSA types. The number 4 indicates that it is flooded domain-wide and is used by External LSAs. Table 5-2 shows the OSPFv3 LSAs.

Table 5-2   OSPFv3 LSAs

Type	Description
0x2001	Router LSA. Advertises the router's links. Generated by each OSPF router. Flooded only within the area.
0x2002	Network LSA. Advertises routers on a multiaccess link. Generated by the DR. Flooded only with the area.
0x2003	Interarea Prefix LSA. Advertises interarea routes. Generated by an ABR. Flooded to adjacent areas.
0x2004	Interarea Router LSA. Advertises the route to an ASBR. Generated by ABRs on behalf of an ASBR. Flooded to adjacent areas.
0x4005	AS-External LSA. Advertises routes in another routing domain. Generated by an ASBR. Flooded to adjacent areas. E1—Metric increased by each router E2—Metric does not increase (the default)
0x2006	Group Membership LSA.
0x2007	NSSA External LSA. Advertises routes in another routing domain. Generated by an ASBR in a not-so-stubby area. Flooded only within the NSSA area. N1—Metric increased by each router N2—Metric does not increase (the default)

Type	Description
0x0008	Link LSA. Advertises the link-local address and all prefixes associated with that link. Generated by each OSPF router. Flooded only on the local link.
0x2009	Intra-area Prefix LSA. Associates routes with a transit network link by referencing a Network LSA or associates routes with a router by referencing a Router LSA. Flooded only within the area.

Traditional OSPFv3 Configuration

There are two sets of commands for configuring OSPFv3. The traditional set includes the term "ipv6" as part of the command. If you are also using OSPFv2 for IPv4, that process runs separately from the IPv6 process and must be configured separately. It can run concurrently with OSPFv2 because each version maintains its own databases and runs a separate SPF calculation.

Assuming that **ipv6 unicast-routing** and interface IPv6 addresses are already in place, the commands to implement traditional OSPFv3 are shown in Example 5-4.

Example 5-4   Example Commands for OSPFv3

```
Router(config)# ipv6 router ospf process-id
Router(config-rtr)# router-id 32bit-address
!
Router(config-rtr)# interface type number
Router(config-if)# ipv6 ospf process-id area area
```

As illustrated in Example 5-5, route summarization is still configured under the OSPF routing process. Note that the router ID is still a 32-bit number, shown here in the form of an IPv4 address. Stub routing is also configured under the routing process, using the same commands as with OSPFv2. The default costs and interface priorities can be overridden at each interface. Example 5-5 shows how these commands might look on an actual router.

Example 5-5   Configuring Traditional IPv6 Routing

```
Router(config)# ipv6 unicast-routing
!
!Create the OSPFv3 process, assign router ID, create a summary
 router, and configure Area 1 as a stub area
Router(config)# ipv6 router ospf 1
Router(config-rtr)# router-id 10.255.255.1
```

Example 5-5 Continued

```
Router(config-rtr)# area 1 range 2001:db8:1::/80
Router(config-rtr)# area 1 stub no summary
!
!Assign interface e0/0 to Area 1 with a cost of 10 and a DR priority
 of 20
Router(config-rtr)# interface e0/0
Router(config-if)# ipv6 address 2001:db8:1:1::2/64
Router(config-if)# ipv6 ospf 1 area 1
Router(config-if)# ipv6 ospf cost 10
Router(config-if)# ipv6 ospf priority 20
!
!Assign interface s1/0/0 to Area 0
Router(config-if)# interface serial 1/0/0
Router(config-if)# ipv6 address 2001:db8:1:5::1/64
Router(config-if)# ipv6 ospf 1 area 0
```

Troubleshooting OSPFv3 is similar to troubleshooting OSPFv2. Start by looking at **show ipv6 route** to verify whether routes have been advertised. Assuming the route is in the routing table, test reachability using **ping ipv6**. You can also look at the OSPF setup using **show ipv6 ospf** *process* **interface**, **show ipv6 ospf**, or **show ipv6 ospf database**.

New OSPFv3 Configuration

The newer method of OSPFv3 configuration runs both protocols in the same OSPF process and enables you to consolidate some of the configuration. Available starting in IOS release 15.1(3)S, it uses the term "ospfv3" in its configuration commands.

The following are some other features:

- A single OSPF process supports both IPv4 and IPv6 routing.

- This process uses a single OSPF database that has both IPv4 and IPv6 information.

- Routing is enabled under the interface for both IPv4 and IPv6—no more **network** commands.

- The **address-family** command is used for v4- or v6-specific configuration.

- Stub area configuration affects both v4 and v6.

Assuming that **ipv6 unicast-routing** and interface addresses are already in place, the commands to implement the new method of OSPFv3 are shown in Example 5-6. You do not actually have to explicitly create the routing process—it is created automatically when you enable OSPFv3 routing on an interface. However, it is useful when you need to add configuration under the process.

Example 5-6 Configuring IPv4 and IPv6 Routing Using OSPFv3

```
!Enable and configure OSPFv3 for both IPv4 and IPv6 routing:
Router(config)# router ospfv3 1
Router(config-router)# router-id 10.10.10.10
Router(config-router)# area 2 stub
!
Router(config-router)# address-family ipv4 unicast
Router(config-router-af)# passive-interface lo0
!
Router(config-router)# address-family ipv6 unicast
Router(config-router-af)# area 1 range 2001:db8:0:110::/60
!
!Enable OSPF for both IPv4 and IPv6 on the interfaces:
Router(config-if)# int e0/0
Router(config-if)# ospfv3 1 ipv4 area 0
Router(config-if)# ospfv3 1 ipv6 area 0
!
Router(config-if)# int e0/1
Router(config-if)# ospfv3 1 ipv4 area 2
Router(config-if)# ospfv3 1 ipv6 area 2
```

Verify many of the same commands as you would normally use with OSPF for IPv4 and IPv6, such as **show ip route** and **show ipv6 route**. However, to see both IPv4 and IPv6 neighbors, you must use **show ospfv3 neighbors,** and to see only IPv4 OSPF routes, use **show ip route ospfv3**. Use the command **show ospfv3 database** to see the combined v4 and v6 database. Example 5-7 shows the OSPFv3 neighbor database—note that it lists both IPv4 and IPv6 neighbors.

Example 5-7 The show ospfv3 neighbors Command

```
Router# show ospfv3 neighbor

      OSPFv3 1 address-family ipv4 (router-id 10.10.10.10)
```

Part I: ROUTE

Example 5-7 Continued

```
Neighbor ID  Pri  State     Dead Time   Interface ID   Interface
4.4.4.4        1  FULL/DR   00:00:31    3              Ethernet0/0
3.3.3.3        1  FULL/BDR  00:00:31    4              Ethernet0/1


        OSPFv3 1 address-family ipv6 (router-id 10.10.10.10)


Neighbor ID  Pri  State     Dead Time   Interface ID   Interface
4.4.4.4        1  FULL/DR   00:00:38    3              Ethernet0/0
3.3.3.3        1  FULL/BDR  00:00:39    4              Ethernet0/1
```

CHAPTER 6

Advanced Routing Techniques

There are times when you need to go beyond just turning on a routing protocol in your network. You might need to control exactly which routes are advertised or redistributed or which paths are chosen. You might also be required to use multiple routing protocols. Network performance can suffer when routing is not optimized. Excessive routing updates lead to extra CPU usage because of the amount of routing information and the frequency of updates. Running multiple protocols requires extra router resources and might result in suboptimal paths. Incorrectly configured route filters can lead to routing issues.

A good routing plan requires a sound design. Design IP addresses that can be summarized, and use techniques such as redistribution and passive interfaces appropriately.

Controlling Routing Updates

When a routing update arrives at a router's interface, the router checks to see whether a route filter is associated with that interface. If not, the update processes normally. If there is a filter, the router checks for an entry matching the update. If there is no matching entry, the update is dropped. If a matching entry exists, the router processes the update based on instructions in the filter.

Cisco IOS provides several ways to control routing updates:

- Route maps
- Prefix lists
- Distribute lists
- Passive interface

Route Maps

Route maps are a bit like programs that use an if/then/else decision-making capability. They match traffic against certain conditions and then set specified options for that traffic. Each statement has a sequence number, statements are read from the lowest number to highest, and the router stops reading when it gets a match. The sequence number can be used to insert or delete statements. Like an access list, there is an implicit "deny" at the end of each route map; any traffic not matched with a route map statement is denied. Some uses for route maps include:

- **Filtering redistributed routes:** Use the **route-map** keyword in the **redistribute** command.

- **Policy-based routing:** To specify which traffic should be policy routed, based on very granular controls.

- **Setting BGP policy:** To control routing updates and manipulate path attributes.

Route Map Syntax

Route maps are created with the global command:

```
Router(config)# route-map {tag} permit | deny [sequence_number]
```

Each statement in a route map begins this same way, with the same route map name but different sequence numbers, and with match and set conditions below it. *Permit* means that any traffic meeting the criteria of the match conditions is processed by the route map statement. *Deny* means that any traffic matching the match conditions is *not* processed by the route map statement; the router simply proceeds to the next route map statement.

Route Map Match and Set Conditions

Each route map statement can have zero to multiple **match** and **set** conditions. If no **match** condition exists, the statement matches anything, similar to a "permit any" in an access list. If there is no **set** condition, the matching traffic is either permitted or denied, with no other conditions being set.

Multiple match conditions on the same line use a logical OR. For example, the router interprets **match a b c** as "match a or b or c." Multiple match conditions on different lines use a logical AND. For example, the router interprets the following route map statement as "match a and b and c":

```
route-map Logical-AND permit 10
 match a
 match b
 match c
```

In route redistribution, some common conditions to match include

- **ip address:** Refers the router to an access list that permits or denies networks.

- **ip address prefix-list:** Refers the router to a prefix list that permits or denies IP prefixes.

- **ip next-hop:** Refers the router to an access list that permits or denies next-hop IP addresses.

- **ip route-source:** Refers the router to an access list that permits or denies advertising router IP addresses.

- **as-path:** Refers the router to an AS-path access list.

- **length:** Permits or denies packets based on their length in bytes.

- **metric:** Permits or denies routes with the specified metric from being redistributed.

- **route-type:** Permits or denies redistribution of the route type listed, such as internal or external.

- **tag:** Routes can be labeled (tagged) with a number, and route maps can look for that number.

In route redistribution, some common conditions to set include

- **metric:** Sets the metric for redistributed routes

- **metric-type:** Sets the type, such as E1 for OSPF

- **tag:** Tags a route with a number that can be matched later by other route maps

Controlling Route Redistribution Using Route Maps

Example 6-1 shows a route map named BGP-LP with three statements that control which routes to redistribute from OSPF into BGP. The router has already been configured with two access lists, numbered 23 and 103 (not shown). The first route map statement, with sequence number 10, is a *permit* statement. The **match** condition orders it to use access list 23. Any traffic permitted by access list 23 matches this statement and is redistributed into BGP. Any traffic explicitly denied by access list 23 is not redistributed into BGP. The **set** condition tells it to set a BGP local preference of 200 for all traffic that matches statement 10. Traffic not matching access list 23 is checked against the second route map statement.

The second route map statement, sequence number 20, is a *deny* statement that matches access list 103. Any traffic permitted by access list 103 is denied by this statement and thus will not be redistributed. Any traffic explicitly denied by access list 103 is ignored by this statement and checked against the next route map statement. This route map statement has no **set** conditions. Traffic not matching route map statements 10 or 20 is checked against statement 30.

The third route map statement, sequence number 30, is a *permit* statement with no **match** or **set** conditions. This statement matches everything and sets nothing, thus permitting all other traffic without changing it. Without this statement, all other traffic is denied.

Finally, the route map is applied to the redistribution command to filter routes redistributed from OSPF into BGP.

Example 6-1   Controlling Redistribution Using a Route Map

```
Router(config)# route-map BGP-LP permit 10
Router(config-route-map)# match ip address 23
Router(config-route-map)# set local-preference 200
Router(config-route-map)# !
Router(config-route-map)# route-map BGP-LP deny 20
Router(config-route-map)# match ip address 103
Router(config-route-map)# !
Router(config-route-map)# route-map BGP-LP permit 30
!
Router(config)# router bgp 65001
Router(config-router)# redistribute ospf 1 route-map BGP-LP
```

Tagging Routes Using a Route Map

Another use for a route map is to tag routes as they are redistributed from one protocol to another. You can then deny tagged routes from being redistributed back into the original protocol. For example, suppose you are mutually redistributing routes between OSPF and EIGRP. You can tag EIGRP routes as you redistribute them into OSPF. Then when you redistribute OSPF routes back into EIGRP, you can deny those tagged routes. Example 6-2 shows the commands to accomplish this.

Example 6-2 Tagging Redistributed Routes

```
Router(config)# route-map EIGRP2OSPF deny 5
Router(config-route-map)# match tag 1
Router(config-route-map)# route-map EIGRP2OSPF permit 10
Router(config-route-map)# set tag 2
!
Router(config)# route-map OSPF2EIGRP deny 5
Router(config-route-map)# match tag 2
!
Router(config-route-map)# route-map OSPF2EIGRP permit 10
Router(config-route-map)# set tag 1
!
Router(config)# router eigrp 1
Router(config-router)# redistribute ospf 2 route-map OSPF2EIGRP
 metric 1 1 1 1 1500
!
Router(config-router)# router ospf 2
Router(config-router)# redistribute eigrp 1 route-map EIGRP2OSPF
subnets
```

Prefix Lists

A prefix list matches both the subnet, or *prefix*, and the number of bits in the subnet mask. Similar to an access list, it consists of one or more statements permitting or denying prefixes. Routers evaluate the prefix statements in order, stopping if they find a match. There is an implicit "deny all" at the end of the prefix list. The command syntax is as follows:

```
ip prefix-list {list-name [seq-number] {permit | deny} network/
 length [ge ge-length] [le le-length]
```

The meaning of each command field is detailed in Table 6-1.

Table 6-1 ip prefix-list Command

Command Field	Meaning
list-name	Gives a name to the prefix list. Prefix lists are named, not numbered.
seq-number	[Optional] Assigns a sequence number to the prefix list statement. Statements are numbered in increments of 5 by default, enabling a statement to be inserted between two others by using the **seq** option.

Table 6-1 Continued

Command Field	Meaning
deny | **permit**	Denies or permits the matching prefix.
network/length	Configures the prefix and number of bits that must be matched. If no **ge** or **le** option is given, the length also equals the length of the subnet mask.
ge *ge-length*	[Optional] Stands for "greater than or equal to." Specifies the minimum number of bits a subnet mask must have to match the statement.
le *le-length*	[Optional] Stands for "lesser than or equal to." Specifies the maximum number of bits a subnet mask can have to match the statement.

Some sample prefix lists include

- **ip prefix-list CCNP permit 0.0.0.0/0:** Permits only a default route.

- **ip prefix-list CCNP permit 0.0.0.0/0 le 32:** Permits all routes (equivalent to a "permit any" in an access list). The prefix 0.0.0.0/0 means that none of the prefix bits must be matched. "Le 32" means that the subnet mask must be less than or equal to 32. Thus, any network will match this statement.

- **ip prefix-list CCNP permit 0.0.0.0/0 ge 32:** Permits only host routes. The prefix 0.0.0.0/0 means that none of the prefix bits must be matched. "Ge 32" means that the subnet mask must be exactly 32 bits, thus this statement matches only host routes.

- **ip prefix-list CCNP permit 10.0.0.0/8 ge 24 le 24:** Permits any route whose first 8 bits equal 10, with a subnet mask of exactly 24 bits.

Prefix lists can also be used within a route map to control redistribution of networks. They can also be applied to a BGP neighbor to filter routing updates to that neighbor.

Distribute Lists

A distribute list enables you to filter both routing updates and routes being redistributed, through the use of an access list. Configure an access list that permits the routes to be advertised or redistributed, and then link that access list to the routing process with the **distribute-list** command, given under router configuration mode. This command has two options:

- **distribute-list** *access-list* **in:** Filters updates as they come into an interface. For OSPF, this controls routes placed in the routing table but not the database. For other protocols, this controls the routes the protocol knows about.

- **distribute-list** *access-list* **out:** Filters updates going out of an interface and updates being redistributed out of another routing protocol into this one.

Passive Interfaces

Using the **passive-interface** command is another way to control routing updates because it prevents any updates from sending out an interface that is marked as passive. OSPF and EIGRP do not send hello messages out a passive interface, and thus do not discover any neighbors. RIP does not send updates out a passive interface but listens for inbound updates. Chapter 4, "EIGRP," and Chapter 5, "OSPF," have more in-depth descriptions of this command.

Using Multiple Routing Protocols

There are several reasons you might need to run multiple routing protocols in your network:

- Migrating from one routing protocol to another, where both protocols will run in the network temporarily

- Applications that run under certain routing protocols but not others

- Areas of the network under different administrative control

- A multivendor environment where not all devices in the network support the desired protocol

Configuring Route Redistribution

Route redistribution is used when routing information must be exchanged among the different protocols or routing domains. Only routes that are in the routing table and learned via the specified protocol are redistributed. Each protocol has some unique characteristics when redistributing, as shown in Table 6-2.

Part I: ROUTE

Table 6-2   Route Redistribution Characteristics

Protocol	Redistribution Characteristics
RIP	Default metric is Infinity. Metric must be set, except when redistributing static or connected routes, which have a metric of 1.
OSPF	Default metric is 20. Can specify the metric type; the default is E2. Must use **subnets** keyword or only classful networks are redistributed.
EIGRP	Default metric is Infinity. Metric must be set, except when redistributing static or connected routes, which get their metric from the interface. Metric value is "bandwidth, delay, reliability, load, MTU." Redistributed routes have a higher administrative distance than internal ones.
Static/Connected	To include local networks not running the routing protocol, you must redistribute connected interfaces. You can also redistribute static routes into a dynamic protocol.
BGP	Metric (MED) is set to IGP metric value.

You can redistribute only between protocols that use the same protocol stack, such as IP. To configure redistribution, issue this command under the routing process that is to receive the new routes:

```
Router(config-router)# redistribute {route-source} [metric metric]
  [route-map tag]
```

The IPv6 commands to redistribute routes between protocols or between multiple instances of a protocol are just like the ones in IPv4. Under the routing protocol configuration mode, issue the command **redistribute** *route-source* and specify any options, such as a route map if desired.

Seed Metric

Redistribution involves configuring a routing protocol to advertise routes learned by another routing process. Normally, protocols base their metric on an interface value, such as bandwidth, but a redistributed route is not associated with an interface. Protocols use incompatible metrics, so the redistributed routes must be assigned a new metric compatible with the new protocol.

A route's starting metric is called its *seed metric*. Set the seed metric for all redistributed routes with the **default-metric** {*metric*} command under the routing process. To set the metric for specific routes, either use the **metric** keyword within the redistribution command or use the **route-map** keyword to link a route map to the redistribution. After the seed metric is specified, it increments normally as the route is advertised through the network (except for certain OSPF routes).

Administrative Distance

Recall that when a router receives routes to the same destination network from more than one routing process, it decides which to put in the routing table by looking at the administrative distance (AD) value assigned to the routing process. The route with the lowest AD is chosen.

The AD can be changed for all routes of a process or only for specific routes within a process. The command for all IGPs except EIGRP is

```
Router(config-router)# distance administrative_distance {address
  wildcard-mask} [access-list-number | name]
```

Using the *address/mask* options in the command changes the AD of routes learned from the neighbor with that IP address. An entry of **0.0.0.0 255.255.255.255** changes the AD of all routes. Specifying an access list number or name changes the AD only on networks permitted in the ACL.

EIGRP and BGP have different AD values for internal and external routes, so you must list those separately when using the command with those protocols. BGP also enables you to change the AD for locally generated routes. For these protocols, the commands are

```
Router(config-router)# distance eigrp internal-distance external-
  distance
Router(config-router)# distance bgp external-distance internal-
  distance local-distance
```

Route redistribution can cause suboptimal routing; one way to correct this is to adjust the AD for redistributed routes. Figure 6-1 shows a network with two routing domains: RIP and OSPF.

Figure 6-1   Controlling Routing with AD

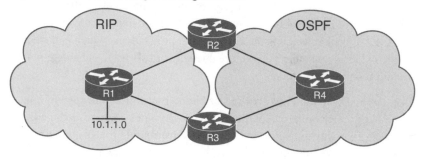

Part I: ROUTE

R2 redistributes its RIP routes into OSPF. These routes inherit OSPF's AD when they are advertised to R4, which then advertises them to R3 as OSPF routes.

R3 now recognizes the 10.1.1.0 network from two routing processes: RIP, with an AD of 120, and OSPF, with an AD of 110. The shortest path is the RIP route through R1. The OSPF path goes through R4 and R2, and then to R1—a much longer path. But, based on AD, R3 puts the OSPF path in its routing table.

To prevent this, increase the AD of the redistributed RIP routes when OSPF advertises them. Note that this doesn't change all OSPF routes, just the ones learned from RIP. The commands given on R2 (the router doing the initial redistribution) are shown in Example 6-3.

Example 6-3   Adjusting Administrative Distance

```
R2(config)# access-list 10 permit 10.1.1.0
!
R2(config)# router ospf 1
R2(config-router)# redistribute rip subnets
R2(config-router)# distance 125 0.0.0.0 255.255.255.255 10
```

The AD is increased to 125 for routes from all neighbors if they match the network permitted in access list 10. Now R3 hears about the 10.1.1.0 network from RIP with an AD of 120 and from OSPF with an AD of 125. The RIP route is put into the routing table based on its lower AD.

Routing protocols that assign a higher AD to external routes, EIGRP and BGP, accomplish a similar result automatically. OSPF can be configured to do so with the **distance ospf external** command.

Planning Route Redistribution

Plan carefully before redistributing routes between protocols. Different protocols have incompatible routing information and unique convergence times. First, decide which is the core or main protocol and which is the edge protocol. Decide whether you require one-way or two-way, and single-point or multipoint redistribution.

One-way redistribution involves redistributing routes from the edge routing protocol into the core protocol. Static or default routes are used in the edge protocol. Two-way redistribution involves redistributing routes mutually between both core and edge protocols. No static routes are needed because both protocols have information about all routes.

One-way and two-way redistribution at just one router within the network is considered safe because traffic between administrative domains has only one exit point, thus routing loops are not a problem. Redistribution at multiple routers within the network can cause routing loops and suboptimal routing.

With multipoint one-way redistribution, the following actions are suggested:

- Use a routing protocol that uses different ADs for external and internal routes (EIGRP, OSPF, and BGP).

- Ensure that the AD of the redistributed external routes is higher than the AD of the protocol where they originated.

Multipoint two-way redistribution adds the following considerations:

- Ensure that only internal routes are redistributed from each protocol. You can do this by tagging the routes and then filtering based on tags when redistributing.

- Adjust the metric of the redistributed routes.

- Consider using a default route to avoid multipoint two-way redistribution.

Redistribution Techniques

Try to design your route redistribution as safely as possible. The options include

- Redistribute all edge information into the core, but send only a default route into the edge.

- Redistribute all edge information into the core, but redistribute multiple static routes into the edge.

- Redistribute routes in both directions, but filter to prevent routes from being redistributed back into their original administrative domain.

- Redistribute all routes in both directions, but increase the AD for external routes.

There are several points to remember when configuring route redistribution:

- A router redistributes only routes learned by the source protocol. When redistributing routes into BGP, use the keyword **include-connected** to get the connected routes into BGP.

- When you redistribute routes between two OSPF processes, the routes are advertised into the new process as Type 2.

- You generally want to include the **subnets** keyword on routes distributed from another routing protocol into OSPF; otherwise, only routes that use their default classful subnet mask are redistributed.

- Be sure to specify a seed metric when redistributing routes into RIP; otherwise, the routes start with a metric of 16, which RIP interprets as "unreachable."

- If you redistribute in multiple places, check the resulting traffic path because you might run into suboptimal routing. One solution is to tune the administrative distance for some of the routes.

- BGP does not redistribute routes learned via iBGP into an IGP by default. To change this behavior, use the router configuration command **bgp redistribute-internal**.

Path Control

In general, link redundancy is desirable, but it can also lead to some network problems. You might want to manually control the route taken by some or all of your traffic to provide a predictable and deterministic traffic flow. Path control can provide the following:

- Prevent suboptimal routing

- Ensure path availability

- Provide optimized performance for specific applications

- Provide load sharing among various paths

A good path control strategy understands that traffic is bidirectional and considers both inbound and outbound traffic. Asymmetric routing—where traffic exits via one link and enters via another—is not inherently bad. But you might need to minimize it when using stateful devices such as firewalls, or with sensitive applications such as voice.

Policy-Based Routing

Policy-based routing (PBR) overrides the normal routing process. Normal routing is performed based on the destination IP address. Policy-based routing is based on source IP address or interface or packet length. It uses a route-map to match traffic and then sets either a next-hop address or an exit interface. It can also mark the traffic that it policy routes. Any traffic not matched in the route map is routed normally. Policy-based routing can be applied both to traffic entering the router and to traffic originated by the router.

Some benefits of policy routing include

- The capability to route based on traffic source and other attributes

- The capability to set QoS markings

- The capability to force load sharing between unequal paths

- The capability to allocate traffic among multiple paths based on traffic attributes

Use the following steps to configure policy-based routing:

Step 1. Configure a route-map that matches the desired traffic and uses the **set** command to define the actions for that traffic.

Step 2. Apply the route map either to an incoming interface or to traffic generated by the router.

Step 3. Verify the configuration.

Some typical attributes to match in the route map include source or destination address with an access list and packet length. If no match criteria are specified, all packets are considered a match.

You can choose to set various options, but the most typical settings determine how the traffic leaves the router. The four most common ways to accomplish this are listed in Table 6-3.

Table 6-3   Policy-Based Routing Options

Command	Description
set ip next-hop *ip-address*	When this command is given, the router checks to see whether the next-hop address is reachable. If so, it forwards the traffic toward that address. If not, it uses the routing table.

Part I: ROUTE

Table 6-3   Continued

Command	Description
set interface *interface-type interface-number*	Multiple interfaces can be listed. When this command is given, the router checks that it has an explicit route for the destination network in its routing table before forwarding the traffic out the specified interface. If it does not, this command is ignored. A default route is not considered an explicit route. Listing multiple interfaces under the **set** command allows for redundancy if the first interface fails or goes down. The router uses the first active interface listed.
set ip default next-hop *ip-address* **[verify-availability]**	If the routing table contains an explicit route for the destination network, that route is used and this command is ignored. If no explicit route exists, this command is executed. A default route is not considered an explicit route. The **verify-availability** option checks the CDP database to ensure the next hop is available.
set default interface *interface-type interface-number*	If the routing table contains an explicit route for the destination network, that route is used and this command is ignored. If no explicit route exists, traffic is forwarded out the specified interface. A default route is not considered an explicit route.

To apply the PBR route-map to an interface, use the interface command **ip policy route-map** *name*. To cause PBR to act on packets originated by the router itself, use the global command **ip local policy route-map** *name*.

Example 6-4 shows a route map named LOCAL that matches the source addresses in access list 1. It assigns a next-hop IP address of 10.1.1.1 to this traffic. Because it is applied to the local router, it is used only for traffic generated by the router itself.

Example 6-4   Applying PBR to Local Router Traffic

```
Router(config)# route-map LOCAL
Router(config-route-map)# match ip address 1
Router(config-route-map)# set ip next-hop 10.1.1.1
!
Router(config)# ip local policy route-map LOCAL
```

Example 6-5 shows a PBR route map that matches traffic in access list 101 and policy routes it to a next hop of 10.1.1.1. The policy is applied to interface Ethernet0/0, so all traffic entering that interface is evaluated against the route-map. Packets not permitted by access list 101 are routed normally (destination routed.)

Example 6-5   Applying PBR to Interface Traffic

```
Router(config)# route-map Policy permit 10
Router(config-route-map)# match ip address 101
Router(config-route-map)# set ip next hop 10.1.1.1
!
Router(config)# interface Ethernet0/0
Router(config-if)# ip policy route-map Policy
```

PBR can also use IP SLA tracking, described in the following IP SLA section. Verify your configuration with the commands **show ip policy** and **show route-map** {*name*}. Use the **debug ip policy** command to see the policy routing in action.

Using IOS IP SLA

IP Service Level Agreement (IP SLA) is a feature that enables a Cisco router or switch to simulate specific types of traffic and send it either to an IP address or to a receiver, called a *responder*. IP SLA probes can simulate various types of traffic, such as

- HTTP
- FTP
- DHCP
- UDP jitter
- UDP echo
- HTTP
- TCP connect
- ICMP echo
- ICMP path echo
- ICMP path jitter
- DNS

Part I: ROUTE

The probes can also report statistics such as path jitter. IP SLA has highly granular application configuration options, such as TCP/UDP port numbers, TOS byte, and IP prefix bits. With IP SLA you can measure network performance and host reachability. This is useful for path control because it enables you to switch to a backup path if network performance on the primary path degrades, or if a link failure occurs someplace in the primary path.

To use IP SLA for path control, you must follow these steps:

Step 1. Create a monitor session on the probe source device.

Step 2. Define the probe by specifying traffic type, destination IP address, and any other desired variables, such as Differentiated Services Code Point (DSCP) value.

Step 3. Schedule the probe beginning and ending times.

Step 4. Define a tracking object that is linked to the monitor session.

Step 5. Link the tracking object to a static route.

The destination can be any trusted device that responds to the traffic you send. To use IP SLA for bringing up a backup link, choose a destination that will reflect problems in the ISP's network. One benefit of using a Cisco device as the responder is that it can add time stamps to help measure latency and jitter. These time stamps take into account the device processing time so that the measurement reflects only network latency. The configuration of a Cisco responder is simple. Use the global command **ip sla responder**.

Figure 6-2 shows a network with two connections to the Internet, one primary and a backup. The edge router has a static default route pointing to each provider. Dynamic failover between the primary and backup path is desired.

Figure 6-2   Using IP SLA for Path Control

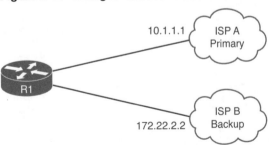

In Example 6-6, router R1 is configured to conditionally announce a default route based on the IP SLA probe response. Two IP SLA monitor sessions are configured to send a ping every 10 seconds to a DNS server within each ISP's network. Separate tracking objects verify reachability to each DNS server. The two default route statements notify the router to give the primary route an administrative distance of 2 if the tracked object is reachable. The backup route is assigned an administrative distance of 3 if its tracked object is reachable.

Example 6-6   Using IP SLA

```
R1(config)# ip sla 1
R1(config-ip-sla)# icmp-echo 10.1.1.50 source-interface e0/0
R1(config-ip-sla-echo)# frequency 10
!
R1(config)# ip sla 2
R1(config-ip-sla)# icmp-echo 171.22.2.52 source-interface e0/1
R1(config-ip-sla-echo)# frequency 10
!
R1(config)# ip sla schedule 1 life forever start-time now
R1(config)# ip sla schedule 2 life forever start-time now
!
R1(config)# track 1 ip sla 1 reachability
R1(config)# track 2 ip sla 2 reachability
!
!Primary route
R1(config)# ip route 0.0.0.0 0.0.0.0 10.1.1.1 2 track 1
!Backup route
R1(config)# ip route 0.0.0.0 0.0.0.0 172.22.2.2 3 track 2
```

Under normal circumstances, the default route with an AD of 2 is installed in the IP routing table instead of the one with an AD of 3. But when the primary DNS server is not reachable, the primary route is withdrawn and the backup route with an AD of 3 is installed in the routing table.

Additionally, you can combine IP SLA tracking with policy-based routing to provide redundancy for specific traffic types on a per-interface basis. For instance, after an access list permitting the interesting traffic is specified, a route-map such as the one shown in Example 6-7 can be configured. In this sample route-map, x.x.x.x and y.y.y.y represent different next hops for the traffic specified in ACL 101. The **track 1** and **track 2** keywords tie the configuration back to the SLA groups configured in Example 6-6. You then apply the policy map under the incoming interfaces, just as with normal policy routing.

Part I: ROUTE

Example 6-7   Using a Route Map with IP SLA

```
route-map REDUNDANT permit 10
 match ip address 101
 set ip next-hop verify-availability x.x.x.x 10 track 1
 set ip next hop verify-availability y.y.y.y 20 track 2
 !

interface Ethernet0/1
 description LAN Interface
 ip policy route-map REDUNDANT
```

VRF-Lite

Virtual routing and forwarding (VRF) is a way to segment traffic and control the path it takes. You might think of it as a Layer 3 VLAN. Just as VLANs create virtual switches with segregated CAM tables, VRFs create virtual routers with segregated routing tables. This enables you to separate guest traffic from employee traffic, for example, and route it over a different path. We usually think of VRFs in association with MPLS, but VRF-Lite lets you create VRFs without using MPLS.

To configure a router for this design, create the necessary VRFs and apply each one to the interfaces to carry traffic for that particular VRF. For example, Figure 6-3 shows a simple network with a switch connected to a router. The router then has two external connections—one to the Internet and the other to the corporate WAN. Internal users' traffic must be separate from guest user traffic and routed to the corporate WAN. Guest users are routed to the Internet. The switch has two VLANs—one for internal users and another for guest users.

In Figure 6-3, two VRFs are created on the router to separate the two types of traffic: INT for internal users and GUEST for guest users. A static default route is created for each VRF. The link between the switch and the router is a trunk, with a subinterface for each of the VRFs. Each subinterface is associated with the appropriate VRF using the command **ip vrf forwarding** *vrf-name*, as are the interfaces to the WAN and to the Internet. Example 6-8 shows this configuration.

Figure 6-3 VRF-Lite

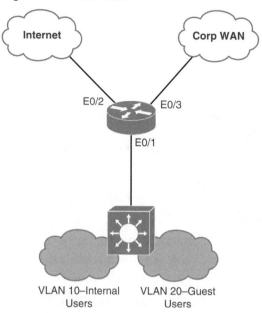

VLAN 10–Internal   VLAN 20–Guest
      Users   Users

Example 6-8 VRF-Lite Configuration

```
R1(config)# ip vrf INT
R1(config-vrf)# description Internal Traffic
!
R1(config-vrf)# ip vrf GUEST
R1(config-vrf)# description Guest Traffic
!
R1(config)# ip route vrf INT 0.0.0.0 0.0.0.0 209.165.201.2
R1(config)# ip route vrf GUEST 0.0.0.0 0.0.0.0 209.165.202.2
!
R1(config)# int e0/1
R1(config-if)# description To SW1
R1(config-if)# int e0/1.10
R1(config-subif)# encapsulation dot1Q 10
R1(config-subif)# ip vrf forwarding INT
R1(config-subif)# ip address 192.168.10.1 255.255.255.0
!
R1(config-subif)# int e0/1.20
R1(config-subif)# encapsulation dot1Q 20
R1(config-subif)# ip vrf forwarding GUEST
R1(config-subif)# ip address 192.168.20.1 255.255.255.0
!
```

Part I: ROUTE

Example 6-8   Continued

```
R1(config)# int e0/2
R1(config-if)# description To Internet
R1(config-if)# ip vrf forwarding GUEST
R1(config-if)# ip address 209.165.202.1 255.255.255.252
!
R1(config)# int e0/3
R1(config-if)# description To WAN
R1(config-if)# ip vrf forwarding INT
R1(config-if)# ip address 209.165.201.1 255.255.255.252
```

Note that the IP address is applied to the interface *after* it is associated with a VRF. If you configure the IP address prior to that, the router removes it when you apply the VRF configuration.

With this configuration, when traffic from VLAN 10 enters the router it is placed into VRF INT and routed to the WAN. The router places traffic from VLAN 20 into VRF GUEST and routes it to the Internet.

To verify your configuration, use the command **show vrf** to check the configured VRFs:

```
R1# show vrf
  Name                        Default RD          Protocols
  Interfaces
  GUEST                       <not set>           ipv4
  Et0/1.20
  INT                         <not set>           ipv4
  Et0/1.10
```

To view the routes for a particular VRF, append the VRF name to the **show ip route** command. Note that only the networks belonging to the "INT" VRF show up in Example 6-9.

Example 6-9   The show ip route vrf Command

```
R1# show ip route vrf INT

Routing Table: INT
Codes: L - local, C - connected, S - static, R - RIP, M - mobile, B
 - BGP
       D - EIGRP, EX - EIGRP external, O - OSPF, IA - OSPF inter
  area
       N1 - OSPF NSSA external type 1, N2 - OSPF NSSA external type
  2
       E1 - OSPF external type 1, E2 - OSPF external type 2
       i - IS-IS, su - IS-IS summary, L1 - IS-IS level-1, L2 - IS-IS
  level-2
```

```
      ia - IS-IS inter area, * - candidate default, U - per-user
static route
      o - ODR, P - periodic downloaded static route, H - NHRP, l -
LISP
      + - replicated route, % - next hop override

Gateway of last resort is 209.165.201.2 to network 0.0.0.0

S*    0.0.0.0/0 [1/0] via 209.165.201.2
      192.168.10.0/24 is variably subnetted, 2 subnets, 2 masks
C        192.168.10.0/24 is directly connected, Ethernet0/1.10
L        192.168.10.1/32 is directly connected, Ethernet0/1.10
      209.165.201.0/24 is variably subnetted, 2 subnets, 2 masks
C        209.165.201.0/30 is directly connected, Ethernet0/3
L        209.165.201.1/32 is directly connected, Ethernet0/3
```

CHAPTER 7

BGP and Internet Connectivity

Planning an Internet Connection

Consider your company's needs when planning your Internet connection. What link type and bandwidth will support all the external connections plus your internal users? Is the company considering any hosted or cloud services that would drive additional bandwidth needs? Will you use static or dynamic routing? How much redundancy will you require, including both link and ISP redundancy?

Types of ISP Connections

A site with a single Internet service provider (ISP) connection is *single homed*, which is sufficient for a site that does not depend heavily on Internet or WAN connectivity. Either use static routes or advertise the site routes to the ISP and receive a default route from the ISP.

A *dual-homed* site has two connections to the same ISP, either from one or two routers. One link might be primary and the other backup, or the site might load balance over both links. Either static or dynamic routing works in this case.

Multihoming means connecting to more than one ISP at the same time. It is done for redundancy and backup in case one ISP fails, and for better performance if one ISP provides a better path to frequently used networks. This also gives you an ISP-independent solution. Border Gateway Protocol (BGP) is typically used with multihomed connections.

You can take multihoming a step further and be *dual-multihomed*, with two connections to multiple ISPs. This gives the most redundancy. BGP is used with dual-multihomed connections.

IP Addressing and AS Numbering

You can choose between provider-assigned and provider-independent IP addressing. If you are connecting to only one ISP, you can use IP addresses owned by that provider. You will either have one edge address or a pool, and use NAT for the inside private addresses. The provider is responsible for advertising your addresses to the Internet.

If your company is multihomed, you will likely acquire your own provider-independent IP address block. IP address allocation is coordinated by Regional Internet Registries (RIR) under the auspices of the Internet Assigned Numbers Authority (IANA). With provider-independent space, you are responsible for the way your routes are advertised to the Internet, giving you more control over routing policies.

To run BGP with an ISP, you need an autonomous system (AS) number. Autonomous systems are explained in the "BGP Overview" section of this chapter. If you are using provider-assigned IP addresses, you will likely use a provider-assigned private AS number. If you plan to use provider-independent addresses then you will need your own public AS number.

BGP Route Options

There are three ways to receive BGP routes from an ISP:

- **Default routes from each provider:** This is simple to configure and results in low use of bandwidth and router resources. The internal network's IGP metric determines the exit router for all traffic bound outside the autonomous system. No BGP path manipulation is possible, so this can lead to suboptimal routing if you use more than one ISP.

- **Default routes plus some more specific routes:** This option results in medium use of bandwidth and router resources. It enables you to manipulate the exit path for specific routes using BGP so that traffic takes a shorter path to networks in each ISP. Thus, path selection is more predictable. The IGP metric chooses the exit path for default routes.

- **All routes from all providers:** This requires the highest use of bandwidth and router resources. It is typically used by large enterprises and ISPs. Path selection for all external routes can be controlled via BGP policy routing tools.

Part I: ROUTE

BGP Overview

BGP is an external gateway protocol, meant to be used between different network entities. It is the protocol used between ISPs and also can be used between an Enterprise and an ISP. BGP was built for reliability, scalability, and control, not speed. Because of this, it behaves differently from the protocols covered so far in this book. Some BGP characteristics are as follows:

- BGP uses the concept of autonomous systems. An *autonomous system* is a group of networks under a common administration. The IANA assigns AS numbers, which are traditionally 16 bits: 1 to 64,511 are public AS numbers and 64,512 to 65,535 are private AS numbers. Since 2007, a 32-bit format can be used: private AS numbers are 4,200,000,000–4,294,967,294 in this format.

- Autonomous systems run Interior Gateway Protocols (IGP) within the system. They run an Exterior Gateway Protocol (EGP) between them. BGP is the only EGP currently in use.

- BGP is a path-vector protocol. Its route to a network consists of a list of autonomous systems on the path to that network.

- Routing between autonomous systems is called *interdomain routing*.

- Routers running BGP are termed *BGP speakers*.

- BGP neighbors are called *peers* and must be statically configured.

- BGP routing with a peer in a different AS is called *external BGP (eBGP)*. With a peer in the same AS it is called *internal BGP (iBGP)*.

- The administrative distance for eBGP routes is 20. The administrative distance for iBGP routes is 200.

- BGP uses TCP port 179. BGP peers exchange incremental, triggered route updates and periodic keepalives.

- Routers can run only one BGP process at a time. Switches with Virtual Device Contexts (VDC) can run one BGP process per VDC. BGP's loop prevention mechanism is an autonomous system number. When an update regarding a network leaves an autonomous system, that AS's number is prepended to the list of autonomous systems that have handled that update. When a BGP router receives an update, it examines the AS list. If it finds its own autonomous system number in that list, the update is discarded.

In Figure 7-1, BGP routers in AS 65100 see network 10.1.1.0 as having an autonomous system path of 65200 65300 65400.

Figure 7-1   BGP AS-Path Advertisement

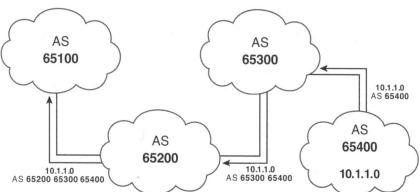

Use BGP when the AS is multihomed, when route path manipulation is needed, or when the AS is a transit AS. (Traffic flows through it to another AS, such as with an ISP.) Do not use BGP in a single-homed AS with a router that does not have sufficient resources to handle it or with a staff that does not have a good understanding of BGP path selection and manipulation.

BGP Databases

BGP uses three databases. The first two listed are BGP-specific; the third is shared by all routing processes on the router.

- **Neighbor database:** A list of all configured BGP neighbors. To view it, use the **show ip bgp summary** command.

- **BGP database:** A list of networks known by BGP, along with their paths and attributes. To view it, use the **show ip bgp** command.

- **Routing table:** A list of the paths to each network used by the router, and the next hop for each network. To view it, use the **show ip route** command.

BGP Message Types

BGP has four types of messages:

- **Open:** After a neighbor is configured, BGP sends an open message to try to establish peering with that neighbor. Includes information such as autonomous system number, router ID, and hold time.

- **Update:** Message used to transfer routing information between peers. Includes new routes, withdrawn routes, and path attributes.

- **Keepalive:** BGP peers exchange keepalive messages every 60 seconds by default. These keep the peering session active.

- **Notification:** When a problem occurs that causes a router to end the BGP peering session, a notification message is sent to the BGP neighbor and the connection is closed.

BGP Next-Hop Selection

The next hop for a route received from an eBGP neighbor is the IP address of the neighbor that sent the update.

When a BGP router receives an update from an eBGP neighbor, it must pass that update to its iBGP neighbors without changing the next-hop attribute. The next-hop IP address is the IP address of an edge router belonging to the next-hop autonomous system. Therefore, iBGP routers must have a route to the network connecting their autonomous system to that edge router. For example, in Figure 7-2, RtrA sends an update to RtrB, listing a next hop of 10.2.2.1, its serial interface. When RtrB forwards that update to RtrC, the next-hop IP address remains 10.2.2.1. RtrC must have a route to the 10.2.2.0 network to have a valid next hop.

Figure 7-2   BGP Next-Hop Behavior

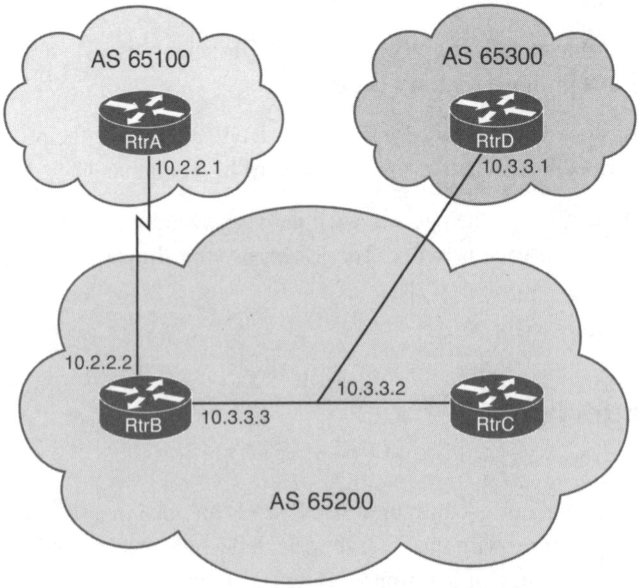

To change this behavior, use the **neighbor** {*ip address* | *peer-group-name*} **next-hop-self** command in BGP configuration mode. In Figure 7-2, this configuration goes on RtrB. After you give this command, RtrB advertises its IP address to RtrC as the next hop for networks from AS 65100 rather than the address of RtrA. Thus, RtrC does not have to know about the external network between RtrA and RtrB (network 10.2.2.0).

BGP Next Hop on a Multiaccess Network

On a multiaccess network, BGP can adjust the next-hop attribute to avoid an extra hop. In Figure 7-2, RtrC and RtrD are eBGP peers, and RtrC is an iBGP peer with RtrB. When RtrC sends an update to RtrD about network 10.2.2.0, it normally gives its interface IP address as the next hop for RtrD to use. But because RtrB, RtrC, and RtrD are all on the same multiaccess network, it is inefficient for RtrD to send traffic to RtrC and RtrC to then send it on to RtrB. This process unnecessarily adds an extra hop to the path. So, by default, RtrC advertises a next hop of 10.3.3.3 (RtrB's interface) for the 10.2.2.0 network. This behavior can also be adjusted with the **neighbor next-hop-self** command.

BGP Synchronization Rule

The BGP synchronization rule requires that when a BGP router receives information regarding a network from an iBGP neighbor, it does not use that information until a matching route is learned via an IGP or static route. It also does not advertise that route to an eBGP neighbor unless a matching route is in the routing table. In Figure 7-2, if RtrB advertises a route to RtrC, then RtrC does not submit it to the routing table or advertise it to RtrD unless it also learns the route from some other IGP source.

Recent IOS versions have synchronization disabled by default. It is usually safe to turn off synchronization when all routers in the autonomous system run BGP. To turn it off in earlier IOS versions, use the command **no synchronization** under BGP router configuration mode.

Configuring Basic BGP

Before configuring BGP, gather the network requirements you need, which should include the following:

- Confirmation as to whether you need to run iBGP for internal connectivity

- External connectivity to the ISP

Part I: ROUTE

- Configuration parameters, such as neighbor IP addresses and their AS number, and which networks you will advertise via BGP

Table 7-1 lists the basic BGP configuration commands and their functions.

Table 7-1   Basic BGP Configuration Commands

Command	Description
router bgp *AS-number*	Starts the BGP routing process on the router.
neighbor *ip-address* **remote-as** *AS-number*	Sets up peering between BGP routers. IP address must match the source of routing updates.
neighbor *peer-group-name* **peer-group**	Creates a peer group to which you can then assign neighbors.
neighbor *ip-address* **peer-group** *peer-group-name*	Assigns a neighbor to a peer group.
neighbor {*ip-address*	*peer-group-name*} **next-hop-self**	Configures a router to advertise its connected interface as the next hop for all routes to this neighbor or peer group.
neighbor {*ip-address*	*peer-group-name*} **update-source** *interface-type number*	Configures a router to use the IP address of a specific interface as the source for its advertisements to this neighbor.
no synchronization	Turns off BGP synchronization.
network *prefix* [**mask** *subnet-mask*]	Initiates the advertisement of a network in BGP.

BGP Network Command

In most IGPs, the **network** command starts the routing process on an interface and causes the protocol to advertise the network associated with that interface. In BGP, the **network** command tells the router to originate an advertisement for that network. The network does not have to be connected to the router; it just has to be in the routing table. In theory, it can even be a network in a different autonomous system (not usually recommended).

When advertising a network, BGP assumes you are using the default classful subnet mask. If you want to advertise a subnet, you must use the optional keyword **mask** and specify the subnet mask to use. Note that this is a subnet mask, not the inverse mask used by OSPF and EIGRP network statements. The routing table must contain an exact match (prefix and subnet mask) to the network listed in the network statement before BGP advertises the route.

BGP Peering

Before any BGP speaker can peer with a neighbor router, that neighbor must be statically defined. A TCP session must be established, so the IP address used to peer with must be reachable. This enables different configuration and policies to be applied to different neighbors. Some BGP routers have many neighbors; because each must be configured separately, the configuration can get unwieldy. To alleviate this, neighbors with the same configuration parameters can be grouped into *peer groups*. This enables the configuration to be entered once, and then applied by joining the neighbor to the peer group. Peer group policies can be overridden by specific neighbor configuration.

BGP assumes that external neighbors are directly connected and that they are peering with the IP address of the directly connected interface of their neighbor. If not, you must tell BGP to look more than one hop away for its neighbor, with the **neighbor** *ip-address* **ebgp-multihop** *number-of-hops* command. You might use this command if you are peering with loopback interface IP addresses, for instance. BGP assumes that internal neighbors might not be directly connected, so this command is not needed with iBGP. If you do peer with loopback IP addresses, you must change the source of the BGP packets to match the loopback address with the **neighbor** *ip-address* **update-source** *interface* command.

To take down the peering session with a neighbor but keep the neighbor configuration, use the **neighbor** *ip-address* **shutdown** command.

BGP Peering States

The command **show ip bgp neighbors** shows a list of peers and the status of their peering session. This status can include the following states:

- **Idle:** No peering; router is looking for neighbor. Idle (admin) means that the neighbor relationship has been administratively shut down.

- **Connect:** A remote peer is trying to initiate a TCP session with the local BGP process.

- **Active:** The local BGP process is trying to establish a TCP session with its remote peer.

- **OpenSent:** TCP session is up, and an Open message has been sent to establish the peering. Router waits for an answering Open message from its peer.

- **OpenConfirm:** Router has sent a Keepalive message to its peer and is waiting to receive a Keepalive message in return.

- **Established:** Routers have a BGP peering session. This is the desired state.

Part I: ROUTE

Troubleshooting BGP

Troubleshoot session establishment with debug commands. Use **debug ip bgp events** or **debug ip bgp ipv4 unicast** to see where the process fails. Some common failure causes include the following:

- AS number misconfiguration

- Neighbor IP address misconfiguration

- A neighbor with no neighbor statement for your router

- A neighbor with no route to the source address of your router's BGP messages

BGP Path Selection

IGPs, such as EIGRP or OSPF, choose routes based on lowest metric. They attempt to find the shortest, fastest way to get traffic to its destination. BGP, however, has a different way of route selection. It assigns various attributes to each path; these attributes can be administratively manipulated to control the path that is selected. It then examines the value of these attributes in order, until it chooses just one path by default. It must be manually configured to choose multiple paths with the command **maximum-paths** *number-of-paths*. BGP can load balance over a maximum of six paths.

BGP Attributes

BGP chooses a route to a network based on attributes included in route advertisements for that network. There are four categories of attributes:

- **Well-known mandatory:** Must be recognized by all BGP routers, present in all BGP updates, and passed on to other BGP routers; for example, AS path, origin, and next hop.

- **Well-known discretionary:** Must be recognized by all BGP routers and passed on to other BGP routers but need not be present in an update; for example, local preference.

- **Optional transitive:** Might or might not be recognized by a BGP router but is passed on to other BGP routers. If not recognized, it is marked as partial; for example, aggregator or community.

- **Optional nontransitive:** Might or might not be recognized by a BGP router and is not passed on to other routers; for example, Multi-Exit Discriminator (MED), or originator ID.

Table 7-2 lists common BGP attributes, their meanings, and their category.

Table 7-2   BGP Attributes

Attribute	Meaning
AS path	An ordered list of all the autonomous systems through which this update has passed. Well-known, mandatory.
Origin	How BGP learned of this network. i = by **network** command, e = from EGP, ? = redistributed from other source. Well-known, mandatory.
Local Preference	A value telling iBGP peers which path to select for traffic leaving the AS. Default value is 100. Well-known, discretionary.
Multi-Exit Discriminator	Suggests to a neighboring autonomous system which of multiple paths to select for traffic bound into your autonomous system. Lowest MED is preferred. Optional, nontransitive.
Weight	Cisco proprietary, to tell a router which of multiple local paths to select for traffic leaving the AS. Highest weight is preferred. Has only local significance.

BGP Path Selection Criteria

BGP attempts to narrow its path selection down to one best path; it does not load balance by default. To do so, it examines the path attributes of any loop-free, synchronized (if synchronization is enabled) routes with a reachable next-hop in the following steps:

Step 1. Choose the route with the highest weight.

Step 2. If weight is not set, select the route with the highest local preference.

Step 3. Choose the route originated by this router.

Step 4. Select the path with the shortest autonomous system path.

Step 5. Choose the path with the lowest origin code (i is lowest, e is next, and ? is last).

Step 6. Select the route with the lowest MED, if the same autonomous system advertises the possible routes.

Step 7. Choose an eBGP route over an iBGP route.

Step 8. Select the route through the nearest IGP neighbor as determined by the lowest IGP metric.

Step 9. Choose the oldest route.

Part I: ROUTE

Step 10. Select a path through the neighbor with the lowest router ID.

Step 11. Choose a path through the neighbor with the lowest IP address.

To enable BGP to load balance over more than one path, you must enter the command **maximum-paths** *number-of-paths*. BGP can load balance over a maximum of six paths.

Influencing BGP Path Selection

BGP was not created to be a fast protocol; it was designed to enable as much administrative control over route path selection as possible. Path selection is controlled by manipulating BGP attributes, usually implementing route maps. You can set a default local preference by using the command **bgp default local-preference** and a default MED for redistributed routes with the **default-metric** command under the BGP routing process. But by using route maps, you can change attributes for certain neighbors only or for certain routes only. Example 6-1 in Chapter 6 shows a route map that sets a local preference of 200 for specific redistributed routes. This is higher than the default local preference of 120, so routers within the AS are more likely to prefer that path than others.

Route maps can also be applied to routes sent to or received from a neighbor. Example 7-1 shows a simple route map that sets an MED value and adds two more copies of its AS number to the AS path on all routes advertised out to an eBGP neighbor.

Example 7-1   Route Map to Set MED and Prepend

```
route-map MED permit 10
 set metric 50
 set as-path prepend 65001 65001
!
router bgp 65001
 neighbor 10.1.1.1 route-map MED out
```

When attributes are changed, you must apply the changes. Either clear the BGP session (**clear ip bgp ***) or do a soft reset (**clear ip bgp * soft in | out**). Routers using recent IOS versions do a route refresh when the session is cleared inbound.

Filtering BGP Routes

BGP provides several ways of controlling the routes advertised to, or received from, a BGP peer. This section discusses prefix lists and AS-path access lists, both of which can be either applied directly to a peer or used in a route map.

Prefix Lists

Prefix lists combined with route maps can be used to filter the routes advertised to or received from a BGP peer, control routes redistributed into BGP, and set BGP attributes for specific routes. Prefix lists also can be applied directly to a neighbor to filter route updates.

Create a prefix list to match the networks to be filtered. Permit the networks you want to allow to be advertised (all others are denied by default), and then apply the prefix list to the BGP neighbor, inbound or outbound. Example 7-2 shows a prefix list that permits only summary routes in the 172.31.0.0 network. All other routes are denied by default. The prefix list is then applied to BGP neighbor 10.1.1.1 outbound, so only these routes are advertised to that peer.

Example 7-2   Configuring a Prefix List

```
ip prefix-list Summary permit 172.31.0.0/16 le 20
!
router bgp 65001
neighbor 10.1.1.1 prefix-list Summary out
```

To verify the results of your configuration use the command **show ip prefix-list**. To clear the counters shown in that command, use the **clear ip prefix-list** command.

You can combine a prefix list with a route map to set attributes on the routes allowed in the prefix list. In Example 7-3, prefix list Summary is used again. Route map CCNP sets the MED for those routes to 100 when they are advertised. It sets a MED of 200 for all other routes advertised. The route map is then applied to BGP neighbor 10.1.1.1 outbound.

Example 7-3   Using a Prefix List with a Route Map

```
route-map CCNP permit 10
match ip address prefix-list Summary
set metric 100
route-map CCNP permit 20
set metric 200
```

Part I: ROUTE

Example 7-3   Continued

```
!
router bgp 65001
neighbor 10.1.1.1 route-map CCNP out
```

AS Path Access List

An AS path access list looks at the AS path portion of route advertisements. The command syntax is **ip as-path access-list** *acl-#* {**permit** | **deny**} *regexp*. It is applied directly to a neighbor using the filter list command **neighbor** *ip-address/peer-group* **filter-list** *acl-#* {**in** | **out**}.

AS path ACLs employ regular expressions (regexp) to identify specific strings of numbers. Regular expressions consist of special characters, numbers, and letters. An explanation of regular expressions is beyond the scope of this book, but some frequently used BGP characters include

- **^** : This signifies the beginning of a string. For example, ^65001 would match an AS path that has AS 65001 as its first entry.

- **$** : This signifies the end of a string. For example, 65001$ would match an AS path that ended in AS 65001.

Local AS path information is added to a route advertisement when it is sent to an eBGP peer. Thus, a route originated within the local AS does not have AS path information attached to it in the BGP database. When the router looks to confirm whether it should be advertised, it sees an empty AS path set. Most companies do not want to ever become a transit AS, so they never want to advertise routes learned from another AS. They only want to advertise locally originated routes. The way this is typically accomplished is with the regular expression ^$—this signifies an empty AS path list. Example 7-4 shows an AS path ACL used to limit route advertisements to local routes only.

Example 7-4   Configuring an AS Path Access List

```
ip as-path access-list 1 permit ^$
!
router bgp 65001
neighbor 10.1.1.1 filter-list 1 out
```

AS path ACLs can also be used in route maps to set attributes on the matching routes. Route map CCNP in Example 7-5 limits the advertised routes to local only and sets a MED of 100 when they are advertised to the BGP neighbor.

Example 7-5   Using an AS Path ACL with a Route Map

```
ip as-path access-list 1 permit ^$
!
route-map CCNP permit 10
match as-path 1
set metric 100
!
router bgp 65001
neighbor 10.1.1.1 route-map CCNP out
```

Order of Operations

As you have seen, multiple filters and policies can be applied to the same BGP neighbor. If you are configuring these, you must understand the order in which they are processed by the router. The order of BGP inbound and outbound policy application has changed over the years and varies based on IOS version. The order given here is based on IOS version 15.2(4)M3.

Note that a distribute list and a prefix list cannot both be applied to the same neighbor in the same direction.

Incoming route advertisements are handled in this order:

1. Filter list

2. Prefix list or distribute list

3. Route map

Outgoing route advertisements are processed in the following order:

1. Filter list

2. Route map or unsuppressed map

3. Advertise map

4. Prefix list or distribute list

5. Outbound route filter (ORF) prefix list

BGP Authentication

BGP supports MD5 authentication between neighbors, using a shared password. It is configured under BGP router configuration mode with the command **neighbor** {*ip-address* | *peer-group-name*} **password** *password.*

Part I: ROUTE

When authentication is configured, BGP authenticates every TCP segment from its peer and checks the source of each routing update. Most ISPs require authentication for their eBGP peers.

Peering succeeds only if both routers are configured for authentication and have the same password. If a router has a password configured for a neighbor, but the neighbor router does not, a message such as the following displays on the console while the routers attempt to establish a BGP session between them:

```
%TCP-6-BADAUTH: No MD5 digest from [peer's IP address]:11003 to
  [local router's IP address]:179
```

Similarly, if the two routers have different passwords configured, a message such as the following will display on the screen:

```
%TCP-6-BADAUTH: Invalid MD5 digest from [peer's IP address]:11004
  to [local router's IP address]:179
```

Verifying BGP

One of the best commands to verify and troubleshoot your BGP configuration is **show ip bgp** [*network*] to see the BGP topology database. **show ip bgp** is such an important command that it's worth looking at in depth. Example 7-6 shows the command output, which lists a table of all the networks BGP knows about, the next hop for each network, some of the attributes for each route, and the AS path for each route.

Example 7-6   Interpreting the BGP Topology Database

```
Router# show ip bgp
BGP table version is 5, local router ID is 192.168.11.1
Status codes: s suppressed, d damped, h history, * valid, > best,
  i - internal,
              r RIB-failure, S Stale, m multipath, b backup-path,
  f RT-Filter,
              x best-external, a additional-path, c RIB-compressed,
Origin codes: i - IGP, e - EGP, ? - incomplete
RPKI validation codes: V valid, I invalid, N Not found

      Network          Next Hop          Metric LocPrf Weight Path
 *>   192.168.11.0     0.0.0.0                0          32768 i
 *>i  192.168.22.0     192.168.2.2            0    100      0 i
 * i  198.51.100.0     209.165.201.6          0    100      0 65200
 65300 i
 *>                    209.165.201.2                        0 65100
 65300 i
```

```
* i 203.0.113.0/22    209.165.201.6         0    100      0 65200
  65300 63000 i
* >                   209.165.201.2                       0 65100
  65300 i
```

Networks are listed in numerical order, smallest to largest. The first three columns list each route's status. An asterisk (*) in the first column means that the route has a valid next hop. Some other options for the first column include the following:

- **"s" for suppressed:** BGP knows about this network but is not advertising it, usually because it is part of a summarized route.

- **"d" for dampened:** BGP can stop advertising a network that flaps (goes up and down) too often until it is stable for a period of time.

- **"h" for history:** BGP knows about this network but does not currently have a valid route to it.

- **"r" for RIB failure:** The route was advertised to BGP but was not installed in the IP routing table. This might be because another protocol has the same route with a better administrative distance.

- **"S" for stale:** Used with nonstop forwarding to indicate that the route is stale and needs to be refreshed when the peer is reestablished.

The second column has a greater-than sign (>) beside the route that was selected as the best path to that network. In the example, there are two routes for network 198.51.100.0 and the router has selected the second one.

The routes learned from an iBGP neighbor have an "i" in the third column. The third column is blank for those routes learned from an eBGP neighbor. Recall that BGP prefers routes through an eBGP neighbor over an internal route.

The fourth column lists the networks. Those without a subnet mask shown use their classful mask. As shown in the example, when the router learns about the same network from multiple sources, it lists only the network once.

The fifth column lists the next-hop address for each route. As you learned in the section on BGP next hops, this might or might not be a directly connected router. A next-hop of 0.0.0.0 means that the local router originated the route.

If a MED value was received with the route, it is listed in the Metric column. This column can also have a value of 0—the default MED—in the Metric column.

Part I: ROUTE

The default Local Preference is 100. This may or may not be displayed in the table. Any nondefault Local Preference value is displayed in that column.

The Weight column always displays a value. The default value is 0 except for locally originated routes, which have a default weight of 32768.

The ninth column shows the AS path for each network. A blank AS path means that the route was originated in the local AS. Reading this field from left to right, the first AS number shown is the adjacent AS this router learned the route from. After that, the autonomous systems that this route traversed are shown in order. The last AS number listed is the originating AS. In the example, our router received an advertisement about network 198.51.100.0 from its neighbor AS 65200, which heard about it from AS 65300. Because AS 65300 is the last one listed, it is where the route advertisement originated.

Note

In the AS Path column, network 203.0.113.0 shows AS 65300 twice in its AS path list. Most likely, AS 65300 has prepended an extra copy of its AS number to make the path through 209.165.201.6 less attractive than the alternative path.

The last column shows how BGP originally learned about the route. All the networks in the example show an "i" for their origin codes. This means that the originating router had a network statement for that route. BGP considers a route with an origin code of "?" as an "incomplete" route. This typically means that the route was redistributed into BGP. You will likely never see the third possibility, an "e," because that means BGP learned the route from the Exterior Gateway Protocol (EGP), which is no longer in use.

Some other useful commands for verifying and troubleshooting BGP include

- **show ip bgp rib-failure:** Displays routes that were not inserted into the IP routing table and the reason they were not used.

- **show ip bgp summary:** Displays the memory used by the various BGP databases, BGP activity statistics, and a list of BGP neighbors.

- **show ip bgp neighbors:** Displays details about each neighbor. Can be modified by adding the neighbor IP address.

- **show ip bgp neighbors** *address* **[received | routes | advertised]:** Lets you monitor the routes received from and advertised to a particular neighbor.

You can search for "public route servers" to find listings of BGP routers that enable public telnet access for viewing their BGP tables. Trying some of these commands on a public route server can help you become familiar with them.

Multiprotocol BGP

Multiprotocol BGP (MP-BGP) involves two extensions to BGP4 that enable BGP to carry reachability information for other protocols, such as IPv6, multicast IPv4, and MPLS. The extensions enable the NEXT_HOP attribute to carry IPv6 addresses and NLRI (network layer reachability information) to an IPv6 prefix. An address-family command is added to the BGP configuration to enable this.

The router ID must be manually configured in an all-IPv6 implementation and is a 32-bit dotted-decimal number. Unlike the IGPs, configuration is done under the BGP router configuration mode, not at the interface. Neighbors are configured under the global BGP configuration mode but must be activated under the IPv6 address family mode. Any policies or networks relevant to this MP-BGP extension are also configured under the address family.

One interesting "feature" is that, because BGP runs over TCP, its advertisements can carry both IPv4 and IPv6 routes regardless of which protocol is used as the transport. You can use IPv4 to carry both IPv4 and IPv6 routes, you can use IPv6 to carry routes from both protocols, or you can use separate BGP sessions for IPv4 and IPv6.

In Example 7-7, an IPv4 BGP session is used to carry both IPv4 and IPv6 routes.

Example 7-7   Carrying IPv6 Routes over an IPv4 BGP Session

```
RouterA(config)# router bgp 65000
RouterA(config-rtr)# neighbor 10.1.1.2 remote-as 65001
!
RouterA(config-rtr)# address-family ipv4 unicast
RouterA(config-rtr-af)# neighbor 10.1.1.2 activate
RouterA(config-rtr-af)# network 10.1.0.0 mask 255.255.0.0
!
RouterA(config-rtr)# address-family ipv6 unicast
RouterA(config-rtr-af)# neighbor 10.1.1.2 activate
RouterA(config-rtr-af)# network 2001:db8:1::/48
```

Part I: ROUTE

Example 7-8 shows using BGP to advertise only IPv6 routes with the session established using IPv6 as the transport protocol. Note that a router ID has been manually configured.

Example 7-8   Using BGP with an IPv6 Session

```
RouterA(config)# router bgp 65000
RouterA(config-rtr)# router-id 10.255.255.1
RouterA(config-rtr)# neighbor 2001:db8:1:1:5::4 remote-as 65001
!
RouterA(config-rtr)# address-family ipv6 unicast
RouterA(config-rtr-af)# neighbor 2001:db8:1:5::4 activate
RouterA(config-rtr-af)# network 2001:db8:1::/48
```

Finally, Example 7-9 shows the BGP commands to run separate BGP sessions for IPv4 and IPv6. The IPv6 neighbor must be manually removed from the IPv4 address family because all neighbors are enabled under the IPv4 address family by default.

Example 7-9   Separate BGP Sessions for IPv4 and IPv6

```
RouterA(config)# router bgp 65000
RouterA(config-rtr)# router-id 10.255.255.1
RouterA(config-rtr)# neighbor 10.1.1.2 remote-as 65001
RouterA(config-rtr)# neighbor 2001:db8:1:1:5::4 remote-as 65001
!
RouterA(config-rtr)# address-family ipv4 unicast
RouterA(config-rtr-af)# no neighbor 2001:db8:1:5::4 activate
RouterA(config-rtr-af)# neighbor 10.1.1.2 activate
RouterA(config-rtr-af)# network 10.1.0.0 mask 255.255.0.0
!
RouterA(config-rtr)# address-family ipv6 unicast
RouterA(config-rtr-af)# neighbor 2001:db8:1:5::4 activate
RouterA(config-rtr-af)# network 2001:db8:1::/48
```

To verify your IPv6 BGP configuration, use the commands **show bgp ipv6 unicast summary** and **show ipv6 route bgp**.

CHAPTER 8

Infrastructure Security

Device Access Control

Because of their importance in packet forwarding, routers make attractive targets for network attacks. This section discusses some of the built-in protections you can enable to secure access to your device.

The most basic type of security is to require a password to access the router. Cisco devices use several types of passwords for access control:

- **Enable password:** Controls access to privileged EXEC mode if the enable secret password is not present. It is stored in clear text in the configuration by default. To configure, use the global command **enable password** *password*.

- **Enable secret:** Controls access to privileged EXEC mode. It is stored in a nonreversible one-way MD5 hash. If present in the configuration, it overrides the enable password. To configure, use the global command **enable secret** *password*. Recent IOS versions can use encryption type 4 (SHA-256). Configure this with the command **enable secret 4** *password*.

- **Line passwords:** Routers have VTY lines for Telnet and SSH access, the console port, the AUX port, and TTY lines that must all be protected. Access to these lines can be controlled either with AAA or with individual passwords applied to them. Line passwords are stored in clear text by default. To configure individual passwords on one of these lines, use the line-configuration mode commands **login** and **password** *password*.

You can encrypt the passwords that are stored in clear text by using the global command **service password-encryption**. However, this uses an encryption method that is easily broken, so do not rely on it to protect highly sensitive passwords.

SSH is more secure than Telnet; use it to access the device's VTY lines. Some Cisco devices have a feature called *Management Plane Protection* that enables you to designate specific interfaces as management interfaces, and only management traffic such as SSH, SNMP, and TFTP is allowed to use these interfaces.

Disable any device services that are not being used. These can include the following, many of which are enabled by default:

- BOOTP server

- CDP

- HTTP/HTTPS

- ICMP Redirects

- IP source routing

- ICMP unreachables

- Proxy ARP

Cisco devices enable you to define up to 16 privilege levels with different command sets assigned to each. Normal user-level privileges are level 0. Standard privileged mode (access to all commands) is level 15. The following configuration shows how to assign the **traceroute** command to level 2, with a separate enable secret password of CCNP. After applying this configuration, users at level 0 can no longer execute traceroutes.

```
Router(config)# privilege exec level 2 traceroute
Router(config)# enable secret level 2 CCNP
```

Router Security Features

In addition to securing access to the router itself, you must consider the security of the data that traverses your network. Cisco devices have some features that can help.

Access Control Lists

An *access control list (ACL)* is an ordered group of statements that permit or deny specified types of traffic. They are used extensively in router security configurations for things such as

- Controlling traffic through the router

- Permitting or denying access to services

- Mitigating address spoofing

- Mitigating attacks

The statements in an ACL are evaluated from the top down, in order. When the router finds a match, it takes the action in the matching statement and does not read the rest of the ACL.

IPv4 can use both standard and extended access lists. Standard ACLs enable filtering based on source IP address only. Extended ACLs permit filtering based on source or destination address as well as most other fields in the IP header. IPv4 access lists can be either numbered or named. Numbered standard ACLs range from 1 to 99 and 1300 to 1999. Numbered extended ACLs range from 100 to 199 and 2000 to 2699. IPv6 uses only named, extended access lists.

You can apply ACLs either inbound or outbound on an interface. Inbound ACLs affect traffic coming in on the interface; outbound ACLs affect traffic leaving out that interface.

All access lists have an implicit "deny any" at the end—any traffic not explicitly permitted by the ACL is denied. IPv6 access lists have two implicit permit statements before the final deny. Because IPv6 relies on the Neighbor Discovery protocol, blocking that would affect function. So IPv6 ACLs end with the following implicit rules:

```
permit icmp any any nd-na
permit icmp any any nd-ns
deny ipv6 any any
```

Configuring IPv4 ACLs

To configure a numbered standard IPv4 access control list, use the global command:

```
access-list number {permit | deny} source-address
 source-wildcard-mask
```

To configure a basic numbered extended IPv4 access control list, use the global command:

```
access-list number {permit | deny} protocol source-address
 source-wildcard-mask destination-address
 destination-wildcard-mask
```

To configure a named ACL, use a global command to create it, and then configure each statement under the access-list configuration submode:

```
ip access-list {standard | extended} name
{permit | deny} protocol source-address source-wildcard-mask
 destination-address destination-wildcard-mask
```

You can also configure an ACL statement that is in effect only during speci-fied times. To do this, first create a time range that lists the times the ACL should be used. Then add the option **time-range** *time-range-name* to the end of your access list statement.

To apply an IPv4 access list to an interface, use the interface command:

```
ip access-group {number | name} {in | out}
```

To verify the ACL configuration and operation, use the command **show access-list**.

Configuring an IPv6 Access List

The commands to create an IPv6 ACL are similar to those for IPv4, except that you use the keyword **ipv6** in the command. Recall that IPv6 uses only named, extended ACLs.

```
ipv6 access-list name
{permit | deny} protocol source-address source-wildcard-mask
 destination-address destination-wildcard-mask
```

The command to apply the access list to an interface is also slightly differ-ent. It uses the keyword **traffic-filter** rather than **access-group**:

```
ipv6 traffic-filter name {in | out}
```

To verify the ACL configuration and operation, use the command **show ipv6 access-list**.

Unicast Reverse Path Forwarding

Unicast Reverse Path Forwarding (uRPF) is a security feature that helps prevent traffic from spoofed addresses being sent through your network. It verifies whether the router can reach the source IP address of the packet. If the source address is not valid, the packet is dropped. There are two modes:

- **Loose mode:** A route for the source address must be in the routing table, but not as a default route or a route pointing to Null0. You can, however, configure the router to accept a default route as valid.

- **Strict mode:** A route for the source address must be in the routing table, and the packet must have come in on the interface associated with that route. In other words, the packet must have come in on the interface the router would use to send traffic out to that source address.

Use loose mode if you have asymmetric routing. uRPF relies on CEF, so make sure it is not disabled. Optionally, use an access list to control which traffic is checked.

uRPF is enabled at each interface with the following command:

```
ip verify unicast source reachable-via {any | rx}[allow-default]
 access-list
```

The **any** keyword enables loose mode, and the **rx** keyword enables strict mode.

To verify whether uRPF is configured on an interface, either check the router configuration or use the command **show cef interface** *type number*. To view uRPF operation, use the command **show ip traffic** to see how many packets have been dropped due to failing the uRPF check.

Tunneling Technologies

Many companies have sites or home offices that connect to the organization's network over the Internet. Because the Internet is inherently insecure, most use some form of a tunneling protocol and encryption to create a virtual private network (VPN). Tunneling protocols encapsulate the original packet in tunnel headers. Other routers along the path from source to destination look only at the tunnel headers and route based on them. The original headers and the data are left intact. The tunnel header is removed at the destination and the traffic is decrypted.

This section discusses three types of tunnels:

- GRE
- DMVPN
- Easy VPN

It also discusses carrying PPP over Ethernet.

Part I: ROUTE

GRE Tunnels

Generic Routing Encapsulation (GRE) is a tunneling protocol that supports multiple Layer 3 protocols. It also enables the use of multicast routing protocols across its tunnel. It adds a 20-byte IP header and a 4-byte GRE header, hiding the existing packet headers. The GRE header contains a flag field and a protocol type field to identify the Layer 3 protocol being transported. It might optionally contain a tunnel checksum, tunnel key, and tunnel sequence number. GRE does not encrypt traffic or use any strong security measures to protect the traffic.

GRE can be used along with IPsec to provide data source authentication and data confidentiality and ensure data integrity. GRE over IPsec tunnels are typically configured in a hub-and-spoke topology over an untrusted WAN to minimize the number of tunnels that each router must maintain.

Figure 8-1 shows how the GRE and IPsec headers work together.

Figure 8-1   GRE over IPsec Headers

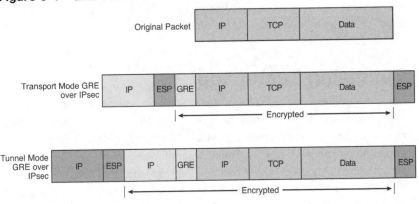

Configuring a GRE Tunnel

To configure GRE using IOS commands, you must first construct a logical tunnel interface. GRE commands are then given under that interface. Specify a source and destination for the tunnel; the source is a local outgoing interface or an interface address. You might also give the tunnel interface an IP address and indicate the tunnel mode. GRE is the default mode.

Example 8-1 shows the commands to configure a GRE tunnel interface.

Example 8-1   GRE Tunnel Configuration Commands

```
interface Tunnel number
 ip address address mask and/or
```

```
ipv6 address address/prefix
tunnel source {interface | address}
tunnel destination {address}
tunnel mode {gre | gre ipv6}
```

Be sure to configure the device on the other end of the tunnel as well. Adjust routing so that traffic uses the tunnel for destinations on the other side—you might want to use a static route for this. Routing protocols can be carried over the tunnel, but be sure that the router does not learn the tunnel destination address through the tunnel itself. Verify the tunnel configuration using **show interface**, or use **traceroute** to confirm whether traffic goes over the tunnel.

DMVPN

Configuring a full mesh of GRE or IPsec tunnels becomes unwieldy as the network grows in size. Dynamic Multipoint Virtual Private Network (DMVPN) dynamically creates IPsec tunnels on demand, thus easing the administrative burden. DMVPN leverages multipoint GRE (mGRE), IPsec, and Next Hop Resolution Protocol (NHRP). The hub site(s) creates an mGRE tunnel interface. Each of the remote sites (spokes) is configured with information about the hub and initiates a tunnel with the hub. The hub uses NHRP to map each spoke's tunnel IP address to its physical address.

When one spoke wants to send traffic to another, it uses an NHRP query to ask the hub for the physical next-hop address of the other spoke. It can then build a dynamic tunnel to that spoke.

DMVPN is a good choice when spoke-to-spoke connections are needed because traffic does not have to traverse the hub. It also supports multicast and routing protocols between the hub and the spokes.

Easy VPN

Cisco Easy VPN simplifies the deployment of services and policies to remote users. Easy VPN enables a server to push down VPN configuration to a client. It is a way to create site-to-site VPNs without manually configuring each remote router, so it is good for remote sites lacking technical support. It also can be used with software clients for remote users.

Cisco Easy VPN dynamically handles the following items:

- Negotiating VPN tunnel parameters

- Establishing the VPN tunnel based on those parameters

Part I: ROUTE

- NAT, PAT, or ACL configuration

- User authentication

- Managing encryption and decryption keys

- Authenticating, encrypting, and decrypting traffic

Cisco Easy VPN has two components: a server and a remote client. The Easy VPN Server can be a Cisco router, ASA Firewall, or Cisco VPN concentrator. It contains security policies and pushes those to remote clients. The Easy VPN Remote can be a Cisco router, ASA Firewall, a hardware client, or a software client. It contacts the server and receives policies from it to establish an IPsec tunnel between the remote site and the central site.

PPPoE

Although not technically a tunneling protocol, Point-to-Point Protocol over Ethernet (PPPoE) is a method used to create logical point-to-point links over a multipoint medium. PPP is a Layer 2 protocol that can be employed to transport many different protocols over point-to-point links. It was originally designed to carry TCP/IP over serial links but is now additionally being used with DSL, SONET, and Metro Ethernet. PPP provides authentication and some other controls that are lacking in these transport mediums.

There are two stages to establishing a PPPoE connection:

- **Active Discovery:** Because PPP was created to be used over a point-to-point connection, and Ethernet is multipoint, PPPoE uses a network-access server discovery process. After a server has been discovered, the client router associates with it and the PPPoE layer is established.

- **PPP Session Setup:** This includes the normal PPP session negotiations and authentication. If this stage succeeds, a virtual point-to-point link is established. Traffic is then sent across the link encapsulated in PPPoE and PPP headers.

Authentication is typically done via the Challenge Handshake Authentication Protocol (CHAP). CHAP uses a three-way handshake to verify the identity of its peer device.

Example 8-2 shows a PPPoE client that receives its outside IP address from the ISP. You can also use statically assigned IP addresses. Note that PPP requires a dialer interface even though nothing is actually being dialed. The IP address and authentication configuration is performed on the dialer interface.

Example 8-2   Configuring PPPoE

```
Router(config)# interface dialer 1
Router(config-if)# mtu 1492
Router(config-if)# encapsulation ppp
Router(config-if)# dialer pool 1
Router(config-if)# ip address negotiated
Router(config-if)# ppp authentication chap
Router(config-if)# ppp chap password CCNP
!
Router(config-if)# int e0/0
Router(config-if)# pppoe-client dial-pool-number 1
```

If you were configuring this router as an edge device for a small or home office, you might also want to add NAT and DHCP server commands to the configuration. Verify the configuration with the command **show pppoe session [all | packets]**. Confirm the PPP negotiations with **debug pppoe {data | errors | events | packets}**.

Part I: ROUTE

CHAPTER 9

Infrastructure Services

Cisco devices have several features and services that are useful for administering, managing, troubleshooting, and optimizing your network. This chapter covers the following subset of these:

- SMTP

- General logging

- Debug

- Syslog

- NTP

- DHCP

- NetFlow

- NAT

The available features and services vary by device, and the commands differ by operating system and version. This book uses commands from IOS version 15.2.

Simple Network Management Protocol

The Simple Network Management Protocol (SNMP) collects information from SNMP agents residing on network devices, either through regular polling or by event-generated traps. The information is stored on the local device in a management information base (MIB). It can then be exported to an SNMP server for analysis. The information that can be collected varies by device but is extensive.

There are three versions of SNMP. Versions 1 and 2c send the community nity strings in clear text. They control access to the MIB by using SNMP community strings, which can be read-only (RO) or read-write (RW). Version 2c is the most widely accepted implementation of version 2. Neither of these can authenticate the source of a message nor encrypt a message; therefore, they should be used only for read-only access. SNMP version 3 adds three security models:

- **noAuthNoPriv:** Neither authenticates nor encrypts; specified by **no auth** during configuration

- **authNoPriv:** Authenticates the sender but does not encrypt the message; specified by **auth** during configuration

- **authPriv:** Both authenticates the sender and encrypts the message; specified by **priv** during configuration

SNMPv2c Configuration

Example 9-1 creates a standard access list that allows SNMPv2 access only to the SNMP manager at 10.1.1.1. Two community strings are created: **ccnp** for read-only access and **c1sc0** for read-write access. Read-write access is permitted only from the host specified in access list 1. Next, the SNMP server address is given, along with the command to send traps messages to that server.

Example 9-1   SNMPv2 Configuration

```
Router(config)# access-list 1 permit 10.1.1.1
Router(config)# snmp-server community ccnp ro
Router(config)# snmp-server community c1sc0 rw 1
Router(config)# snmp-server host 10.1.1.2 traps
```

SNMPv3 Configuration

SNMPv3 configuration can be more complex because you have the option to configure authentication and encryption. The basic items that you need to configure in SNMP version 3 are as follows:

- Create an access list for limiting SNMP access, if desired.

- Create an SNMPv3 group, assign it one of the three security models, and optionally a security level.

- Create an SNMPv3 user, link it with a group, and optionally configure authentication and encryption parameters.

- Specify an SNMP host or hosts.

- Enable SNMP traps.

In Example 9-2, an access list is created to restrict SNMP access to hosts on the management subnet of 192.168.1.0/24. An SNMPv3 group named CCNP

Part I: ROUTE

is configured to use security model authNoPriv, meaning that it authenticates but does not encrypt SNMP traffic. Access list 1 is linked to the group. An SNMPv3 user named admin1 is created and linked to the CCNP group. User admin1 will have an authentication password of Secret and use HMAC SHA for authentication. (Note the router's message after the user is configured.) The SNMP server address is added and linked to user admin1, and the collection of traps is enabled.

Example 9-2   Configuring SNMPv3

```
Router(config)# access-list 1 permit 192.168.1.0 0.0.0.255
Router(config)# snmp-server group CCNP v3 auth access 1
Router(config)# snmp-server user admin1 CCNP v3 auth sha Secret

*Jun 14 19:37:07.930: Configuring snmpv3 USM user, persisting
 snmpEngineBoots. Please Wait...

Router(config)# snmp-server host 192.168.1.1 traps version 3 auth
 admin1
Router(config)# snmp-server enable traps
!
Router# show snmp
<output omitted>
SNMP global trap: enabled
SNMP logging: enabled
    Logging to 192.168.1.1.162, 0/10, 260 sent, 0 dropped.
```

Additional verification commands include **show snmp group**, **show snmp user**, and **show snmp host**.

Logging

Logging is an essential network management tool, providing insight into network traffic and device failures or critical events. Routers can gather information from various sources, such as debugs, Simple Network Management Protocol (SNMP) traps, system logging (syslog), and NetFlow. This information can be stored on the buffer of the local device, but this is not scalable and is erased if the device reloads. Sending it to a remote server or collection device is usually preferable.

By default, all logging is displayed on the device's console. You can stop this with the command **no logging** console or control it with the **logging console** *level* command. There are other options, such as

- **Terminal line:** Enable this with the command **terminal monitor**. Disable it with the command **terminal no monitor**.

- **Internal buffer:** Enable this with the command **logging buffered**.

- **Syslog server:** This is detailed in the "Syslog" section of this chapter.

- **SNMP server:** This is detailed in the "Simple Network Management Protocol" section of this chapter.

You will likely want to record the time the log message was sent. The command to enable this is **service timestamps {debug | log}**.

Debug

Debug is a useful troubleshooting tool, with the caveat that it can produce large amounts of traffic because it displays the device's internal processes. The command to enable debugging is **debug** *action-to-be-displayed*. You can view many actions with debug, and they vary by device; use the **debug ?** command to see them all. To turn off debugging, use either the same command preceded by **no** or the command **undebug all** (the short version of this command is **u all**).

When you give the **debug** command, it applies to all traffic that matches; for example, debugging AAA looks at AAA traffic. You can limit it for some protocols to traffic matching certain conditions, such as an interface, by using *conditional debug*. The generic command to enable conditional debugging is **debug condition** *condition modifier*. For example, to restrict the debug output to a specific interface, use **debug condition interface** *interface*.

Syslog

Cisco devices produce system logging (or *syslog*) messages that can be output to the device console, VTY connection, system buffer, or remote syslog server. You are probably familiar with the following syslog message, for example:

```
%SYS-5-CONFIG_I: Configured from console by console
```

If sent to a syslog server, messages are sent on UDP port 514. A syslog message always starts with the percent sign and has the following format:

```
%FACILTY-SUBFACILITY-SEVERITY-MNEMONIC: message text
```

Part I: ROUTE

Each portion of a syslog message has a specific meaning:

- **FACILITY-SUBFACILITY:** This reports the protocol, module, or process that generated the message. Some examples are SYS for the operating system, OSPF, IF for an interface, and IP.

- **SEVERITY:** A number from 0 to 7 designating the importance of the action reported. Enabling logging of any of these levels also enables all levels above it. For instance, enabling level 4 also enables levels 0 through 3. The logging levels are

  — Emergency—0

  — Alert—1

  — Critical—2

  — Error—3

  — Warning— 4

  — Notice—5

  — Informational— 6

  — Debugging— 7

- **MNEMONIC:** A code that identifies the action reported.

- A plain-text description of the event that triggered the syslog message.

Configuring Syslog

Configuring a Cisco device to send syslog messages to an external server is fairly simple. The server itself must, of course, also be configured to receive those messages. Example 9-3 shows the configuration to send syslog messages of level 3, Error, or worse to a server located at 192.168.1.1. Because there might be several ways to reach that server, the source interface of Lo0 is specified.

Example 9-3   Configuring Syslog

```
Router(config)# logging 192.168.1.1
Router(config)# logging trap 3
Router(config)# logging source-interface lo0
Router(config)# logging on
```

Network Time Protocol

The Network Time Protocol (NTP) is a client/server protocol that enables network devices to dynamically synchronize their internal clocks with a common external source. Clock synchronization is important for correlating syslog messages, authentication key expiration, certificate-based encryption, and other features. Cisco devices can act either as an NTP peer or an NTP server. In a peer association, the local system can either synchronize to another device or the other device can synchronize to it. In a server association, the local device can only synchronize to an NTP server.

NTP Version 3 supports IPv4, and clients can use broadcasts for clock updates. Version 4 adds IPv6 support, is backward compatible with v3, and messages are sent via multicast. NTP uses the concept of "stratum" to designate the reliability of a clock source, with 1 being the best. A stratum 1 clock is an authoritative source such as an atomic clock. Stratum 2 is one hop away from that, and so on.

Time is tracked internally using universal coordinated time (UTC). You can configure a time zone and daylight saving time so that time is displayed in local format.

Because time synchronization is a security-related feature, configuring authentication for NTP information is wise. This prevents an attacker from spoofing NTP packets to corrupt the system clock. For added security, you can add an access list to restrict the IP addresses with which the router can synchronize time.

Example 9-4 shows a router configured to get its time from an authenticated NTP version 3 server located at 10.1.1.1. The time zone is set to Eastern Standard Time and is adjusted for daylight saving time.

Example 9-4 NTP Configuration

```
Router(config)# ntp authenticate
Router(config)# ntp authentication-key 1 md5 my_ntp_key
Router(config)# ntp trusted-key 1
Router(config)# ntp server 10.1.1.1 key 1
Router(config)# clock timezone EST -5
Router(config)# clock summertime EDT recurring
```

The command for IPv6 routers to synchronize their time with an NTPv4 server is

```
Router(config)# ntp server ipv6-address version 4
```

Verify your NTP configuration with the commands **show clock**, **show ntp status**, and **show ntp associations**.

Part I: ROUTE

DHCP

DHCP automates the assignment of IP addresses to network hosts. DHCP addresses can be allocated in the following ways:

- **Manually:** A specific IP address is assigned to a MAC address.

- **Automatic:** An IP address is permanently assigned to a host.

- **Dynamic:** The IP address is assigned for a limited amount of time or until the client releases it.

DHCP for IPv4

The process of acquiring an IP address from a DHCP server has four steps:

Step 1.   The host broadcasts a DHCPDISCOVER message.

Step 2.   The server responds with a DHCPOFFER message containing the IP address and optionally other settings.

Step 3.   The client broadcasts a DHCPREQUEST message, requesting the offered IP address.

Step 4.   The server sends a DHCPACK confirming the address assignment.

Configuring DHCP for IPv4

Cisco routers can be DHCP clients, servers, or relay agents. To configure an IOS device as a DHCP client, use the **ip address dhcp** command on the interface that needs to obtain the DHCP address. To configure a router as a DHCP server, you must create an IP address pool and assign a network or subnet to that pool. Exclude any static IP addresses within the pool, such as the router's address.

You can optionally add information, such as default gateway, DNS server, domain name, or lease duration. The Option statement provides additional information to clients; some typical options include Option 150 to locate a TFTP server for Cisco IP phones and Option 43 to locate a Wireless LAN Controller for access points.

Example 9-5 shows a router configured as a DHCP server, giving addresses from the 10.6.3.0/24 network. The IP address range of 10.6.3.1–10.6.3.5 is excluded from the pool. The clients' default gateway is 10.6.3.1. Option 150 tells the phones the address of the TFTP server where they will download their configuration.

Part I: ROUTE

Example 9-5 Configuring a DHCP Server

```
Router(config)# ip dhcp excluded-address 10.6.3.1 10.6.3.5
!
Router(config)# ip dhcp pool PHONES
Router(dhcp-config)# network 10.6.3.0 /24
Router(dhcp-config)# default-router 10.6.3.1
Router(dhcp-config)# option 150 10.6.2.2
```

IPv4 DHCP Relay Agent

Hosts discover their DHCP server by sending broadcasts. If the DHCP server is on a different subnet, those broadcasts must be routed to the server as unicasts. You can configure a router to relay DHCP messages with the **ip helper-address** interface command. It is important to understand that this command must be given on the interface that receives the host broadcasts. A Cisco DHCP relay agent functions as follows:

Step 1. A client broadcasts a DHCP request, which is seen by the IOS device (a router, for instance).

Step 2. The router changes the destination address of the packet to the unicast address of the server. It optionally adds option 82 (relay agent option) information.

Step 3. The router sends the unicast packet to the server.

Step 4. The server responds with the IP address and other parameters, such as the default gateway assigned to the client.

Step 5. The router gets the packet from the server, removes any option 82 information, and forwards it to the client.

Verify your DHCP configuration with the commands **show ip dhcp database**, **show ip dhcp server statistics**, and **show ip dhcp binding**. Delete address assignments with the **clear ip dhcp binding** {*address* | ***} command.

DHCP for IPv6

As described in Chapter 2, "IPv6 Overview," clients can use stateless autoconfiguration to obtain their network prefix and then use that prefix plus their MAC address to create a unique IPv6 address. DHCPv6 can be used instead of or in addition to stateless autoconfiguration. Two types of DHCPv6 are

- **Stateful DHCP:** When you need to control the prefixes given to clients

Part I: ROUTE

- **Stateless DHCP:** Used with stateless autoconfiguration to provide more information, such as domain name, DNS server, NTP server, or other options

---

Note

One big difference between DHCPv4 and DHCPv6 is that DHCPv6 servers do not give out IP addresses. They give out prefixes. The client then uses its MAC address along with the prefix to create its IPv6 address, just as it would with stateless autoconfiguration.

DHCPv6 Process

IPv6 clients first listen for router advertisement (RA) to determine whether they should use DHCP. If there is no router on the link, or if the RA specifies the use of DHCP, clients begin this process:

Step 1. The client sends a SOLICIT message to the all-DHCP-agents multicast address.

Step 2. All DHCP servers receiving the multicast answer with a unicast ADVERTISE message. This contains prefix and any other configured information, such as DNS server.

Step 3. The client responds to one of the DHCP servers (if there are multiple) with a REQUEST message, confirming its configuration parameters.

Step 4. The DHCP server responds with a REPLY message.

As with DHCPv4, there is a time limit on the prefix lease, and clients must renew the lease periodically.

A faster, two-step process called Rapid-Commit does exist that uses only SOLICIT and REPLY messages. This is useful when there is only one DHCP server or users are highly mobile. Rapid-Commit must be enabled on both clients and servers before it is used.

Configuring Stateful DHCPv6

The steps to configure DHCPv6 are similar to those for configuring DHCPv4. You create a pool, and specify all the configuration parameters under that pool. However, you do not specify a range of address—you configure a network prefix. There is no "excluded address" command because actual addresses are not given out. Another difference is that you must associate the pool with an interface. In Example 9-6, a pool named CCNP is configured to provide prefix and DNS server information, and the lease length is set to 2 days. The DHCP pool is applied to e0/0, which is the client-facing interface on which requests will come in.

Example 9-6   Configuring Stateful DHCPv6

```
Router(config)# ipv6 dhcp pool CCNP
Router(config-dhcpv6)# address prefix 2001:db8:1::/64
Router(config-dhcpv6)# dns-server 2001:db8:2::1
Router(config-dhcpv6)# information refresh 2
!
Router(config)# int e0/0
Router(config-if)# ipv6 dhcp server CCNP
```

Configuring Stateless DHCPv6

Stateless DHCPv6, or DHCPv6 Lite, does not distribute either IP address or prefixes—clients obtain those via another method, usually by stateless auto-configuration. Stateless DHCP is used to provide other information, such as DNS server address or options. You still must configure a DHCP pool and associate it with an interface. However, there is an additional line of inter-face configuration to let clients know to look to the pool for additional infor-mation. That command is **ipv6 nd other-config-flag**. Example 9-7 shows a DHCP pool that furnishes DNS server and domain name information. The pool is then linked to the incoming interface.

Example 9-7   Configuring Stateless DHCPv6

```
Router(config)# ipv6 dhcp pool STATELESS
Router(config-dhcpv6)# dns-server 2001:db8:2::1
Router(config-dhcpv6)# domain-name ccnp.com
!
Router(config)# int e0/0
Router(config-if)# ipv6 dhcp server STATELESS
Router(config-if)# ipv6 nd other-config-flag
```

IPv6 DHCP Relay Agent

Hosts discover their DHCPv6 server by sending link-scoped multicasts, not broadcasts. However, if the DHCP server is on a different subnet, those multi-casts must still be routed to the server as unicasts. Configure a router to relay DHCPv6 messages with the interface command **ipv6 dhcp relay destination** *address* [*source interface*]. Source interface must be specified in the com-mand if the destination address given is a link-local address. If it is a global address, then no source interface is needed. As with DHCPv4, this command must be configured on the interface that receives the host broadcasts.

Part I: ROUTE

The following configuration shows the router configured to forward DHCPv6 multicasts from interface e0/1 to a DHCPv6 server at 2001:db8:3::1:

```
Router(config)# int e0/1
Router(config-if)# ipv6 dhcp relay destination 2001:db8:3::1
```

NetFlow

NetFlow is an IOS feature that captures statistics on IP traffic flows through Cisco devices. It is beneficial in monitoring applications and users, which helps in such tasks as identifying security risks, network optimizing, troubleshooting, chargeback billing, and data mining. NetFlow collects data about unidirectional flows of traffic between sources and destinations. It uses the following seven fields to identify a unique flow:

- Source IP address

- Source port number

- Destination IP address

- Destination port number

- Layer 3 protocol type

- Type of service

- Logical input interface

NetFlow creates a flow record for each traffic flow. There have been several formats for flow records, but the current ones in use are version 5 and version 9. Version 5 added BGP support. Version 9, which supports IPv6, is the basis for an IETF standard for information export and is based on a template that makes it easily adaptable to new protocols. However, it is not backward compatible with any previous version.

Two main components of NetFlow are

- **NetFlow cache:** The flow record for each active flow is maintained in the cache.

- **NetFlow export:** Information about flows that are no longer active are grouped into export datagrams to be exported via UDP to an external NetFlow collector.

To begin collecting NetFlow data, enable it to capture ingress and/or egress traffic on at least one interface. Then configure a destination for exporting the data to, the UDP port number to use, and optionally set the version number. Example 9-8 shows a basic IPv4 NetFlow configuration.

Example 9-8   NetFlow Configuration

```
Router(config)# int e0/0
Router(config-if)# ip flow ingress
Router(config-if)# ip flow egress
!
Router(config)# ip flow-export destination 10.1.1.1 2000
Router(config)# ip flow-export version 9
```

Verify NetFlow configuration and action with the commands **show ip flow interface**, **show ip cache flow**, and **show ip flow export**.

Network Address Translation

Network Address Translation (NAT) replaces the original IP address in the IP header with a different one on outgoing traffic and then places the original IP address into the header on incoming traffic. This hides actual device IP addresses from the world outside the NAT device. It is commonly used to translate the private IP addresses used inside a network to global, public addresses for Internet access. It can also be used to translate internal network addresses when there is an overlapping IP address range in two portions of the same network. There is even a type of NAT, called NAT64, that can translate between IPv4 and IPv6 addresses.

NAT performs three types of translation:

- **Static NAT:** Each device has a manually configured one-to-one mapping between its inside and outside address.

- **Dynamic NAT:** Each device gets a unique outside address from a pool of many addresses.

- **PAT (Port Address Translation):** Each inside device gets translated to the same (or one of a few) outside address. PAT uses different port numbers to distinguish between the inside hosts.

NAT uses four terms to refer to host addresses:

- **Inside local:** The IP address assigned to a host on the internal network. This is the address that is typically translated.

Part I: ROUTE

- **Inside global:** The IP address of the internal host as it appears to the external network; what the rest of the world thinks is the host's address.

- **Outside local:** What an internal device thinks is the IP address of an external device; it might have been translated or it might actually be the device's address.

- **Outside global:** The IP address actually assigned to the external device.

Configuring Traditional NAT for IPv4

The first step in configuring traditional NAT is to identify which interfaces the traffic to be translated will come in on, and which interface it will exit. The ingress interfaces are designated as "inside" and the egress interface is designated as "outside." You use the interface command **ip nat [inside | outside]** to configure this, as shown in Example 9-9. Interface Ethernet 0/0 is the ingress interface, where the traffic to be translated enters the router. Interface Ethernet 0/2 is the egress interface, where that traffic will exit the router.

Example 9-9   Configuring NAT Inside and Outside Interfaces

```
interface Ethernet0/0
 description LAN Interface
 ip address 192.168.10.1 255.255.255.0
 ip nat inside
!
interface Ethernet0/2
 description WAN Interface
 ip address 209.165.201.1 255.255.255.224
 ip nat outside
```

Static NAT

In static NAT, one inside local address is mapped to one inside global address. This might be used when you have a server with an inside address that must be reached from the outside. You always want it to have the same global IP address. Once you have the inside and outside interfaces configured, use the global command:

```
ip nat inside source static inside-local-adddr inside-global addr
```

Dynamic NAT

Use Dynamic NAT when you have a pool of global addresses that will be used by local hosts. One global address is assigned to each local host, but it is done dynamically. As before, identify the inside and outside interfaces. Then create an access list that permits the inside local address range to be translated. Then create a pool that lists the starting and ending addresses to be used as inside global addresses. Link the two together with the **ip nat inside source** command.

The following example assumes that the inside and outside interfaces have been configured. It shows an access list that permits the range 192.168.10.0/24—these are the local addresses to be translated. The NAT pool named DYNAMIC specifies 11 addresses to be used as global addresses. They are assigned to the first 11 hosts that send traffic from inter-face e0/0 bound out of interface e0/2. The third command tells the router to translate traffic with source addresses matching access list 1, coming in the interfaces marked as "inside," to an address in the pool DYNAMIC.

```
Router(config)# access-list 1 permit 192.168.10.0 0.0.0.255
Router(config)# ip nat pool DYNAMIC 209.165.201.10 209.165.201.20
 prefix-length 26
Router(config)# ip nat inside source list 1 pool DYNAMIC
```

PAT

PAT is also called *NAT overload*. Instead of only translating IP addresses, PAT also translates the source port as necessary. Each translation is identi-fied by both its IP address and its port number. Thus, one global address can represent multiple local hosts. The keyword **overload** tells the router to use PAT.

Start by identifying the inside and outside address as was done previously. You can create an address pool and translate multiple hosts to them, but typi-cally you use the address of the Internet-facing interface instead.

The following example assumes that the inside and outside interfaces have been configured. It shows an access list that permits the range 192.168.10.0/24—these are the local addresses to be translated. No pool is created; all traffic uses the IP address of interface e0/2 as its source address.

```
Router(config)# access-list 1 permit 192.168.10.0 0.0.0.255
Router(config)# ip nat inside source list 1 int e0/2 overload
```

Verify your NAT and PAT configurations with the commands **show ip nat translations** and **show ip nat statistics**.

Configuring NAT Virtual Interface

In more recent IOS versions, you do not have to identify the inside and outside interfaces. Instead, just enable interfaces for NAT. The router creates a NAT Virtual Interface (NVI). When traffic comes in a NAT-enabled interface it is checked against the NAT translation table. If there is a match, then the traffic is routed to the NVI interface where it is translated. It is then routed to its exit interface.

Enable an interface to use NVI with the interface command **ip nat enable**. The actual translation commands are slightly different also, in that they omit the **inside** and **outside** keywords.

The NVI command equivalent to the static NAT command shown in the "Static NAT" section is

```
ip nat source static inside-local-adddr inside-global-addr
```

The NVI command to use an access list and a NAT pool to do the dynamic NAT translation shown in the "Dynamic NAT section is

```
Router(config)# ip nat source list 1 pool DYNAMIC
```

Example 9-10 shows the configuration for NVI with PAT, using source addresses from access list 1 and translating to the IP address of interface e0/2. Note that the router has automatically created an NVI interface and given it the IP address of interface e0/0.

Example 9-10   Configuring NVI with PAT

```
Router(config)# access-list 1 permit 192.168.10.0 0.0.0.255
Router(config)# ip nat source list 1 int e0/2 overload
!
Router(config)# int e0/0
Router(config-if)# ip nat enable
Router(config)# int e0/2
Router(config-if)# ip nat enable
!
Router# show ip interface brief
Interface       IP-Address      OK? Method Status   Protocol
Ethernet0/0     192.168.10.1    YES NVRAM  up       up
Ethernet0/1     unassigned      YES NVRAM  down     down
Ethernet0/2     209.165.201.1   YES NVRAM  up       up
NVI0            192.168.10.1    YES unset  up       up
```

Verify your NVI configuration with the commands **show ip nat nvi translations** and **show ip nat nvi statistics** (notice the addition of the keyword **nvi**).

NAT64

Network Address Translation IPv6 to IPv4 (NAT64) enables IPv6 hosts to communicate with IPv4 hosts, and vice versa. This is accomplished by translating between IPv6 and IPv4 addresses, and also between the IPv4 and IPv6 header formats. It supports two types of translation:

- **Stateless NAT64:** Performs one-to-one IP address mapping of IPv6 addresses to IPv4 addresses

- **Stateful NAT64:** Performs one-to-many IP address mapping, similar to PAT in NAT for IPv4

NAT64 provides a migration path for enterprises building out IPv6 sections of their network. Hosts running either protocol can reach the same services without requiring them to be dual-stacked and without running IPv6 routing in the whole network .

PART II
SWITCH

CHAPTER 1

LAN Switching Basics

Switches were developed from hubs, by way of bridges. In a hub, all ports share access to the backplane so that if multiple ports forward data at the same time, a collision occurs. The Carrier Sense Multiple Access with Collision Detection (CSMA/CD) process attempts to correct for this by detecting a collision and backing off before resending the data. Ports on hubs operate at half-duplex mode; they can either send or receive but cannot do both at the same time. The entire hub is said to be in one collision domain.

On a switch, each port is its own collision domain. Traffic is not forwarded to all ports, only to the port where the destination device is located. Switch ports can operate in full-duplex mode, sending and receiving data at the same time because access to the backplane is controlled by intelligence within the switch.

Switches traditionally operate at Layer 2 of the OSI model. They make forwarding decisions based on the information contained in the Layer 2 header—for Ethernet switches, this is the destination Media Access Control (MAC) address. Multilayer, or Layer 3, switches add routing functionality to this so that they can make forwarding decisions based on information contained in both the Layer 2 and the Layer 3 headers.

Access switches typically have limited resources that are allocated to provide the appropriate levels for typical uses. Resource allocations are described in Switch Database Management (SDM) templates. View the current template and settings with the command **show sdm prefer**. To see all the templates that a particular switch supports, use the global configuration mode command **sdm prefer ?**. To change SDM templates, use the global configuration mode command **sdm prefer** *template-name*. You must then reload the switch for it to take effect. Do not change the SDM template lightly because you might inadvertently starve one process while enabling another.

MAC Address Operation

Switches learn MAC addresses by examining the source MAC address field of incoming frames. They save a mapping of MAC address to switch port in the content-addressable memory (CAM). The CAM table is optimized for fast lookup of two variables: fixed-length address, such as a MAC address, which is always 6 bytes, and port number. Forwarding or filtering decisions are made based on the CAM information. Switches can also have ternary content-addressable memory (TCAM) tables. TCAM is optimized for three variables that might change in length. It is used for access control list (ACL), quality of service (QoS), and other upper-layer processing.

MAC Address Learning

Consider the network shown in Figure 1-1. Some hosts are connected to Switch1. Switch1 has a Layer 2 connection to Switch2. Assume that all ports in both switches are in the same VLAN.

Figure 1-1   Layer 2 Network

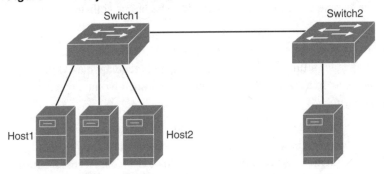

When Switch1 first boots up, the CAM table is empty of dynamic addresses, as shown in Example 1-1. Note that the command to view this table is **show mac address-table**.

Example 1-1   Empty Switch CAM Table

```
Switch1# show mac address-table
          Mac Address Table
---------------------------------------------


Vlan    Mac Address      Type        Ports
----    -----------      --------    -----
```

Suppose that Host1 on Switch1 wants to communicate with Host2. Suspend reality for a moment and assume that the host already knows the MAC address it needs to reach. The frame header lists both the destination and the source MAC addresses. Switch1 examines its CAM table and does not find the destination address listed, so it *floods* the frame to all ports within the VLAN except the incoming port. The switch can, however, look at the source MAC address and map that to the incoming port. When Host2 replies, the switch can then map its source MAC address to the incoming port. The

MAC address of Host1 is in the CAM table now, so the switch forwards the frame only out the port where Host1 is connected. This process continues as traffic flows through the switch. The default aging time for a MAC address to stay in the CAM table without any activity is 300 seconds. That can be manually adjusted with the global command **mac address-table aging-time** *seconds*.

Example 1-2 shows Switch1's CAM table after a few minutes.

Example 1-2 Populated Switch CAM Table

```
Switch1# show mac address-table
          Mac Address Table
-------------------------------------------

Vlan    Mac Address      Type        Ports
----    -----------      --------    -----
   1    aabb.cc00.8d00   DYNAMIC     Et0/1
   1    aabb.cc00.8e00   DYNAMIC     Et0/2
   1    aabb.cc00.8f00   DYNAMIC     Et0/3
   1    aabb.cc00.9000   DYNAMIC     Et1/1
   1    aabb.cc00.9100   DYNAMIC     Et1/1
Total Mac Addresses for this criterion: 5
```

Notice in Example 1-2 that there are two entries for port Ethernet 1/1. In Figure 1-1, notice that two devices are reachable out that interface—Switch2 and the host connected to it. One port can have multiple MAC addresses associated with it.

Frame Forwarding

In Figure 1-1, the initial frame from Host1 was a *unicast* frame—its destination was one specific MAC address. However, it was flooded to all the ports because Switch1 did not have a mapping for that destination MAC address in its CAM table. Therefore, it was an *unknown unicast*. Unknown unicasts are flooded to all ports in the VLAN except the port where the frame originated.

Suppose the message had been a multicast or broadcast frame. ARP is one example of this. It is sent from a specific host to a broadcast address. The broadcast MAC address is FFFF.FFFF.FFFF. This will never be a source host address, thus the switch has no way of learning an association between it and a port. Switches flood broadcasts to all ports within the VLAN except the port where the frame originated. The same is true for multicasts, although switches have other ways to limit the scope of those.

Part II: SWITCH

The forwarding process is different for multilayer switches. Multilayer switches make forwarding decisions based on both MAC address and IP address. If the frame is bound for a host on the same Layer 2 network, then the destination MAC address is that host and the multilayer switch forwards it accordingly.

The destination MAC address might be that of the switch itself. This can happen when the traffic is bound for the switch or if a multilayer switch is the default gateway. In this case, the switch removes the Layer 2 header and examines the IP header following it. If the IP address is one assigned to an interface on the switch, it processes the data internally. If the IP address is that of a remote host, the multilayer switch uses its routing logic to forward the packet. It changes the source MAC address to its own address and the destination MAC address to that of the next Layer 2 hop.

Figure 1-2 shows Host 1 communicating with Host 2 on a separate subnet. Relevant parts of the frame and IP headers are also shown. Host 1 places its own IP address and the IP address of Host 2 in the IP header. It places its own MAC address in the Ethernet header but uses the MAC address of the switch as the destination MAC because that is its default gateway. When the switch forwards the frame, it does not change the IP address information. However, in the Layer 2 header, the switch lists its own MAC address as the source and the MAC address of Host 2 as the destination. (It also recalculates the checksum information in the IP and Ethernet headers and decrements the Time to Live count.)

Figure 1-2   Multilayer Frame Forwarding

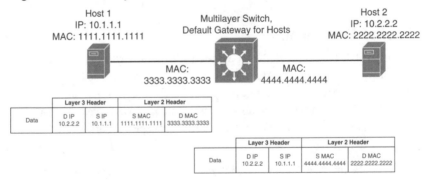

Neighbor Discovery Protocols

Cisco switches support two Layer 2 protocols for neighbor discovery: Cisco Discovery Protocol (CDP) and Link Layer Discovery Protocol (LLDP). These operate at Layer 2 to exchange information about directly connected peer devices, so they are not dependent on upper-layer protocols to operate. These protocols are useful for troubleshooting and mapping the network.

Cisco Discovery Protocol

Cisco Discovery Protocol (CDP) is a Cisco proprietary protocol. It is enabled by default on Cisco switches and runs independent of physical media or network connectivity. CDP sends advertisements every 60 seconds to the multicast address 0100.0CCC.CCCC. It gathers quite a bit of information on its neighbors, as you can see in Examples 1-3, 1-4, and 1-5. The current version is version 2, which added enhanced error reporting, including native VLAN ID mismatch and duplex mismatch. These errors appear as console messages by default.

You might want to disable CDP on interfaces connected to non-Cisco devices or at a security boundary. Use the command **no cdp enable** at the interface configuration mode. To disable CDP on an entire device, use the global command **no cdp run**.

Examples 1-3, 1-4, and 1-5 illustrate the output from some of the most widely used CDP commands. Example 1-3 shows the default settings for CDP.

Example 1-3   CDP Default Settings

```
DSW1# show cdp
Global CDP information:
        Sending CDP packets every 60 seconds
        Sending a holdtime value of 180 seconds
        Sending CDPv2 advertisements is enabled
```

Example 1-4 illustrates the list of directly connected neighbors. Notice that switch DSW1 is directly connected to two devices: SW1 and R1. The output shows the local interface connected to each device, and also the remote interface (Port ID) that connects back to this switch. The Capability column shows that SW1 is a switch running IGMP and R1 is a router.

Example 1-4   Using the show cdp neighbors Command

```
DSW1# show cdp neighbors
Capability Codes: R - Router, T - Trans Bridge, B - Source Route
  Bridge
                  S - Switch, H - Host, I - IGMP, r - Repeater, P -
  Phone,
                  D - Remote, C - CVTA, M - Two-port Mac Relay
```

Part II: SWITCH

Example 1-4   Continued

Device ID	Local Intrfce	Holdtme	Capability	Platform
Port ID				
SW1	Eth 0/3	131	S I	Linux Uni
Eth 0/0				
R1	Eth 0/2	129	R	Linux Uni
Eth 0/1				

To gain even more information about the directly connected neighbors, use the command **show cdp neighbors detail** as shown in Example 1-5. The **detail** keyword provides VTP, native VLAN, and IOS version information, as well as IP addresses.

Example 1-5   Using the show cdp neighbors detail Command

```
DSW1# show cdp neighbors detail
-------------------------
Device ID: SW1
Entry address(es):
Platform: Linux Unix,  Capabilities: Switch IGMP
Interface: Ethernet0/3,  Port ID (outgoing port): Ethernet0/0
Holdtime : 162 sec

Version :
Cisco IOS Software, Solaris Software (I86BI_LINUXL2-
  ADVENTERPRISEK9-M), Experimental Version 15.1(20130726:213425)
  [dstivers-july26-2013-team_track 104]
Copyright (c) 1986-2013 by Cisco Systems, Inc.
Compiled Fri 26-Jul-13 15:56 by dstivers

advertisement version: 2
VTP Management Domain: ''
Native VLAN: 1
Duplex: full
Management address(es):

-------------------------
Device ID: R1
Entry address(es):
  IP address: 10.0.99.2
Platform: Linux Unix,  Capabilities: Router
Interface: Ethernet0/2,  Port ID (outgoing port): Ethernet0/1
Holdtime : 160 sec
```

```
Version :
Cisco IOS Software, Solaris Software (I86BI_LINUX-ADVENTERPRISE-M),
  Experimental Version 15.1(20130726:213425) [dstivers-july26-2013-
  team_track 106]
Copyright (c) 1986-2013 by Cisco Systems, Inc.
Compiled Fri 26-Jul-13 16:24 by dstivers

advertisement version: 2
Duplex: full
Management address(es):
  IP address: 10.0.99.2
```

Two other commands that are useful for troubleshooting switch connections
and monitoring CDP operation are **show cdp traffic** and **show cdp
interface**. The output from those commands is shown in Example 1-6.

Example 1-6   Monitoring CDP Operation

```
DSW1# show cdp traffic
CDP counters :
        Total packets output: 16, Input: 8
        Hdr syntax: 0, Chksum error: 0, Encaps failed: 0
        No memory: 0, Invalid packet: 0,
        CDP version 1 advertisements output: 0, Input: 0
        CDP version 2 advertisements output: 16, Input: 8

DSW1# show cdp interface
Ethernet0/0 is up, line protocol is up
  Encapsulation ARPA
  Sending CDP packets every 60 seconds
  Holdtime is 180 seconds
Ethernet0/1 is up, line protocol is up
  Encapsulation ARPA
  Sending CDP packets every 60 seconds
  Holdtime is 180 seconds
<output omitted>
```

LLDP

Link Layer Discovery Protocol is a standards-based neighbor discovery
protocol similar to CDP and is described by IEEE 802.1AB. It is a good
choice in a multivendor environment. Whether it is enabled by default
depends on the hardware and IOS version. LLDP sends advertisements every
30 seconds by default, rather than 60 seconds as with CDP, to one of three
multicast addresses (0180.C200.0000, 0180.C200.0003, or 0180.C200.0003).
LLDP is a bit more customizable than CDP.

Part II: SWITCH

If LLDP is not running, enable it with the command **lldp run**. Optionally, you can choose to only receive or transmit advertisements with the interface configuration command **lldp receive** or **lldp transmit**. To disable LLDP on the entire device, use the global command **no lldp run**.

Examples 1-7, 1-8, and 1-9 illustrate the output from some of the most widely used LLDP commands. Example 1-7 enables LLDP globally and shows the default settings for LLDP.

Example 1-7   LLDP Default Settings

```
DSW1(config)# lldp run
!
DSW1# show lldp

Global LLDP Information:
    Status: ACTIVE
    LLDP advertisements are sent every 30 seconds
    LLDP hold time advertised is 120 seconds
    LLDP interface reinitialisation delay is 2 seconds
```

Example 1-8 illustrates the list of directly connected neighbors. It uses the same network as the previous CDP examples; switch DSW1 is directly connected to two devices: SW1 and R1. As with CDP, the output shows the local interface connected to each device and also the remote interface (port ID) that connects back to this switch. The Capability codes are different from those for CDP, however.

Example 1-8   Using the show lldp neighbors Command

```
DSW1# show lldp neighbors
Capability codes:
    (R) Router, (B) Bridge, (T) Telephone, (C) DOCSIS Cable Device
    (W) WLAN Access Point, (P) Repeater, (S) Station, (O) Other

Device ID          Local Intf    Hold-time  Capability     Port
    ID
R1                 Et0/2         120        R              Et0/1
SW1                Et0/3         120                       Et0/0

Total entries displayed: 2
```

To gain even more information about the directly connected neighbors, use the command **show lldp neighbors detail**, as shown in Example 1-9. The **detail** keyword provides VTP, native VLAN, and IOS version information, as well as IP addresses. In addition, LLDP lists such useful information as the remote interface description, VLAN number, chassis MAC address, and physical media type.

Example 1-9   Using the show lldp neighbors detail Command

```
DSW1# show lldp neighbors detail
--------------------------------------------------
Chassis id: aabb.cc00.5700
Port id: Et0/1
Port Description: Link to DSW1
System Name: R1

System Description:
Cisco IOS Software, Solaris Software (I86BI_LINUX-ADVENTERPRISE-M),
  Experimental Version 15.1(20130726:213425) [dstivers-july26-2013-
  team_track 106]
Copyright (c) 1986-2013 by Cisco Systems, Inc.
Compiled Fri 26-Jul-13 16:24 by dstivers

Time remaining: 94 seconds
System Capabilities: B,R
Enabled Capabilities: R
Management Addresses:
    IP: 10.0.99.2
Auto Negotiation - not supported
Physical media capabilities - not advertised
Media Attachment Unit type - not advertised
Vlan ID: - not advertised


--------------------------------------------------
Chassis id: aabb.cc00.8100
Port id: Et0/0
Port Description: Link to DSW1
System Name: SW1

System Description:
Cisco IOS Software, Solaris Software (I86BI_LINUXL2-
  ADVENTERPRISEK9-M), Experimental Version 15.1(20130726:213425)
  [dstivers-july26-2013-team_track 104]
Copyright (c) 1986-2013 by Cisco Systems, Inc.
Compiled Fri 26-Jul-13 15:56 by dstivers

Time remaining: 118 seconds
System Capabilities: B,R
Enabled Capabilities - not advertised
Management Addresses - not advertised
Auto Negotiation - not supported
```

Example 1-9   Continued

```
Physical media capabilities - not advertised
Media Attachment Unit type - not advertised
Vlan ID: - not advertised


Total entries displayed: 2
```

Similar to CDP, two other commands that are useful for troubleshooting switch connections and monitoring CDP operation are **show lldp traffic** and **show lldp interface**. The output from those commands is shown in Example 1-10.

Example 1-10   Monitoring LLDP Operation

```
DSW1# show lldp traffic

LLDP traffic statistics:
    Total frames out: 193
    Total entries aged: 0
    Total frames in: 17
    Total frames received in error: 0
    Total frames discarded: 0
    Total TLVs discarded: 0
    Total TLVs unrecognized: 0

DSW1# show lldp interface

Ethernet0/0:
    Tx: enabled
    Rx: enabled
    Tx state: IDLE
    Rx state: WAIT FOR FRAME

Ethernet0/1:
    Tx: enabled
    Rx: enabled
    Tx state: IDLE
    Rx state: WAIT FOR FRAME
```

Switch Traffic Monitoring

Because switches forward unicast traffic only to the port listed in their MAC address tables, an administrator who needs to sniff network traffic

would have to place a sniffer on each interface. A better option is to configure the switch to send a copy of some or all traffic out the interface where
a sniffer is connected. This is called *port mirroring* or *port monitoring*
and is the basis of the Switched Port Analyzer (SPAN) and Remote SPAN
(RSPAN) features.

SPAN

SPAN causes the switch to make copies of all traffic from a specific *source*
port or VLAN and send the copies to a destination or monitor port. Both
source and destination must be on the same switch. SPAN can make copies
of inbound traffic, outbound traffic, or both. A *SPAN session* associates
source port(s) or VLAN(s) with a destination port. Some rules about destination ports are as follows:

- After a port is configured as a destination port, only mirrored traffic is
  forwarded to it.

- The number of destination ports available is platform-dependent.

- Destination ports cannot also be source ports.

Configure SPAN by creating a monitor session and then associating source
and destination ports with that session. Example 1-11 shows the configuration to set up monitor session 1, using interface e0/0 as the source port and
interface e1/1 as the destination port. Because neither received nor transmitted traffic is specified, the switch monitors both by default. The **show
monitor** command verifies the configuration.

Example 1-11   Configuring SPAN

```
Switch(config)# monitor session 1 source interface e0/0
Switch(config)# monitor session 1 destination interface e1/1
!
Switch# show monitor
Session 1
---------
Type : Local Session
Source Ports :
Both : e0/0
Destination Ports : e1/1
Encapsulation : Native
Ingress : Enabled
```

RSPAN

RSPAN overcomes SPAN's requirement to have both the source and destination ports on the same switch. It enables the final destination to be on a separate switch from the source ports. RSPAN consists of the following components:

- Switches that are connected via trunk links

- A VLAN that is designated as an RSPAN VLAN and configured on all source, destination, and intermediate switches

- A source session, defined on the local switch, that is associated with the RSPAN VLAN

- A destination session, defined on the remote switch, that is associated with the RSPAN VLAN

Figure 1-3 shows a simple RSPAN design. Switch1 has a host that will be monitored on its e0/0 interface, and Switch2 has a monitoring device on its e1/1 interface. The link between the switches is a trunk link that is allowed to carry VLAN 900.

Figure 1-3   Network for RSPAN Session

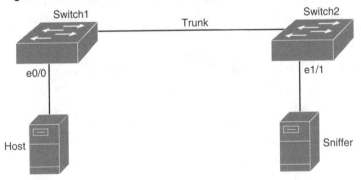

Example 1-12 illustrates the configuration to establish an RSPAN session between the two switches. First, VLAN 900 is configured on both switches and designated as an RSPAN VLAN. Then the monitor session is established on Switch1 with a source of e0/0 and a destination of the RSPAN VLAN 900. On Switch2, the monitor session is configured with a source of the RSPAN VLAN 900 and a destination of interface e1/1.

Part II: SWITCH

Example 1-12   Configuring RSPAN

```
!Configuration on Switch1
Switch(config)# vlan 900
Switch(config-vlan)# remote-span
!
Switch(config)# monitor session 1 source interface e0/0
Switch(config)# monitor session 1 destination remote vlan 900

!Configuration on Switch2
Switch(config)# vlan 900
Switch(config-vlan)# remote-span
!
Switch(config)# monitor session 1 source remote vlan 900
Switch(config)# monitor session 1 destination interface e1/1
```

CHAPTER 2

VLANs

VLAN Overview

A physical network segment is a group of devices that shares the same physical wire. They can communicate directly with each other. A virtual LAN (VLAN) is a logical network segment. It is a way to group devices so that they can communicate at Layer 2 even though they might be physically separate. Switch ports assigned to the same VLAN create a virtual LAN, sharing a broadcast (and multicast) domain regardless of their physical locations in the switched network. A switch can have multiple VLANs, in which case frames are only forwarded to other ports within the same VLAN. For traffic to move between VLANs requires a Layer 3 process, and thus either a router or a multilayer switch. VLAN membership can be assigned either statically by port or dynamically by MAC address or username.

Two types of VLANs are end-to-end and local.

End-to-end VLANs enable VLAN members to reside on different switches throughout the network. They are used when hosts are assigned to VLANs for policy reasons rather than physical location. This provides users a consistent policy and access to resources regardless of their location. Avoid end-to-end VLANs if possible. They make troubleshooting more complex because so many switches can carry traffic for a specific VLAN, broadcasts can traverse many switches, and a failure on any of the switches affects many others. Figure 2-1 shows end-to-end VLANs.

Figure 2-1   End-to-End VLANs

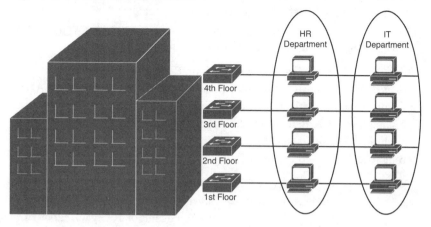

Local VLANs are used when hosts are assigned to VLANs based on their locations, such as a floor in a building. This design is more scalable and easier to troubleshoot because the traffic flow is more deterministic. It enables more redundancy and minimizes failure domains. It does require a routing function to share resources between VLANs. Figure 2-2 shows an example of local VLANs.

Figure 2-2   Local VLANs

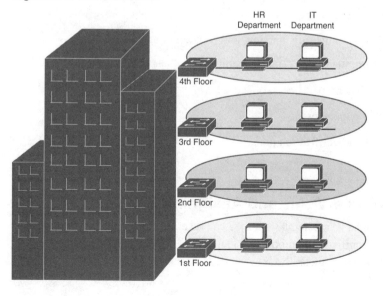

When planning a VLAN structure, consider traffic flows and link sizing. Take into account the entire traffic pattern of applications found in your network. For example, IP voice media traffic travels directly between phones, but signaling traffic must pass to the Unified Communications Manager. Multicast traffic is required to communicate back to the routing process and possibly call upon a rendezvous point. Various user applications, such as email and Citrix, place different demands on the network.

Application flow influences link bandwidth. Remember that uplink ports need to handle all hosts communicating concurrently, and although VLANs logically separate traffic, the traffic in different VLANs still travels over the same trunk line. Benchmark throughput for critical application and user data during peak hours, and then analyze the results for any bottlenecks throughout the layered design.

User access ports are typically Gigabit Ethernet. Access switches must have the necessary port density and can be either Layer 2 or Layer 3. Ports from user access to the Distribution layer must be Gigabit or 10Gigabit Ethernet, with an oversubscription ratio of no more than 20:1. Distribution switches must be multilayer or Layer 3. Links from distribution to the core must be Gigabit or 10-Gigabit Ethernet, using either EtherChannels or virtual port channels, with an oversubscription of no more than 4:1.

VLAN Planning

Before beginning a VLAN implementation, you must determine the following information:

- VLAN numbering, naming, and IP addressing scheme.

- VLAN placement—local or multiple switches.

- Are any trunks necessary and where?

- VTP parameters.

- Test and verification plan.

Creating a VLAN and Assigning Ports

VLANs must be created before they can be used. Creating VLANs is easy—in global configuration mode, just identify the VLAN number and optionally name it. When you create a VLAN, its information is stored in a database on the switch.

VLANs are identified by number and name. Numbers must be between 1 and 4094. The original VLAN range was 1–1005, with VLANs 1002–1005 reserved for legacy protocols. The VLAN range of 1006–4094 is called the *extended range*. VLAN number 1 is always present, and all ports are assigned to it by default.

If you do not specify a name, the switch names it VLAN*number*. In Example 2-1 in the next section, VLAN 20 uses the default name and VLAN 21 has been manually given a name. The following commands create VLAN 12 and assign it the name MYVLAN:

```
Switch(config)# vlan 12
Switch(config-vlan)# name MYVLAN
```

Delete a VLAN by using the same command with **no** in front of it. There is no need to include the name when deleting.

When statically assigning ports to VLANs, first make the interface an access port and then assign the port to a VLAN. An access port is one connected to just one VLAN, usually a user or perhaps an end device such as a printer. The following configuration shows an interface configured to be an access port and placed into VLAN 12:

```
Switch(config-if)# switchport mode access
Switch(config-if)# switchport access vlan 12
```

There is an exception to the rule of an access port being connected to just one VLAN. Some Cisco switches enable you to configure a voice VLAN on an access port. After an IP phone is connected, the switch discovers it via CDP and phone traffic is put into the voice VLAN. If a computer is daisy-chained to the phone, the computer's traffic is put into the configured access (or data) VLAN. To configure this, add the command **switchport voice vlan** *vlan*. If data traffic should be in VLAN 12 and voice traffic in VLAN 22, the configuration looks like this:

```
Switch(config-if)# switchport mode access
Switch(config-if)# switchport access vlan 12
Switch(config-if)# switchport voice vlan 22
```

Verifying VLAN Configuration

To see a list of all the VLANs and the ports assigned to them, use the command **show vlan**. To narrow down the information displayed, use these keywords after the command **brief**, *vlan-number*, or **name** *vlan-name*. Example 2-1 shows the output from this command with the **brief** keyword added. Note that VLANs 1 and 1002–1005 are created by default and are reserved for certain legacy protocols.

Part II: SWITCH

Example 2-1   Using the show vlan brief Command

```
Switch# show vlan brief
VLAN Name                      Status     Ports
---- ---------------------- ---------- ----------------------------
1    default                active     E0/1, E0/2, E0/3,
                                        E0/10,E0/11,E0/12

20   VLAN0020               active     E0/5,E0/6,E0/7
21   Servers                active     E0/8,E0/9
1002 fddi-default           active
1003 trcrf-default          active
1004 fddinet-default        active
1005 trbrf-default          active
```

Other verification commands include

- **show running-config interface** *interface*: Verifies the VLAN configured on the port:

  ```
  Switch# show run interface e0/1
  Building configuration...
  Current configuration 64 bytes
  interface Ethernet 0/1
   switchport access vlan 10
   switchport mode access
  ```

- **show mac address-table interface** *interface* **vlan** *vlan*: Shows the MAC addresses learned through that port for the specified VLAN:

  ```
  Switch# show mac address-table interface e0/1
        Mac Address Table
  -------------------------------------------
  Vlan  Mac Address    Type    Ports
  ----  -----------    ----    -----
  10    0030.b656.7c3d DYNAMIC    E0/1
  Total Mac Addresses for this criterion: 1
  ```

- **show interfaces** *interface* **switchport**: Displays detailed information about the port configuration, such as entries in the Administrative mode and Access mode VLAN fields:

  ```
  Switch# show interfaces e0/1 switchport
  Name: E0/1
  Switchport: Enabled
  Administrative Mode: dynamic desirable
  Operational Mode: static access
  Administrative Trunking Encapsulation: negotiate
  ```

```
Operational Trunking Encapsulation: native
Negotiation of Trunking: On
Access Mode VLAN: 1 (default)
Trunking Native Mode VLAN: 1 (default)
Trunking VLANs Enabled: ALL
Pruning VLANs Enabled: 2-1001
Protected: false
Unknown unicast blocked: false
Unknown multicast blocked: false
Broadcast Suppression Level: 100
Multicast Suppression Level: 100
Unicast Suppression Level: 100
```

VLAN Trunking

A *trunk* is a link that carries traffic for more than one VLAN. Trunks multiplex traffic from various VLANs. They typically connect switches and enable ports on multiple switches to be assigned to the same VLAN.

802.1Q is a standards-based protocol that defines how trunks operate and maintain VLAN separation as a frame traverses a trunk link. 802.1Q tags Ethernet frames by inserting a field into the original frame immediately after the source MAC address field.

When a frame comes into a switch port, the frame is tagged internally within the switch with the VLAN number of the port. After it reaches the outgoing port, the internal tag is removed. If the exit port is a trunk port, an 802.1 tag is inserted that identifies its VLAN. The switch on the other end of the trunk removes the 802.1Q information, checks the VLAN of the frame, and adds an internal tag. If the exit port is a user port, the original frame is sent out unchanged, making the use of VLANs transparent to the user.

If a nontrunking port receives an 802.1Q frame, the source and destination MAC addresses are read, the tag field is ignored, and the frame is switched normally at Layer 2.

802.1Q uses the concept of a *native VLAN*. Frames from the native VLAN are sent over the trunk link untagged and the native VLAN setting must match on both sides of the trunk link. VLAN 1 is the default native VLAN for all ports, but best practice is to set it to a VLAN not assigned to users. This method also decreases the danger of having a large spanning tree instance in VLAN 1.

Part II: SWITCH

Configuring a Trunk Link

Ports can become trunk ports either by static configuration or dynamic negotiation using Dynamic Trunking Protocol (DTP). A switch port can be in one of five DTP modes:

- **Access:** The port is a user port in a single VLAN and does not become a trunk.

- **Trunk:** The port negotiates trunking with the port on the other end of the link.

- **Non-negotiate:** The port does not do DTP negotiation with the other side of the link.

- **Dynamic desirable:** It actively negotiates trunking with the other side of the link. It becomes a trunk if the port on the other switch is set to **trunk**, **dynamic desirable**, or **dynamic auto** mode.

- **Dynamic auto:** It passively waits to be contacted by the other switch. It becomes a trunk if the other end is set to **trunk** or **dynamic desirable** mode.

Configure a port for trunking at the interface configuration mode:

```
Switch(config-if)# switchport mode {dynamic {auto | desirable} | trunk}
```

If a dynamic mode is used, DTP negotiates the trunking state and encapsulation. If trunk mode is used, you must specify encapsulation, and you can disable all DTP negotiation:

```
Switch(config-if)# switchport trunk encapsulation dot1q
Switch(config-if)# switchport nonegotiate
```

Specify a native VLAN for the trunk link with the following command:

```
Switch(config-if)# switchport trunk native vlan vlan
```

Pruning VLANs on a Trunk

By default, a trunk carries traffic for all VLANs. You can change that behavior for a particular trunk link by giving the following command at the interface config mode:

```
switchport trunk allowed vlan vlans
```

Make sure that both sides of a trunk link enable the same VLANs.

Verifying a Trunk Link

Two useful commands to verify your trunk configuration are

```
show running-config
show interfaces interface {switchport | trunk}
```

Using the **trunk** keyword with the **show interfaces** command gives information about the trunk link, as shown in Example 2-2.

Example 2-2   Verifying Trunk Interfaces

```
Switch# show interfaces e0/1 trunk
Port    Mode         Encapsulation   Status       Native vlan
E0/1    desirable    802.1q          trunking     1


Port    Vlans allowed on trunk
E0/1    1-150
<further output omitted>
```

Best Practices for Trunking

Change the native VLAN to one not assigned to any users.

On links that should be trunks, turn off trunking negotiation by setting the mode to **trunk**, specifying the encapsulation type, and adding the **switchport nonegotiate** command. On links that should never be trunks, turn off trunking negotiation by setting the switchport mode to **access** or **host**. This sets it as an access port, enables PortFast, and disables EtherChannel negotiation.

Limit the VLAN traffic carried by the trunk to only those VLANs it needs to carry.

VLAN Trunking Protocol

VLAN Trunking Protocol (VTP) is a Cisco-proprietary protocol that runs over trunk links and synchronizes the VLAN databases of all switches in the VTP domain. A VTP domain is an administrative group; all switches within that group must have the same VTP domain name configured, or they do not synchronize databases.

Part II: SWITCH

VTP works by using configuration revision numbers and VTP advertisements:

- All switches send out VTP advertisements every 5 minutes or when there is a change to the VLAN database (when a VLAN is created, deleted, or renamed).

- Advertisements are sent as multicasts over the native VLAN.

- VTP advertisements contain a configuration revision number. This number is increased by one for every VLAN change.

- When a switch receives a VTP advertisement, it compares the configuration revision number against the one in its VLAN database.

- If the new number is higher, the switch overwrites its database with the new VLAN information and forwards the information to its neighbor switches.

- If the number is the same, the switch ignores the advertisement.

- If the new number is lower, the switch replies with the more up-to-date information contained in its own database.

VTP Switch Roles

A switch can have one of several roles within VTP, depending on the VTP version:

- **Server:** The default VTP role. Servers create, delete, and rename VLANs. They originate both periodic and triggered VTP advertisements and synchronize their databases with other switches in the domain. VLAN information is stored in the vlan.dat file in NVRAM, and so survives a switch reload. You must delete the vlan.dat file and reload the switch to delete its VLAN and VTP information.

- **Client:** Clients cannot make VLAN changes. They originate periodic VTP advertisements and synchronize their databases with other switches in the domain. VLAN information is stored in the vlan.dat file in NVRAM, and so survives a switch reload. You must delete the vlan.dat file and reload the switch to delete its VLAN and VTP information.

- **Transparent:** The switch creates, deletes, and renames VLANs, but its VLANs are only local. It does not originate advertisements or synchronize its database with any other switches. It does pass along

VTP advertisements out its trunk links, however. VLAN information is stored in the switch configuration file. If you erase the startup-config then you will delete a transparent switch's VLANs. VTP transparent is the recommended mode for today's networks.

■ **Off:** Off mode is available only in VTP version 3. Like a Transparent mode switch, it does not originate advertisements or synchronize its database with any other switches. However, unlike a Transparent mode switch, it terminates any VTP advertisements it receives, rather than passing them along.

Configuring VTP

There are three versions of VTP. The default version is Version 1. To use Versions 2 or 3, all switches in the domain must be capable of using it. Configure one server for the new version, and the information is propagated through VTP.

VTP Version 2 added the following features:

■ Token Ring VLAN support.

■ Transparent switches able to pass along messages from all versions of VTP.

■ Consistency checks are performed only when changes are configured through the CLI or SNMP.

VTP Version 3 is not backward compatible with Version 1, but it can work with Version 2 if you are not using extended or private VLANs. Version 3 added the following features:

■ Supports extended and private VLANs.

■ Concept of a primary server. This is the only device allowed to update the other switches in the domain.

■ MST support.

■ VTP password security.

■ No automatic learning of domain name. With previous VTP versions, if a switch with no VTP configuration heard a VTP advertisement, it adopted the VTP domain name in the advertisement. This could lead to problems. Version 3 requires manual configuration of the domain name.

VTP configuration is accomplished at the global config mode. To configure the switch's VTP mode:

```
Switch(config)# vtp mode {server | client |transparent | off}
```

To configure the VTP domain name:

```
Switch(config)# vtp domain name
```

To configure a VTP password (all switches in the domain must use the same password):

```
Switch(config)# vtp password password
```

To configure the switch to use a different VTP version:

```
Switch(config)# vtp version version
```

Verifying and Monitoring VTP

To obtain basic information regarding the VTP configuration, use **show vtp status**. Example 2-3 shows the default settings. Note that there is no default VTP domain name and the configuration revision number is zero because no VLANs have been manually configured. However, five VLANs already exist on the switch. These are VLAN 1 and VLANs 1002–1005, which are there by default.

Example 2-3   Verifying VTP Status

```
Switch# show vtp status
VTP Version   : 1
Configuration Revision  : 0
Maximum VLANs supported locally  : 1005
Number of existing VLANs  : 5
VTP Operating Mode  : Server
VTP Domain Name  :
VTP Pruning Mode  : Disabled
VTP V2 Mode  : Disabled
VTP Traps Generation  : Disabled
MD5 digest  :
```

Adding a New Switch to a VTP Domain

Adding a new switch in client mode does not prevent it from propagating its VLAN information. A server synchronizes to a client if the client has the higher configuration revision number. You must reset the revision number back to 0 on the new switch. To be safe, follow these steps:

Step 1. With the switch disconnected from the network, set it as VTP transparent and delete the vlan.dat file from its flash memory.

Step 2. Set it to a fake VTP domain name and into client mode.

Step 3. Reboot the switch.

Step 4. Configure the correct VTP settings, such as domain, password, mode, and version.

Step 5. Connect the switch to the network, and verify that it receives the correct information.

Troubleshooting VLAN Issues

Configuration problems can arise when user traffic must traverse several switches. The following sections list some common configuration errors. But before you begin troubleshooting, create a plan. Check for any changes recently made, and determine likely problem areas.

Troubleshooting User Connectivity

User connectivity can be affected by several things:

- **Physical connectivity:** Make sure the cable, network adapter, and switch port are good. Check the port's link LED.

- **Switch configuration:** If you see FCS errors or late collisions, suspect a duplex mismatch. Check configured speed on both sides of the link. Be sure the port is enabled and set as an access port.

- **VLAN configuration:** Make sure the hosts are in the correct VLAN.

- **Allowed VLANs:** Be sure that the user VLAN is allowed on all appropriate trunk links.

Troubleshooting Trunking

When troubleshooting trunking, ensure that physical layer connectivity is present before moving on to search for configuration problems, such as the following:

- Are both sides of the link in the correct trunking mode?
- Is the same trunk encapsulation on both sides?

Part II: SWITCH

- If using 802.1Q, is the same native VLAN on both sides? Look for CDP messages warning of this error.

- Are the same VLANs permitted on both sides?

- Is a link trunking that should not be?

Troubleshooting VTP

The following are some common things to check when troubleshooting problems with VTP:

- Make sure you are trunking between the switches. VTP is sent only over trunk links.

- Confirm that the domain name matches on both switches. (The name is case sensitive.)

- Confirm that the VTP version matches on all switches.

- If the switch is not updating its database, ensure it is not in transparent or off mode.

- If using passwords, make sure they all match. To remove a password, use the command **no vtp password**.

- If VLANs are missing, check the revision number for a possible database overwrite. Also examine the number of VLANs in the domain. There might be too many VLANs for VTP to update properly.

- In a network with many broadcasts, you might want to implement *VTP pruning*. By default, all switches in a Layer 2 network receive all broadcasts, whether or not they have any ports assigned to the VLAN for which the broadcast is bound. VTP pruning sends broadcasts only to switches with ports assigned to the broadcast's VLAN.

CHAPTER 3

EtherChannels

EtherChannel Overview

An EtherChannel is a method of combining several physical links between switches into one logical connection. This is typically used when you need increased bandwidth between switches and also provides link redundancy. As illustrated in Figure 3-1, Spanning Tree normally blocks redundant links to avoid loops; EtherChannels circumvent that and enable load balancing across those links. A logical interface called the *Port Channel interface* is created. Spanning Tree then acts as if the port channel interface were a single physical interface.

Figure 3-1   Spanning Tree Versus EtherChannel

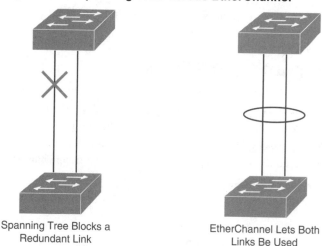

Spanning Tree Blocks a
Redundant Link

EtherChannel Lets Both
Links Be Used

Configuration can be applied to both the logical and the physical interfaces. Configuration applied to the port channel interface is inherited by the physical interfaces that are part of the channel bundle. Configuration applied to a physical interface affects that interface only.

The following are some guidelines for EtherChannels:

- Interfaces in the channel do not have to be physically next to each other or on the same module.

- All ports must be the same speed and duplex.

- For Layer 2 EtherChannels, all ports in the bundle must be in the same VLAN, or the channel must be configured as a trunk. If they are trunks, they must all carry the same VLANs and use the same trunking mode.

- An EtherChannel trunk should be configured to allow the same VLANs on both sides of the link.

- For optimal operation, use an even number of links.

- All ports in the bundle must be enabled.

- None of the bundle ports can be a SPAN port.

- If you are using a Layer 3 EtherChannel, the IP address must be assigned to the logical Port-Channel interface, not the physical ones.

- Put all bundle ports in the same VLAN, or make them all trunks.

Configuring an EtherChannel

Basic EtherChannel configuration is fairly easy. Simply configure the logical interface, and then link the physical interfaces to it. Notice that the logical interface is called a *Port-Channel interface*, not EtherChannel. The number assigned to the Port-Channel interface determines the channel group; this is the number you use to configure an interface to be part of the EtherChannel.

```
(config)# interface port-channel number
![any additional configuration, such as trunking for a Layer 2
  EtherChannel]
```

The preceding command creates a Layer 2 EtherChannel. If you need a Layer 3 EtherChannel, add the following:

```
(config-if)# no switchport
(config-if)# ip address address mask
```

The next step is to assign ports to the EtherChannel. At each port that should be part of the EtherChannel, use the following command:

```
(config)# interface { number | range interface - interface}
(config-if)# channel-group number mode {auto | desirable | active
  | passive | on}
```

To make the configuration even easier, simply put interfaces into a channel group to create a Layer 2 EtherChannel, and the logical interface is automatically created.

Example 3-1 shows a switch configured with a Layer 2 EtherChannel. Ports e0/0 through e0/3 are part of channel group number 1. Notice that the Port-Channel interface was created automatically when these interfaces were placed into the EtherChannel. However, because this channel must be a trunk, configure trunking under the Port-Channel interface so that it will then be inherited by the physical interfaces that are part of the channel bundle.

Example 3-1   Configuring a Layer 2 EtherChannel

```
Switch(config)# interface range e0/0-3
Switch(config-if-range)# channel-group 1 mode active
Creating a port-channel interface Port-channel 1
!
Switch(config-if-range)# interface port-channel 1
Switch(config-if)# switchport trunk encapsulation dot1q
Switch(config-if)# switchport mode trunk
```

Example 3-2 shows a switch configured with a Layer 3 EtherChannel. Ports e1/0 through e1/3 are configured to be part of the channel bundle. In this case, it is more efficient to first create and configure the logical Port-Channel interface and then add the physical interfaces to the channel group. Because this is a Layer 3 EtherChannel, the **no switchport** command is necessary on both the Port-Channel interface and the physical interfaces. Without it, you get an error message similar to the following:

> Command rejected (Port-channel2, Et1/0): Either port is L2 and port-channel is L3, or vice versa

Example 3-2   Configuring a Layer 3 EtherChannel

```
Switch(config-if)# interface port-channel 2
Switch(config-if)# no switchport
Switch(config-if)# ip address 192.168.3.1 255.255.255.0
!
Switch(config)# interface range e1/0-3
Switch(config-if-range)# no switchport
Switch(config-if-range)# channel-group 2 mode active
```

Part II: SWITCH

Channel Negotiation Protocols

The **mode** keyword shown in Example 3-2 refers to protocols used to dynamically negotiate the formation of an EtherChannel. Two protocols are supported by most Cisco switches: the Cisco proprietary Port Aggregation Protocol (PAgP) and the standards-based Link Aggregation Control Protocol (LACP). LACP is IEEE standard 802.3ad.

If **mode** is set to **on**, the link acts as part of the channel group and does not use either of the protocols to negotiate with the switch on the other end of the link. The port on the other side must also be set to **on**.

The two PAgP modes are

- **Auto:** Responds to PAgP messages but does not initiate them. Port channels if the port on the other end is set to Desirable. This is the default mode.

- **Desirable:** Port actively negotiates channeling status with the interface on the other end of the link. Port channels if the other side is Auto or Desirable.

The two LACP modes are

- **Active:** Port actively negotiates channeling with the port on the other end of the link. A channel forms if the other side is Passive or Active.

- **Passive:** Responds to LACP messages but does not initiate them. A channel forms only if the other end is set to Active.

Verifying EtherChannel Configuration

Probably the most useful command for verifying your EtherChannel configuration and operation is **show etherchannel summary**. This command provides information about all the EtherChannels configured on the switch. Example 3-3 shows the output from this command, given on the switch where the two EtherChannels in Examples 3-1 and 3-2 were configured.

Example 3-3   Using the show etherchannel summary Command

```
Switch# show etherchannel summary
Flags:  D - down          P - bundled in port-channel
        I - stand-alone s - suspended
        H - Hot-standby (LACP only)
        R - Layer3       S - Layer2
        U - in use        f - failed to allocate aggregator
```

```
           M - not in use, minimum links not met
           u - unsuitable for bundling
           w - waiting to be aggregated
           d - default port


Number of channel-groups in use: 2
Number of aggregators:            2

Group  Port-channel  Protocol    Ports
------+-------------+-----------+-----------------------------------
------------
1      Po1(SU)        LACP        Et0/0(P)    Et0/1(P)    Et0/2(P)
  Et0/3(P)
2      Po2(RU)        LACP        Et1/0(P)    Et1/1(P)    Et1/2(P)
Et1/3(P)
```

The output from Example 3-3 is worth understanding. Fortunately, the meaning of most of the codes is given in the output. Group 1 is Port-Channel interface 1. The codes (SU) denote that it is a Layer 2 EtherChannel and it is in use. The channel negotiation protocol used is LACP because the **active** mode was configured. The four interfaces included in the EtherChannel are each successfully bonded to the channel, as denoted by the (P) beside each one.

Group 2 is similar except that it has the code (RU). R denotes that it is a Layer 3 EtherChannel, and U denotes that it is in use.

The **show interfaces** *number* **etherchannel** command gives information pertaining to both the local port and the remote port. This is useful for verifying your configuration and troubleshooting problems. In Example 3-4, note that the local port, Ethernet0/1, is configured as LACP active mode while the remote port, Ethernet 1/1, is configured as LACP passive.

Example 3-4 Using the show interfaces etherchannel Command

```
Switch# show interfaces e0/1 etherchannel
Port state     = Up Mstr Assoc In-Bndl
Channel group = 1    Mode = Active        Gcchange = -
Port-channel  = Po1  GC   =    -          Pseudo port-channel = Po1
Port index    = 0    Load = 0x00          Protocol =    LACP

Flags:  S - Device is sending Slow LACPDUs   F - Device is sending
  fast LACPDUs.
        A - Device is in active mode.        P - Device is in pas-
  sive mode.
```

Example 3-4 Continued

```
Local information:
                    LACP port    Admin    Oper   Port      Port
Port  Flags  State  Priority     Key      Key    Number    State
Et1/1 SA     bndl   32768        0x1      0x1    0x102     0x3D


Partner's information:

             LACP port                  Admin Oper   Port     Port
Port  Flags  Priority Dev ID        Age  key   Key    Number   State
Et0/1 SP     32768    aabb.cc00.7600 14s 0x0   0x1    0x3      0x3C
```

Other useful verification and troubleshooting commands include

- **show running-config** *interface*: Shows the switch interface configuration

- **show etherchannel** *number* **port-channel:** Shows information about the EtherChannels in a specific group

EtherChannel Load Balancing

Traffic is balanced between the physical links in a channel based on an algorithm that takes into account such things as source or destination MAC address or IP address. The default load-balancing algorithm for most switches is source and destination IP address. The types of load balancing available vary by switch platform, but most support the following:

- Source MAC address

- Source IP address

- Destination MAC address

- Destination IP address

- Source and destination MAC address

- Source and destination IP address

To see which load-balancing options are available on your particular switches, use the **port-channel load-balance ?** command. The EtherChannel load-balancing method is configured at global configuration mode using the command **port-channel load-balance** *type*. Note that because this command is given at *global* configuration mode, it affects all EtherChannels on the switch.

Verify with the command **show etherchannel load-balance**. The output of this command and the default load-balancing configuration are shown in Example 3-5.

Example 3-5   Verifying EtherChannel Load Balancing

```
Switch# show etherchannel load-balance
EtherChannel Load-Balancing Configuration:
        src-dst-ip

EtherChannel Load-Balancing Addresses Used Per-Protocol:
Non-IP: Source XOR Destination MAC address
  IPv4: Source XOR Destination IP address
  IPv6: Source XOR Destination IP address
```

EtherChannel Guard

Cisco switches have a feature that helps detect when an EtherChannel has been misconfigured, called *EtherChannel Guard*. This might occur if the interfaces on both sides of the link are not configured in the same way. The channel configuration might be different, or one side might be configured as a channel and the other one might not be. If an issue is detected, EtherChannel Guard places the interfaces into an error-disabled state. It also displays an error message in the system log.

EtherChannel Guard is enabled by default on most current switches. To verify this, use the command **show spanning-tree summary**, as shown in Example 3-6. To disable it, use the command **no spanning-tree etherchannel guard misconfig**.

Example 3-6   Verifying EtherChannel Misconfiguration Guard

```
Switch# show spanning-tree summary
Switch is in pvst mode
Root bridge for: VLAN0001
Extended system ID            is enabled
Portfast Default              is disabled
PortFast BPDU Guard Default   is disabled
Portfast BPDU Filter Default  is disabled
Loopguard Default             is disabled
EtherChannel misconfig guard is enabled
Configured Pathcost method used is short
UplinkFast                    is disabled
BackboneFast                  is disabled
```

MEC and vPC

Traditional EtherChannels are formed between two neighboring, directly connected devices. Two special technologies enable channels to be formed between one end device and two neighboring devices: MEC and vPC. Cisco Catalyst switches that use the Virtual Switching System (VSS) act as one switch. A neighboring device can have one or more uplinks to each of the switches in a VSS pair, and combine them into an EtherChannel. This is called a *Multichassis EtherChannel (MEC)*. The downstream switch does not know that its channel is connected to two physical switches; it acts as if all links in the channel were connected to the same switch. Configuration on the downstream switch is exactly the same as a normal EtherChannel.

Cisco Nexus switches use *virtual Port Channel (vPC)* technology to create an EtherChannel that spans two chassis. Although Nexus switches have independent control planes, they exchange channel information over a peer link between them. Again, configuration of the EtherChannel on the downstream device is the same as for a normal EtherChannel. It does not have to support MEC or vPC—it only needs to support the appropriate channel negotiation protocol.

CHAPTER 4

Spanning Tree Protocol

Ethernet network design balances two separate imperatives. First, having multiple ways to reach a destination is generally a good thing. Redundant links proactively prepare the network for inevitable link failure. Second, Ethernet has no way to detect circular paths. If such paths exist, traffic loops around until it is stopped by some external force (such as a network admin pulling out a cable) because there is no Time-to-Live field in an Ethernet header.

Spanning Tree Protocol (STP) prevents loop formation by detecting redundant links and disabling them until needed. Designers can therefore build networks with redundant connections, and the protocol enables one link to pass traffic while keeping the other in reserve. When the active link fails, Spanning Tree enables the secondary link. This sounds like a good idea and might lead you to wonder why Spanning Tree is so vilified and why network engineers try so hard to design around it. Spanning Tree can be a useful tool within a network when it is used in appropriate areas and properly configured by someone with a good understanding of the protocol. Unfortunately, that is not always the case.

The Spanning Tree Protocol has had several modifications over the years. This chapter examines the original version, known as *Common Spanning Tree (CST)* and described in IEEE standard 802.1D. Also note the following versions:

- **Per-VLAN Spanning Tree (PVST+):** This is a Cisco implementation of STP that runs a separate instance of STP for each VLAN.

- **Rapid Spanning Tree (RSTP):** This is the IEEE standard 802.1w that provides faster convergence time than original STP. The Cisco implementation of this is *Rapid PVST+*, sometimes abbreviated as *RPVST+* and sometimes as *PVRSTP+*.

- **Multiple Spanning Tree (MST):** Also called *MSTP*, this is the IEEE 802.1s standard. It maps multiple VLANs into a single STP instance.

Understanding Basic Spanning Tree Protocol

Switches either forward or filter Layer 2 frames. They make forwarding and filtering decisions based on the information contained in the Layer 2 header—for Ethernet switches this is the destination MAC address. Switches function in the following ways:

- They learn MAC (Media Access Control) addresses by looking at the source address of incoming frames. They build a table mapping MAC address to port number.

- They forward known unicasts out the port associated with the destination MAC address. A known unicast has a mapping associating the destination MAC address with a switch port.

- They forward unknown unicasts out all ports except the one in which they came. An unknown unicast is a message bound for a unicast MAC address that is not in the switch's table of addresses and ports.

- They forward broadcasts and multicasts out all ports except the one in which they came. (This is called *flooding*.)

Note

A switch does not make any changes to the frames as it forwards them.

Suppose there were two switches with redundant links between them. If a broadcast frame was sent from one switch to the other, it would be flooded and thus go down the second link right back to the switch that sent it. This broadcast frame would again be flooded out the first link, and this would continue because the redundant links have created a loop.

Spanning Tree Protocol works by electing one switch to act as root bridge and then selecting one loop-free path from the root bridge to every other switch. (STP uses the term *bridge* because it was written before there were switches.)

Spanning Tree must elect:

- One root bridge
- One root port per every nonroot bridge
- One designated port per network segment

Part II: SWITCH

Spanning Tree Election Criteria

Spanning Tree builds paths out from a central point along the fastest available links. It selects paths according to the following criteria:

1. Lowest root bridge ID (BID)

2. Lowest path cost to the root

3. Lowest sender bridge ID

4. Lowest sender port ID (PID)

The following are some important terms to remember:

- **Bridge ID (BID):** An 8-byte value that combines bridge priority and bridge MAC address. For example, a switch with a priority of 8000 hex and a MAC address of 1111.1111.1111 would have a BID of 8000.1111.1111.1111.

- **Bridge priority:** A 2-byte value, 0–65,535 (0–0xFFFF).

- **Default bridge priority:** 32,768 (0x8000 in hexadecimal).

- **Port ID (PID):** Port priority and port number.

- **Port priority:** A 6-bit value, 0–63; the default is 32.

- **Path cost:** The cumulative value of the cost of each link between the bridge and the root. Path cost values have changed over the years as link bandwidths have changed. The actual cost used by a particular switch depends on its IOS version. Table 4-1 shows the cost values used by recent IOS versions.

Table 4-1 Spanning Tree Link Costs

Link Speed	Cost
10 Gbps	2 (some switches assign a cost of 1)
1 Gbps	4
100 Mbps	19
10 Mbps	100

STP Election

Spanning Tree builds paths out from a starting point, the "root" of the tree. The first step in selecting paths is to identify this root device. Then, each device selects its best path back to the root, according to the criteria laid out

Part II: SWITCH

in the previous sections (lowest root BID, lowest cost, lowest advertising BID, lowest port ID).

Root Bridge Election

The first task is to elect a root bridge. Each switch starts out assuming it is the root and sending Bridge Protocol Data Units (BPDU) with its BID listed as the root. It looks at BPDUs received from its neighbors. If a switch receives a BPDU with a better (meaning lower) root BID than its own, it recognizes that it is not the root and uses the root bridge listed in that BPDU. At some point, the switches all converge on one root bridge. Note that if a new switch is introduced to the Layer 2 network, the election must take place again.

Consider the switched network illustrated in Figure 4-1. Assume each switch uses the default priority. Which switch will be elected as root?

Figure 4-1   Example Switched Topology

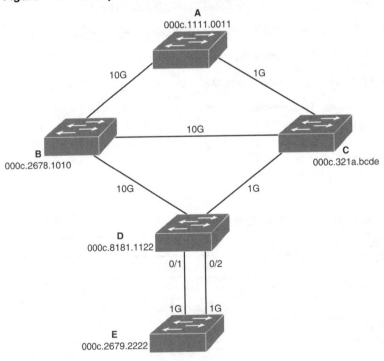

The Bridge IDs for each of the switches in Figure 4-1 are as follows:

Switch A BID = 8000.000c.1111.0011

Switch B BID = 8000.000c.2678.1010

Switch C BID = 8000.000c.321a.bcde

Switch D BID = 8000.000c.8181.1122

Switch E BID = 8000.000c.2679.2222

Switch A has the lowest BID, so it is the root. Each nonroot switch must now select a root port.

Root Port Election

The *root port* is the port that provides the lowest-cost path back to the root. Continuing on with the example in Figure 4-1, when A is acknowledged as the root, the remaining bridges sort out their lowest-cost path back to A, as explained here:

- **Switch B:** Uses the direct link to Switch A with a cost of 2 (link speed of 10 Gbps) because the other option, the link to C and then A, has a higher path cost of 6 (one 10 Gbps and one 1 Gbps link).

- **Switch C:** The link directly connected to Switch A has a cost of 4 (1 Gbps), and the link through B has a path cost of 4 (two 10 Gbps links). Because the costs are the same, the next step is to look at sender Bridge ID. Switch A's BID is lower than Switch B's BID, so Switch C designates the port connecting to Switch A as the root port.

- **Switch D:** Switch B's BPDUs indicate it has a root path cost of 2. Switch D adds its link cost to that, with a result of a cost of 4 for the path through B. The path cost through C to A is 8 (two 10 Gbps links and one 1 Gbps link), so the port connecting to Switch B is chosen as the root port.

- **Switch E:** Switch E has two links to Switch D, and thus two choices for root port. The lowest path cost is the same for both ports (the path through D to C to B to A with a cost of 8). The next step is to check the sender's BID—the sender for both ports is Switch D, so that does not break the tie. Next, the switch checks the sender Port ID. Assuming default port priority, the PID for interface 0/1 is lower than the PID for 0/2, so the port on the left is the root port.

Designated Port Election

Designated ports lead away from the root. Obviously, all ports on the root bridge are designated ports (A–B and A–C as shown in Figure 4-1).

Part II: SWITCH

- **Segment B–D:** B has the lowest path cost to root (2 versus 4), so it is designated for this segment.

- **Segment C–D:** Both C and D have the same path cost to the root (4), so the next step is to look at sender bridge ID. Because Switch C has a lower bridge ID than Switch D, it is designated for this segment.

- **Segment B–C:** B has the lowest path cost to the root (2 versus 4), so it is designated for this segment.

- **Both segments D–E:** D has the lowest cost to the root (4 versus 8), so it is designated for both segments.

Now the looped topology has been turned into a tree with A at the root, as illustrated in Figure 4-2. Notice that no more redundant links exist.

Figure 4-2   Active Topology After Spanning Tree Is Complete

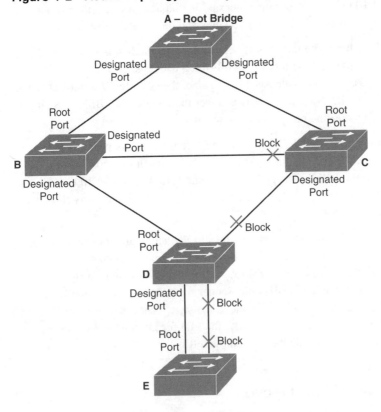

Bridge Protocol Data Units

Switches exchange STP BPDUs. The two types of BPDUs are *configuration* and *topology change notification (TCN)*. Configuration BPDUs are sent every 2 seconds from the root toward the downstream switches. Configuration BPDUs are used for the following:

- To aid in the election process

- To maintain connectivity between switches

- To send timer information from the root

TCN BPDUs are sent for the following reasons:

- There is a link failure.

- A port starts forwarding, and a designated port already exists.

- The switch receives a TCN from a neighbor.

When a switch receives a TCN BPDU, it acknowledges that with a configuration BPDU that has the TCN Acknowledgment bit set.

When the root bridge receives a TCN, it starts sending configuration BPDUs with the TCN bit set for a period of time equal to max age plus forward delay. Switches that receive this notification change their MAC table aging time to the Forward Delay time, causing MAC addresses to age faster. The topology change also causes an election of the root bridge, root ports, and designated ports.

The following are some important fields in the BPDU:

- **Root bridge ID:** The BID of the current root

- **Sender's root path cost:** The cost to the root

- **Sender's bridge ID:** Sender's priority concatenated to MAC

- **Sender's port ID:** The port number, transmitted as final tie-breaker

- **Max Age:** 20 seconds by default

- **Hello time:** 2 seconds by default

- **Forward Delay:** 15 seconds by default

Part II: SWITCH

Spanning Tree Port States

When a port is first activated, it transitions through the stages shown in Table 4-2. If you add the times together, you will see that in original Spanning Tree, it can take 50 seconds before the port is active and capable of forwarding frames.

Table 4-2   Spanning Tree Port States

Port State	Timer	Action
Blocking	Max Age (20 sec)	Discards frames, does not learn MAC addresses, receives BPDUs
Listening	Forward Delay (15 sec)	Discards frames, does not learn MAC addresses, receives BPDUs to determine its role in the network
Learning	Forward Delay (15 sec)	Discards frames, does learn MAC addresses, receives and transmits BPDUs
Forwarding		Accepts frames, learns MAC addresses, receives and transmits BPDUs

Configuring and Verifying Spanning Tree

Spanning Tree is enabled by default on all Cisco switches. Certain commands enable you to change its default behavior and verify its actions

To change the STP priority value, use the following global command. Note that the value must be between 0 and 65,535 and in increments of 4096.

```
Switch (config)# spanning-tree vlan vlan_no. priority value
```

To configure a switch as root using a built-in macro, use the following global command. The **primary** keyword sets the priority value to 4096 less than the current root. The **secondary** keyword sets the value to 28,672.

```
Switch (config)# spanning-tree vlan vlan_no. root {primary |
  secondary}
```

To change the STP port cost for an access port, use the following interface command:

```
Switch(config-if)# spanning-tree cost value
```

To change the STP port cost for a VLAN on a trunk port, use the following interface command:

```
Switch(config-if)# spanning-tree vlan vlan_no. cost value
```

To change the STP port priority, use the interface command:

```
Switch (config-if)# spanning-tree vlan vlan_no. port-priority
  value
```

To display general Spanning Tree information for all VLANs on the switch, use the command:

```
Switch# show spanning-tree
```

Example 4-1 illustrates the output for the **show spanning tree** command.

Example 4-1   The show spanning-tree Command Output

```
VLAN0001
  Spanning tree enabled protocol rstp
  Root ID    Priority    28673
             Address     aabb.cc00.7600
             This bridge is the root
             Hello Time   2 sec  Max Age 20 sec  Forward Delay 15 sec

  Bridge ID Priority    28673   (priority 28672 sys-id-ext 1)
            Address     aabb.cc00.7600
            Hello Time   2 sec  Max Age 20 sec  Forward Delay 15 sec
            Aging Time  300 sec

Interface         Role Sts Cost     Prio.Nbr Type
----------------  ---- --- -------- -------- ------------------------
Et0/0             Desg FWD 4        128.1    Shr
Et0/1             Desg FWD 4        128.2    Shr
<output omitted>
```

To limit the displayed STP information to just a specific VLAN, use the following:

```
Switch# show spanning-tree vlan vlan_no.
```

To display the STP information for an interface, use the following:

```
Switch # show spanning-tree interface interface_no. [detail]
```

```
Vlan                Role Sts Cost      Prio.Nbr Type
------------------- ---- --- --------- -------- --------------------
----------
VLAN0001            Desg FWD 4         128.1    Shr
```

Part II: SWITCH

To verify STP timers, use the following command. Note the highlighted timers in the output.

```
Switch # show spanning-tree bridge
                                        Hello  Max  Fwd
Vlan                      Bridge ID      Time  Age  Dly
  Protocol
---------------- ------------------------------- ----- --- ---
--------
VLAN0001    28673 (28672,  1) aabb.cc00.7600    2    20   15
  rstp
```

Per-VLAN Spanning Tree

The IEEE's version of STP assumes one common Spanning Tree instance (and thus one root bridge) regardless of how many VLANs are configured. With the Cisco Per-VLAN Spanning Tree (PVST+) there is a different instance of STP for each VLAN. To derive the VLAN BID, the switch picks a different MAC address from its base pool for each VLAN. Each VLAN has its own root bridge, root port, and so on. You can configure these so that data flow is optimized, and traffic load is balanced among the switches by configuring different root bridges for groups of VLANs. In a Cisco Layer 2 network, using the Rapid version of PVST+ is more common, as the following section describes.

Rapid Spanning Tree

Rapid Spanning Tree Protocol (RSTP), described in IEEE standard 802.1w, is a standards-based, nonproprietary way of speeding STP convergence. Switch ports exchange an explicit handshake when they transition to forwarding. RSTP uses different port states than regular STP, as shown in Table 4-3. A version of PVST+ is used with Rapid Spanning Tree; this is called *Per-VLAN Rapid Spanning Tree* (PVRST+). It is sometimes also referred to as *Rapid Per-VLAN Spanning Tree* (RPVST+).

Table 4-3   Comparing 802.1d and 802.1w Port States

STP Port State	Equivalent RSTP Port State
Disabled	Discarding
Blocking	Discarding
Listening	Discarding
Learning	Learning
Forwarding	Forwarding

RSTP Port Roles

RSTP also defines different Spanning Tree roles for ports:

- **Root port:** The best path to the root (same as STP).

- **Designated port:** Same role as with STP.

- **Alternate port:** A backup to the root port.

- **Backup port:** A backup to the designated port. Seeing a backup port in a production network is unlikely because it occurs when two switches are connected to the same segment, such as when they have a hub between them.

- **Disabled port:** Not used in Spanning Tree.

- **Edge port:** Connected only to an end user. If this port ever receives a BPDU, it stops being an edge port.

Figure 4-3 shows the same topology as used in Figure 4-2, but with RSTP port roles. Note that alternate ports do not forward frames but continue to send and receive BPDUs and transition to forwarding if needed.

Part II: SWITCH

Figure 4-3   RSTP Topology

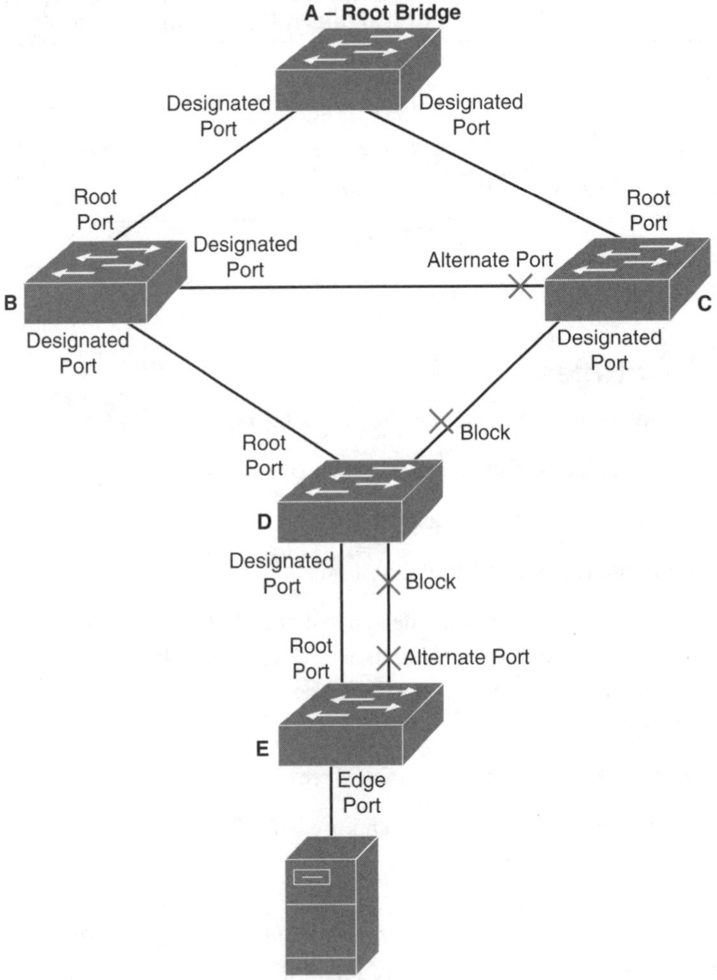

BPDU Differences in RSTP

In regular STP, BPDUs are originated by the root and relayed by each switch. In RSTP, each switch originates BPDUs, whether or not it receives a BPDU on its root port. All eight bits of the BPDU type field are used by RSTP. The Topology Change (TC) and TC Ack bits are still utilized. The other six bits specify the port's role and its RSTP state and are employed in the port handshake. The RSTP BPDU is set to Type 2, Version 2.

RSTP Fast Convergence

The Rapid Spanning Tree process understands and incorporates topology changes much quicker than the previous version:

- **RSTP uses a mechanism similar to BackboneFast:** When an inferior BPDU is received, the switch accepts it. If the switch has another path to the root, it uses that and informs its downstream switch of the alternative path.

- **Edge ports work the same as Portfast ports:** They automatically transition directly to forwarding.

- **Link type:** If you connect two switches through a point-to-point link and the local port becomes a designated port, it exchanges a handshake with the other port to quickly transition to forwarding. Full-duplex links are assumed to be point-to-point; half-duplex links are assumed to be shared.

- **Backup and alternate ports:** These ports can transition to forwarding when BPDUs are not received from a neighbor switch (similar to UplinkFast).

If an RSTP switch detects a topology change, it sets a TC timer to twice the Hello time and sets the TC bit on all BPDUs sent out its designated and root ports until the timer expires. It also clears the MAC addresses learned on these ports. Only changes to the status of non-edge ports cause a TC notification.

If an RSTP switch receives a TC BPDU, it clears the MAC addresses on that port and sets the TC bit on all BPDUs sent out its designated and root ports until the TC timer expires. Rapid PVST+ is the default mode on most Cisco switches. Verify which version of Spanning Tree your switch is running with the command **show spanning-tree**. If the switch is not running RPVST+, enable it with the following global command:

```
Switch(config)# spanning-tree mode rapid-pvst
```

You should still configure root and secondary root bridges for each VLAN when using RSTP.

Multiple Spanning Tree

With Multiple Spanning Tree (MST), you can group VLANs and run one instance of Spanning Tree for a group of VLANs. This cuts down on the number of root bridges, root ports, designated ports, and BPDUs in your network. For instance, assume you had a network with 1,000 VLANs; 1,000 sets of BPDUs are sent every two seconds, and 1,000 elections are held for root bridge and all the other STP settings. Combining these into just a few instances of Spanning Tree might be more efficient—MST enables you to do that. MST is compatible with other versions of STP, so you can use MST in one part of the network and Rapid PVST+ in another part.

A group of VLANs is called an *MST region*. MST regions use a special STP instance to carry BPDUs, numbered instance 0 and called the *Internal Spanning Tree (IST)*. The IST appears as one bridge to other STP areas, enabling it to interact with other versions of STP. A region can contain other instances, each with their own instance number. VLANs are grouped into an instance, and each instance elects a root bridge. The IST represents the entire region to the rest of the network.

Example 4-2 shows the commands used to configure and verify MST. Perform the MST configuration before changing the Spanning Tree mode to MST; otherwise, each STP will have to reconverge each time you assign VLANs to an instance. MST configuration does not take effect until you give the **end** command under MST configuration mode. Before committing a change, you can use the **show pending** command to see the configuration that will take effect after you type **end**. To see the current MST configuration, use the **show current** command under MST configuration mode.

Example 4-2   Configuring MST

```
Switch(config)# spanning-tree mst configuration
Switch(config-mst)# name region_name
Switch(config-mst)# revision number
Switch(config-mst)# instance number vlan vlan_range
Switch(config-mst)# end
!
Switch(config)# spanning-tree mode mst
!
Switch# show spanning-tree mst
```

Any VLANs on the switch that are not assigned to an MST instance are automatically assigned to instance 0. Cisco recommends that you place all VLANs in an instance other than 0. MST instances run Rapid STP by default. You can change root and port priorities as with other versions of Spanning Tree. STP stability mechanisms, such as those described in the following section, should still be used.

Part II: SWITCH

Spanning Tree Improvements

Spanning Tree has several additional tools for tuning STP to protect the network and keep it operating properly. They can be divided into two groups, those that improve STP performance and those that improve STP stability. Some of these are not needed when using RSTP because they are integrated into the protocol.

Performance-improving mechanisms include

- PortFast

- UplinkFast (not needed with RSTP)

- BackboneFast (not needed with RSTP)

Stability improving mechanisms include

- BPDU Guard

- BPDU Filter

- Root Guard

- UDLD

- Loop Guard

PortFast

PortFast is a Cisco-proprietary enhancement to Spanning Tree that helps speed up the time for a port to become active. PortFast causes the port to transition directly to forwarding, bypassing the other STP states. Alterations in port state do not cause topology change notifications to be sent. It is for access (user) ports only—connecting a switch to a PortFast port could cause loops to develop. Configure PortFast on an interface or interface range with the following:

```
Switch(config-if)# spanning-tree portfast
```

It can also be configured globally with

```
Switch(config)# spanning-tree portfast default
```

UplinkFast

UplinkFast is for speeding convergence when a direct link to an upstream switch fails. The switch identifies backup ports for the root port. (These are called an *uplink group*.) If the root port fails, one of the ports in the uplink group is unblocked and transitions immediately to forwarding; it bypasses the listening and learning stages. It should be used in wiring closet switches with at least one blocked port.

UplinkFast is enabled globally, so the command affects all ports and VLANs. The command to enable UplinkFast is **spanning-tree uplinkfast**.

BackboneFast

BackboneFast is used for speeding convergence when a link fails that is not directly connected to the switch. It helps the switch detect indirect failures. If a switch running BackboneFast receives an inferior BPDU from its designated bridge, it recognizes that a link on the path to the root has failed. (An inferior BPDU is one that lists the same switch for the root bridge and designated bridge.)

The switch then tries to find an alternative path to the root by sending a Root Link Query (RLQ) frame out all alternate ports. The root then responds with an RLQ response, and the port receiving this response can transition to forwarding. Alternate ports are determined in this way:

- If the inferior BPDU was received on a blocked port, the root port and any other blocked ports are considered alternates.

- If the inferior BPDU was received on the root port, all blocked ports are considered alternates.

- If the inferior BPDU was received on the root port and there are no blocked ports, the switch assumes it has lost connectivity with the root and advertises itself as root.

Configure BackboneFast by giving this global command on all switches in the network: **spanning-tree backbonefast**.

BPDU Guard

BPDU Guard prevents loops if another switch is attached to a PortFast port. When BPDU Guard is enabled on an interface, the port is put into an error-disabled state (basically, shut down) if a BPDU is received on the interface. BPDU Guard can be enabled at either global config mode—in which case it affects all PortFast interfaces—or at interface mode. PortFast does not need to be enabled for BPDU Guard to be configured at a specific interface.

Example 4-3 shows BPDU Guard being enabled, first at the global configuration mode and then at the interface configuration mode. Verify its operation with the command **show spanning-tree summary totals**.

Example 4-3   Configuring BPDU Guard

```
Switch(config)# spanning-tree portfast bpduguard default
!
Switch(config)# interface e0/0
Switch(config-if)# spanning-tree bpduguard enable
!
Switch# show spanning-tree summary totals
```

BPDU Filter

BPDU Filter can be a dangerous tool because it prevents BPDUs from being sent out a port. In normal circumstances, even blocked or alternate ports send and receive BPDUs so that they know whether they should become active. Filtering BPDUs can inadvertently cause loops to form. Do not try to enable both BPDU Guard and BPDU Filter on the same interface; only BPDU Filter will be active.

Configure BPDU Filter for the entire switch with the global command **spanning-tree portfast bpdufilter default** or for a specific port with the interface command **spanning-tree bpdufilter enable**. BPDU Filter functions differently depending on whether it is enabled globally or at the interface level. When applied at global configuration mode, it causes an interface to be taken out of PortFast status if the interface receives any BPDUs. When applied at interface configuration mode, it prevents the port from sending or receiving BPDUs.

Root Guard

Root Guard is meant to prevent the wrong switch from becoming the Spanning Tree root. It is enabled on ports other than the root port and on switches other than the root switch (or the secondary root). Root Guard should not be configured on interfaces that connect to the root switch or backup root. If a Root Guard port receives a BPDU that might cause it to become a root port, the port is put into "root-inconsistent" state and does not

Part II: SWITCH

pass traffic through it. If the port stops receiving these BPDUs, it automatically reenables itself. To enable and verify Root Guard, use the following commands:

```
Switch(config-if)# spanning-tree guard root
!
Switch# show spanning-tree inconsistentports
```

Unidirectional Link Detection

A switch notices when a physical connection is broken by the absence of Layer 1 electrical keepalives. (Ethernet calls this a *link beat*.) However, sometimes a cable is intact enough to maintain keepalives but not to pass data in both directions. It has become a *unidirectional* link. This could interfere with routing and create a loop by interfering with Spanning Tree. Operating at Layer 2, Unidirectional Link Detection (UDLD) detects a unidirectional link by sending periodic hellos out to the interface. It also uses probes, which must be acknowledged by the device on the other end of the link.

UDLD has two modes: normal and aggressive. In normal mode, the link status is changed to undetermined state if the hellos are not returned. The port still passes traffic. In aggressive mode, the port is error-disabled if a unidirectional link is found. UDLD aggressive mode is typically configured on all fiber interfaces. On most Cisco switches it is enabled by default on Ethernet fiber interfaces.

To enable UDLD on all fiber-optic interfaces, use the global command:

```
Switch(config)# udld {enable | aggressive}
```

Although this command is given at global config mode, it applies only to fiber ports.

To enable UDLD on nonfiber ports, give the same command at the port interface configuration mode.

To control UDLD on a specific fiber port, use the following command:

```
Switch(config-if)# udld port [aggressive | disable]
```

To reenable all interfaces shut by UDLD, either shut the interface and then reenable it or use the following command:

```
Switch# udld reset
```

To verify UDLD status, use the following:

```
Switch# show udld
```

Loop Guard

Loop Guard prevents loops that might develop if a port that should be blocking inadvertently transitions to the forwarding state. This happens if the port stops receiving BPDUs (perhaps because of a unidirectional link or a software/configuration problem in its neighbor switch). When one of the ports in a physically redundant topology stops receiving BPDUs, STP thinks the topology is loop-free. Eventually, the blocking port becomes designated and moves to forwarding state, thus creating a loop. With Loop Guard enabled, an additional check is made.

If no BPDUs are received on a blocked port for a specific length of time, Loop Guard puts that port into "loop inconsistent" blocking state, rather than transitioning to forwarding state. It is most effective when used with UDLD. Configure Root Guard on designated ports (downlinks to lower-level switches) and Loop Guard on all nondesignated ports (the uplinks of those switches), or all root and alternate ports.

To enable Loop Guard for all point-to-point links on the switch, use the global version of the command:

```
Switch(config)# spanning-tree loopguard default
```

To enable Loop Guard on a specific interface, use the following:

```
Switch(config-if)# spanning-tree guard loop
```

Loop Guard automatically reenables the port if it starts receiving BPDUs again.

Using Spanning Tree Improvements

You can use the **show spanning-tree summary** command to view which of the Spanning Tree improvement tools described in the previous sections are enabled globally. In Example 4-4, only EtherChannel Misconfiguration Guard (which is enabled by default) is turned on.

Example 4-4   Verifying Global STP Configurations

```
Switch# show spanning-tree summary
Switch is in rapid-pvst mode
Root bridge for: VLAN0001
```

Part II: SWITCH

Example 4-4   Continued

```
Extended system ID          is enabled
Portfast Default            is disabled
PortFast BPDU Guard Default is disabled
Portfast BPDU Filter Default is disabled
Loopguard Default           is disabled
EtherChannel misconfig guard is enabled
Configured Pathcost method used is short
UplinkFast                  is disabled
BackboneFast                is disabled


Name              Blocking Listening Learning Forwarding STP Active
----------------- -------- --------- -------- ---------- ----------
1 vlan                   0         0        0         24         24
```

To see which STP tools are configured on a specific interface, either examine the running configuration or use the command **show spanning-tree interface** *interface* **detail**. The output in Example 4-5 shows that Root Guard is configured on this interface.

Example 4-5   **Verifying Interface STP Configurations**

```
Switch# show spanning-tree interface e0/0 detail
 Port 1 (Ethernet0/0) of VLAN0001 is designated forwarding
   Port path cost 100, Port priority 128, Port Identifier 128.1.
   Designated root has priority 28673, address aabb.cc00.7600
   Designated bridge has priority 28673, address aabb.cc00.7600
   Designated port id is 128.1, designated path cost 0
   Timers: message age 0, forward delay 0, hold 0
   Number of transitions to forwarding state: 1
   Link type is shared by default
   Root guard is enabled on the port
   BPDU: sent 468, received 37
```

Confused by all the acronyms and STP features? Figure 4-4 shows the STP tools you can use in your network and where to implement them.

Figure 4-4   Sample STP Improvements Use

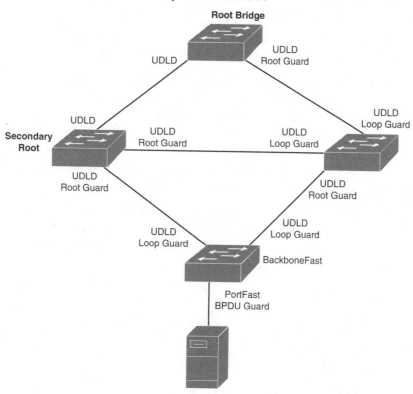

Troubleshooting STP

Spanning Tree problems frequently come as a surprise—you enable a port on one switch, and it brings down part of your network. It's very important to have complete, accurate documentation of a Layer 2 network. Using the tools listed in previous sections and following the best practices listed in the following section will lessen the chances of a Spanning Tree issue. But if one occurs, the following are some common things to look for when trouble-shooting Spanning Tree Protocol:

- **Duplex mismatch:** This occurs when one side of a link is half-duplex and the other is full-duplex. This causes late collisions and FCS errors.

- **Unidirectional link failure:** The link is up, but data flows only in one direction. It can cause loops.

- **Frame corruption:** Physical errors on the line cause BPDUs to be lost, and the port incorrectly begins forwarding. This is caused by duplex mismatch, bad cable, or when the cable is too long.

- **Resource errors:** STP is implemented in software, so a switch with an overloaded CPU or memory might neglect some STP duties.

- **PortFast configuration errors:** This occurs when you connect a switch to two ports that have PortFast enabled. It can cause a loop.

- **STP tuning errors:** Max Age or Forward Delay set too short can cause a loop. A network diameter that is set too low causes BPDUs to be discarded and affects STP convergence.

Suspect a loop if there is abnormally high port utilization, you capture traffic on a link and see the same frames multiple times, or all users in a bridging domain have connectivity problems at the same time.

To remedy a loop quickly, shut redundant ports and then enable them one at a time. Some switches enable debugging of STP to help in diagnosing problems. The following commands are useful for isolating a bridging loop and for troubleshooting and verifying Spanning Tree operation in general:

- **show interfaces**
- **show spanning tree**
- **show process cpu**
- **debug spanning tree**
- **show mac address-table aging-time** *vlan#*
- **show spanning-tree vlan** *vlan#* **detail**

Spanning-Tree Best Practices

To optimize data flow in the network, design and configure Spanning Tree in the following ways:

- Statically configure switches to be the primary and secondary root bridges by setting priority values.

- Consider which interfaces will become designated and root ports (possibly set port priorities/path cost).

- Tune STP using the improvements and tools detailed in this chapter.

- Enable UDLD aggressive mode on all fiber interfaces.

- Design STP domains that are as simple and contained as possible by using multilayer switches and routed links.

- Use PVRST+ or MST for the fastest convergence times.

CHAPTER 5

First Hop Redundancy Protocols

Layer 2 devices, such as end hosts and switches, need to go through a Layer 3 device to communicate with hosts on different VLANs or subnets. This Layer 3 device is called a *default gateway*. In Figure 5-1, the end hosts are connected to a Layer 2 switch. If one of them needs to reach a server in another part of the network, it must go through either Router A or Router B.

Figure 5-1   Layer 2 and Layer 3 Network

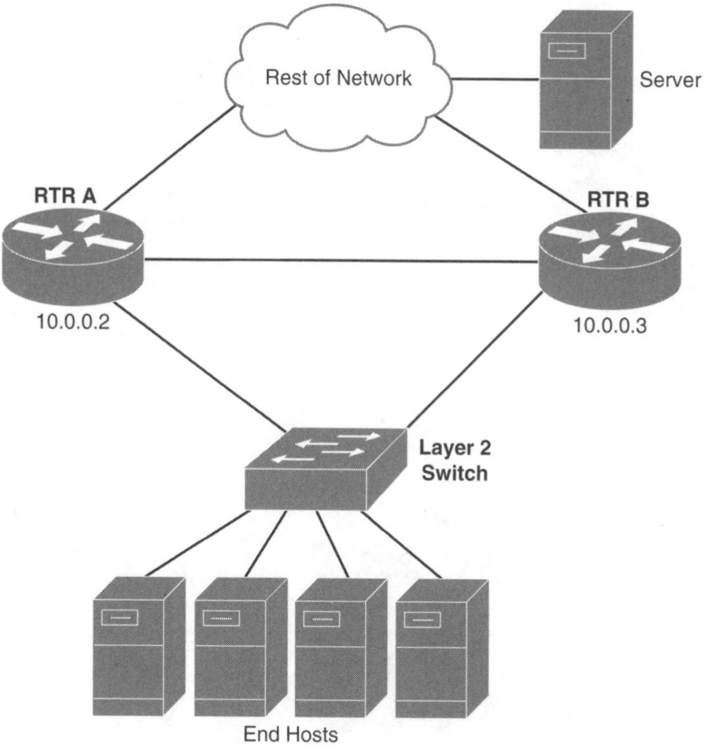

You can manually configure hosts to use a specific default gateway, but that leads to a single point of failure. Suppose the end hosts had RTR A's IP address hard-coded as their default gateway, but then RTR A failed? Proxy Address Resolution Protocol (ARP) is one method for hosts to dynamically discover gateways, but it has issues in a highly available environment. With

Proxy ARP, hosts send an ARP broadcast for all destinations, even remote ones. A router (or Layer 3 gateway) responds with its own MAC address. One problem with this solution is its slow failover because ARP entries in a host take minutes to timeout so it sends traffic to the router even if the router is no longer available.

Instead of making the host responsible for choosing a new gateway, first hop redundancy protocols (FHRP) enable two or more routers to support a shared MAC address. With FHRPs, two or more devices support a "virtual router" with a fictitious MAC address and unique IP address. One of the actual routers responds to ARP requests with the information of the virtual router. Hosts use this IP address as their default gateway and the MAC address for the Layer 2 header. All traffic from that host is then forwarded through the router that responded to the ARP request, as shown in Figure 5-2.

Figure 5-2   Using a First Hop Redundancy Protocol

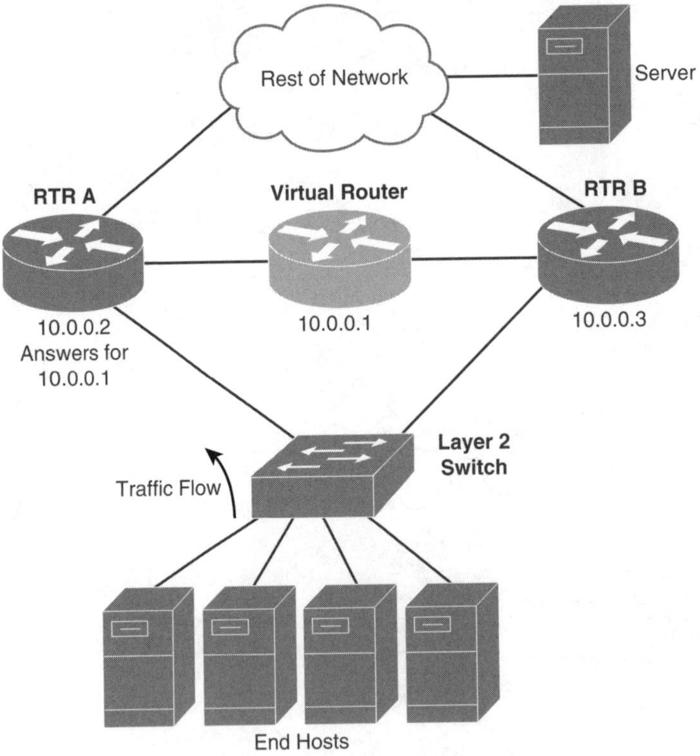

If the primary router is lost, the backup router dynamically assumes control of traffic forwarded to that MAC and begins answering ARP requests for that IP address, as shown in Figure 5-3.

Figure 5-3   FHRP Failure

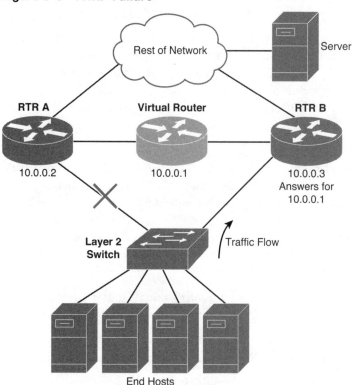

This chapter examines three first hop redundancy protocols: HSRP, VRRP, and GLBP. It also looks at using HSRP and GLBP for IPv6 first hop redundancy. IPv6 uses router advertisements to dynamically assign default gateways, but the failover is moderately slow. Additionally, router advertisements do not have as many control features as do FHRPs. For these reasons, HSRP, VRRP, and GLBP all have versions that support IPv6. However, there is currently very little support for IPv6 VRRP in Cisco devices.

Note

This chapter refers to *routers*, but this term also refers to those multilayer switches that can implement Layer 3 redundancy.

Part II: SWITCH

Hot Standby Router Protocol

Hot Standby Router Protocol (HSRP) is a Cisco proprietary first-hop redundancy protocol. With HSRP, the virtual router's MAC address is based on the HSRP group number; HSRPv1 uses 0000.0C07.AC*xx*, where *xx* is the

HSRP group number, and HSRPv2 uses 0000.0C09F.FXXX, where XXX is the HSRP group number. Multiple groups (virtual routers) are allowed.

The active router forwards traffic. The standby is backup. The standby monitors periodic hellos to detect a failure of the active router. These hellos are multicast to 224.0.0.2 or 224.0.0.102 depending on HSRP version. When the standby router detects a failure, the standby device starts answering messages sent to the IP and MAC addresses of the virtual router. When using Layer 3 switches, configure the same switch to be the primary HSRP router and the Spanning Tree root.

The active router is chosen because it has the highest HSRP priority (default priority is 100). In case of a tie, the router with the highest configured IP address wins the election. A new router with a higher priority does not cause an election unless it is configured to *preempt*—that is, take over from a lower-priority router. Configuring a router to preempt also ensures that the highest-priority router regains its active status if it goes down but then comes back online again.

Interface tracking reduces the active router's priority if a specified circuit is down. This enables the standby router to take over even though the active router is still up.

There are two versions of HSRP; currently version 1 is the default.

Table 5-1 compares the two versions of HSRP.

Table 5-1   Comparison of HSRP Versions

HSRP Version 1	HSRP Version 2
Group numbers 0–255	Group numbers 0–4095
Virtual MAC address = 0000.0C07.ACXX	Virtual MAC address = 0000.0C9F.FXXX
Multicast address = 224.0.0.2	Multicast address = 224.0.0.102
No IPv6 support	Supports IPv6

HSRP States

HSRP devices move between these states:

- **Initial:** HSRP is not running.
- **Learn:** The router does not know the virtual IP address and is waiting to hear from the active router.

- **Listen:** The router knows the IP and MAC of the virtual router, but it is not the active or standby router.

- **Speak:** The router sends periodic HSRP hellos and participates in the election of the active router.

- **Standby:** The router monitors hellos from the active router and assumes responsibility if the active router fails.

- **Active:** The router forwards packets on behalf of the virtual router.

Note

The Learn state is not actually seen in debugs of HSRP.

Configuring HSRP

One thing to remember about HSRP is that its commands use the keyword **standby** rather than "HSRP" or something else logical. To begin configuring HSRP, use the **standby** *group-no.* **ip** *virtual-IP-address* command in interface configuration mode. Routers in the same HSRP group must belong to the same subnet/virtual LAN (VLAN). Give this command under the interface connecting to that subnet or VLAN. For instance, use the following to configure the router as a member of HSRP group 2 with virtual router IP address 10.0.0.1:

```
Router(config-if)# standby 2 ip 10.0.0.1
```

HSRP authentication helps prevent unauthorized routers from seeing user traffic. The protocol supports both plain text and MD5 authentication, but MD5 is preferred because it is more secure. Make sure all HSRP peers use the same authentication settings.

```
Router(config-if)# standby group-no. authentication md5 key-string
  password
```

Rather than accepting the defaults, you might want to tune HSRP with three options: priority, preemption, and timers. You can manually designate the router to be elected as the active router by configuring its priority higher than the default of 100. If the Spanning Tree root bridge is also one of the default gateways, it is important to align FHRPs and STP. Use the **priority** command to ensure that the STP root is always the active router when it is available and the secondary root as the standby router. Recall that the highest priority device is selected.

```
Router(config-if)# standby group-no. priority priority
```

Part II: SWITCH

Along with configuring priority, configure **preempt** to enable a router to take over if the active router has lower priority, as shown in the following commands. This helps lead to a predictable data path through the network. The first command activates preemption. The second command delays preemption to give the router or switch time to fully boot and the routing protocol time to converge. A good rule for this is to time how long it takes to boot and add about 50 percent to get the delay value in seconds.

```
Router(config-if)# standby group-no. preempt
Router(config-if)# standby group-no. preempt delay minimum seconds
```

Speed convergence by changing the hello and hold times. The default hello is 3 seconds, and hold time is 10 seconds. These timers can be set between 1–255 seconds and by default are specified by second in the command. However, if the **msec** keyword is used, they must be specified in milliseconds.

```
Router(config-if)# standby group-no. timers [msec] hello [msec]
  hold
```

Example 5-1 shows the commands for configuring HSRP on RTR A and RTR B in Figure 5-1. RTR A is configured as the active HSRP router for Group 2, and RTR B is configured as the standby. RTR A is set to preempt so that it reclaims active status when it comes back online after a failure. Both routers use HSRP MD5 authentication with a password of C1sco. The configuration sets the hello interval to 1 second and the hold time to 3 seconds on both routers.

Example 5-1   Configuring HSRP

```
!Configuration for RTR-A
RTR-A(config)# int e0/1
RTR-A(config-if)# ip address 10.0.0.2 255.255.255.0
RTR-A(config-if)# standby 2 ip 10.0.0.1
RTR-A(config-if)# standby 2 priority 125
RTR-A(config-if)# standby 2 preempt delay minimum 90
RTR-A(config-if)# standby 2 authentication md5 key-string C1sco
RTR-A(config-if)# standby 2 timers 1 3

!Configuration for RTR-B
RTR-B(config)# int e0/1
RTR-B(config-if)# ip address 10.0.0.3 255.255.255.0
RTR-B(config-if)# standby 2 ip 10.0.0.1
RTR-B(config-if)# standby 2 authentication md5 key-string C1sco
RTR-B(config-if)# standby 2 timers 1 3
```

The **show standby [brief]** command verifies the configuration as shown in Example 5-2. It first shows the output from **show standby brief** on both RTR-A and RTR-B. This is a good command to get a quick picture of the status of HSRP on each router. Note that RTR-A shows that it is the active router for group 2, it has a priority of 125, and it is configured to preempt. The output from RTR-B shows that it is the standby router for group 2 and is using the default priority of 100. The command **show standby** (without the **brief** keyword) gives much more detail, such as virtual MAC address, timers, and authentication type.

Example 5-2   Verifying HSRP Configuration

```
RTR-A# show standby brief
                    P indicates configured to preempt.
                    |
Interface   Grp  Pri P State   Active     Standby       Virtual IP
Et0/1       2    125 P Active  local      10.0.0.3      10.0.0.1

RTR-B# show standby brief
                    P indicates configured to preempt.
                    |
Interface   Grp  Pri P State   Active     Standby       Virtual IP
Et0/1       2    100   Standby 10.0.0.2   local         10.0.0.1

RTR-A# show standby
Ethernet0/1 - Group 2
  State is Active
    2 state changes, last state change 00:12:40
  Virtual IP address is 10.0.0.1
  Active virtual MAC address is 0000.0c07.ac02
    Local virtual MAC address is 0000.0c07.ac02 (v1 default)
  Hello time 1 sec, hold time 3 sec
    Next hello sent in 0.400 secs
  Authentication MD5, key-string
  Preemption enabled, delay min 90 secs
  Active router is local
  Standby router is 10.0.0.3, priority 100 (expires in 2.128 sec)
  Priority 125 (configured 125)
  Group name is "hsrp-Et0/1-2" (default)
```

HSRP with Tracking

Tracking an interface triggers an election if the active router is still up, but a critical interface (such as the one to the Internet) is down. In the following command, the router's HSRP priority is decremented by 100 if interface e1/1 goes down (the default value to decrement is 10).

```
Router(config-if)# standby 2 track e1/1 100
```

Another way to track an indirect connection is to use IP SLA. With IP SLA tracking, HSRP can failover to the standby router if any connection on the path to a remote location fails or exceeds link-quality thresholds. Example 5-3 shows how to add tracking an IP SLA session number 5 to an existing HSRP interface configuration for group 2. The IP SLA session tracks the jitter on a connection to 172.17.1.2; tracking can be much more complex than what's shown in Example 5-3. IP SLA is covered in detail in the ROUTE exam.

Example 5-3   Configuring HSRP with SLA Object Tracking

```
Router(config)# ip sla 5
Router(config-ip-sla)# udp-jitter 172.17.1.2 16000
!
Router(config)# track 10 ip sla 5
Router(config-if)# int e1/1
Router(config-if)# standby 2 track 10 decrement 50
```

Note

The standby router must be configured with the **preempt** command for it to take control.

It might seem that all traffic uses one router and the other one is idle. Fortunately, that does not have to be the case. Recall that priorities are configured per HSRP group. You can configure multiple HSRP standby groups, and each router can be active for some groups and standby for others by adjusting priorities. Place the interfaces for different VLANs into the corresponding HSRP groups. You can have a maximum of 255 groups. HSRP load sharing is illustrated in Figure 5-4.

Figure 5-4   HSRP Load Sharing

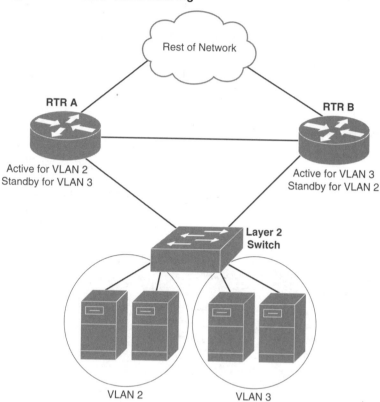

HSRP for IPv6

HSRP version 2 supports IPv6 addresses. Configuration and operation is similar to version 1. The virtual MAC address is derived from the HSRP group number, and the virtual IPv6 link-local address is derived from that MAC address. The router sends router advertisements for that virtual IPv6 link-local address. Versions 1 and 2 cannot be enabled for the same HSRP group at the same time; you must put IPv4 hosts and IPv6 hosts in different groups.

Example 5-4 shows a router configured for HSRP version 2. In this example, the IPv6 virtual router address is created using autoconfiguration. Notice that the same commands are used to verify HSRPv2—**show standby** and **show standby brief**.

Example 5-4   Configuring HSRP for IPv6

```
RTR-A(config)# int e0/0
RTR-A(config-if)# ipv6 address 2001:db9:0::2/64
RTR-A(config-if)# standby version 2
RTR-A(config-if)# standby 3 ipv6 autoconfig
RTR-A(config-if)# standby 3 priority 125
RTR-A(config-if)# standby 3 preempt


RTR-A# show standby brief
                        P indicates configured to preempt.

                        |
Interface   Grp  Pri P State   Active   Standby          Virtual IP
Et0/0        3   125 P Active  local    FE80::A8BB:CCFF:FE00:8800


FE80::5:73FF:FEA0:3

RTR-A# show standby
Ethernet0/0 - Group 3 (version 2)
  State is Active
    2 state changes, last state change 00:01:15
  Virtual IP address is FE80::5:73FF:FEA0:3
  Active virtual MAC address is 0005.73a0.0003
    Local virtual MAC address is 0005.73a0.0003 (v2 IPv6 default)
  Hello time 3 sec, hold time 10 sec
    Next hello sent in 2.208 secs
  Preemption enabled
  Active router is local
  Standby router is FE80::A8BB:CCFF:FE00:8800, priority 100 (expires
in 8.000 sec)
  Priority 125 (configured 125)
  Group name is "hsrp-Et0/0-3" (default)
```

Virtual Router Redundancy Protocol

Virtual Router Redundancy Protocol (VRRP) is similar to HSRP, but it is an open standard (RFC 2338). Two or more devices act as a virtual router. With VRRP, however, the IP address used can be either a virtual one or the actual IP address of the primary router. There are two versions of VRRP; version 2 is most commonly used and provides support for IPv4 only. VRRP version 3 supports both IPv4 and IPv6. VRRP version 2 is the default version. VRRPv3 is not supported on all Cisco devices.

The VRRP master router forwards traffic. The master is chosen either because it owns the real address or it has the highest priority (the default priority is 100). A backup router takes over if the master fails, and there can be multiple backup routers. They monitor periodic hellos multicast by the master to 224.0.0.18 IPv6 FF02:0:0:0:0:0:0:12 to detect a failure of the master router. Multiple VRRP groups are allowed, just as with HSRP. Routers in the same VRRP group must belong to the same subnet/VLAN.

Configuring VRRPv2

VRRP does not use the keyword **standby**; instead, its commands begin with **vrrp**. To enable VRRP, give this command **vrrp** *group-number* **ip** *virtual-IP-address* under the interface connecting to that subnet or VLAN:

```
Router(config-if)# vrrp 2 ip 10.0.0.1
```

Control the master and backup elections by configuring priority values from 1–255. If a master VRRP router is shut down, it advertises a priority of 0. This triggers the backup routers to hold an election without waiting for the master's hellos to time out.

```
Router(config-if)# vrrp 2 priority 125
```

VRRP uses the following timers:

- Advertisement, or hello, interval in seconds. Default is 1 second.

- Master-down interval. Equals 3 × advertisement interval plus skew time. Similar to a hold or dead timer.

- Skew time. (256–priority) / 256. This is meant to ensure that the highest-priority backup router becomes master because higher-priority routers have shorter master-down intervals.

To change the timers on the master, use the following command. The **advertise** keyword is used because the master is the router that advertises hellos.

```
Router(config-if)# vrrp 2 timers advertise 5
```

To change the timers on the backup routers, use the following command. The **learn** keyword is used because backup routers hear the hellos from the master.

```
Router(config-if)# vrrp 2 timers learn
```

Part II: SWITCH

VRRP cannot track interfaces but can track IP SLA object groups. The following command configures tracking of IP SLA object 1 for VRRP group 2. It decrements the router's priority by 50 based on the status of the object tracked.

```
Router(config-if)# vrrp 2 track 1 decrement 50
```

Example 5-5 shows a router configured to be VRRP master using the **priority** option. VRRP MD5 authentication is also configured. Notice the steps that the protocol goes through in electing a master router. The example also shows output from the verification commands **show vrrp brief** and **show vrrp** on both the master and the backup router. In the **show** output, notice that preemption is enabled even though no command was given for it—preemption is enabled by default for VRRP routers.

Example 5-5   Configuring VRRP

```
RTR-A(config)# int e0/1
RTR-A(config-if)# ip address 10.0.0.2 255.255.255.0
RTR-A(config-if)# vrrp 2 ip 10.0.0.1
RTR-A(config-if)#
*Jul 13 20:06:36.675: %VRRP-6-STATECHANGE: Et0/1 Grp 2 state Init ->
  Backup
*Jul 13 20:06:36.679: %VRRP-6-STATECHANGE: Et0/1 Grp 2 state Init ->
  Backup
*Jul 13 20:06:40.295: %VRRP-6-STATECHANGE: Et0/1 Grp 2 state Backup
  -> Master
RTR-A(config-if)#
RTR-A(config-if)# vrrp 2 priority 125
RTR-A(config-if)# vrrp 2 timers advertise 1
RTR-A(config-if)# vrrp 2 authentication md5 key-string C1sco

RTR-A# show vrrp brief
Interface   Grp Pri Time  Own Pre State   Master addr     Group addr
Et0/1        2   125 3609      Y   Master  10.0.0.2        10.0.0.1

RTR-A# show vrrp
Ethernet0/1 - Group 2
  State is Master
  Virtual IP address is 10.0.0.1
  Virtual MAC address is 0000.5e00.0102
  Advertisement interval is 1.000 sec
  Preemption enabled
  Priority is 125
  Authentication MD5, key-string
```

```
Master Router is 10.0.0.2 (local), priority is 125
Master Advertisement interval is 1.000 sec
Master Down interval is 3.511 sec

RTR-B# show vrrp
Ethernet0/1 - Group 2
  State is Backup
  Virtual IP address is 10.0.0.1
  Virtual MAC address is 0000.5e00.0102
  Advertisement interval is 1.000 sec
  Preemption enabled
  Priority is 100
  Authentication MD5, key-string
  Master Router is 10.0.0.2, priority is 125
  Master Advertisement interval is 1.000 sec
  Master Down interval is 3.609 sec (expires in 2.974 sec)
```

Configuring VRRPv3

VRRPv3 operates similarly to version 2. Advertisements are sent to either
the IPv4 or the IPv6 multicast address, depending on which protocol the
VRRP group is configured to use. One difference is that VRRPv3 allows
millisecond timers, whereas VRRPv2 does not. Preemption is enabled by
default.

Enable VRRPv3 with the global command **fhrp version vrrp v3**. Because
this is a global command, it affects all VRRP sessions configured on the
switch. VRRPv2 is disabled by default after you enable VRRPv3.

Separate VRRPv3 groups must be configured for IPv4 and IPv6 using
address families. Enable VRRPv3 on an interface with the command **vrrp**
group-id **address-family** {**ipv4** | **ipv6**}. You can then configure a virtual IP
address and optional items, such as priority and preemption delay, under the
group.

GLBP

One issue with both HSRP and VRRP is that only the primary router is in
use; the others must wait for the primary to fail before they are employed.
These two protocols use groups to get around that limitation. However,
Gateway Load Balancing Protocol (GLBP) enables the simultaneous use of
up to four gateways, thus maximizing bandwidth. With GLBP, there is still
one virtual IP address. However, each participating router has a virtual MAC

Part II: SWITCH

address, and different routers' virtual MAC addresses are sent in answer to ARPs for the virtual IP address. The virtual MAC address has the format 0007.b4YY.YYXX, where the first 6 bits of YYYY are zeros and the last 10 bits are the GLBP group number. XX represents the AVF number of that particular router. Load sharing is accomplished in one of three ways:

- **Weighted load balancing:** Traffic is balanced proportional to a configured weight.

- **Host-dependent load balancing:** A given host always uses the same router.

- **Round-robin load balancing:** Each router MAC is used to respond to ARP requests in turn.

GLBP routers elect an Active Virtual Gateway (AVG). This is the only router to respond to ARPs. It uses this capacity to balance the load among the GLBP routers. The highest-priority router is the AVG; the highest configured IP address is used in case of a tie. The AVG assigns each router in the group a virtual MAC address, numbered sequentially.

The actual router used by a host is its Active Virtual Forwarder (AVF). GLBP group members multicast hellos every 3 seconds to IP address 224.0.0.102, UDP port 3222. If one router goes down, another router answers for its MAC address.

Configure GLBP with the interface command **glbp** *group-number* **ip** *virtual-IP-address*, as shown:

```
Router(config-if)# glbp 39 ip 10.0.0.1
```

To ensure deterministic AVG elections, each router can be configured with a priority. The default priority is 100:

```
Router(config-if)# glbp 39 priority 150
```

Hello and hold (or dead) timers are configured for each interface with the command **glbp** *group-number* **timers** [**msec**] *hello-time* [**msec**] *hold-time*. Values are in seconds unless the **msec** keyword is used.

GLBP uses weighting to indicate the forwarding ability of each router in the group. You can set thresholds so that if a router's weight drops below a certain amount, it will no longer be an AVF. Use object tracking to decrement the weights based on criteria such as network access or interface status.

Verify GLBP configuration and status with the command **show glbp**.

GLBP for IPv6

Most recent IOS versions support GLBP for IPv6 without having to specify a different version. The configuration and operation are similar to GLBP for IPv4, with a few differences. GLBP routers track their group members by using Neighbor Discovery messages rather than a specific multicast address. When enabling GLBP on an interface, you can either configure a virtual IP address or direct the router to configure it automatically.

AVFs are assigned a virtual MAC address by the AVG. AVGs answer Neighbor Discovery requests for the virtual IP address and reply with the virtual MAC of an AVF. As with GLBP for IPv4, you can configure priority, tracking, weighting, and other parameters.

Use the interface command **glbp** *group* **ipv6** {*ipv6-address* | **autoconfig**} to enable GLBP for IPv6.

Planning Router Redundancy Implementation

Before configuring first-hop redundancy, determine which protocol is best in your network. If you have the same VLAN on multiple access switches, use HSRP or VRRP. If you use local VLANs contained to a single switch, GLBP is an option.

Before configuring HSRP or VRRP on a multilayer switch, determine which switch is the root bridge for each VLAN. The root bridge should be the active HSRP/VRRP router. Determine priorities to be used and whether you need tracking or timer adjustment.

After your implementation, verify and test using the commands for the specific FHRP.

Part II: SWITCH

CHAPTER 6

InterVLAN Routing

VLANs divide the network into smaller broadcast domains but also block communication between domains. A Layer 3 device, such as a router or multilayer switch, enables communication between users in different VLANs or subnets.

InterVLAN Routing Using an External Router

A Layer 2 switch connects to a router to provide reachability between VLANs. This is accomplished either via separate physical links for each VLAN or a trunk link from the switch to the router. A trunk link is most common, and this type of setup is frequently called *router on a stick*. When using a trunk link you must create separate subinterfaces on the router's physical interface—one subinterface for each VLAN plus one for the native VLAN. The router is the default gateway for the users.

A router on a stick is shown in Figure 6-1. Users in VLANs 2 and 3 are connected to the same Layer 2 switch. When the user in VLAN 2 needs to communicate with the user in VLAN 3, her traffic is sent through the switch and up the trunk link to the router. It is received by a logical subinterface configured on the physical interface Ethernet 0/1. This logical interface is linked to VLAN 2 and has been assigned the subinterface number e0/1.2. The router directs the traffic to its subinterface associated with VLAN 3— subinterface e0/1.3. The traffic travels back down the trunk link and through the switch, to the user on VLAN 3.

Figure 6-1   Router on a Stick

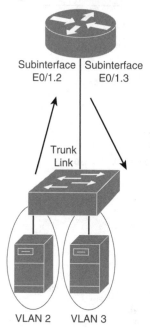

This process works with any kind of Layer 2 switch. The router on a stick can be either an actual router or a switch with Layer 3 capability. The implementation is straightforward, but the router becomes a single point of failure for all users. Notice that all traffic between VLANs must traverse the trunk link, so that link might become congested.

Example 6-1 shows the configuration for a Layer 2 switch and the directly connected router acting as a router on a stick. Interface e0/2 on the switch connects to interface e0/1 on the router. The switch just needs the interface configured as a normal trunk, with VLAN 20 designated as the native VLAN. Three interfaces are configured on the router and associated with VLANs 2, 3, and 20. VLAN 20 is the native VLAN for the 802.1Q trunk. The router's configuration is verified with the **show ip interface brief** command.

Example 6-1   Configuring Router on a Stick

```
Layer 2 Switch Configuration
Switch(config)# int e0/2
Switch(config-if)# switchport trunk encapsulation dot1q
Switch(config-if)# switchport mode trunk
Switch(config-if)# switch trunk native vlan 20
```

Part II: SWITCH

Example 6-1 Continued

```
Router Configuration
Router(config)# int e0/1.2
Router(config-subif)# description Data VLAN
Router(config-subif)# encapsulation dot1q 2
Router(config-subif)# ip address 10.2.2.1 255.255.255.0
!
Router(config-subif)# int e0/1.3
Router(config-subif)# description Voice VLAN
Router(config-subif)# encapsulation dot1q 3
Router(config-subif)# ip address 10.3.3.1 255.255.255.0
!
Router(config-subif)# int e0/1.20
Router(config-subif)# description Native VLAN
Router(config-subif)# encapsulation dot1q 20 native
Router(config-subif)# ip address 10.20.20.1 255.255.255.0
!
Router# show ip interface brief
Interface        IP-Address       OK? Method Status    Protocol
Ethernet0/0      209.165.201.2    YES NVRAM  up        up
Ethernet0/1      10.0.99.2        YES NVRAM  up        up
Ethernet0/1.2    10.2.2.1         YES manual up        up
Ethernet0/1.3    10.3.3.1         YES manual up        up
Ethernet0/1.20   10.20.20.1       YES manual up        up
```

InterVLAN Routing Using Multilayer Switches

A multilayer switch can perform both Layer 2 switching and Layer 3 routing. It is sometimes called a *Layer 3 switch*. Routing is disabled by default on switches. Enable it using the global command **ip routing**.

Figure 6-2 shows a multilayer switch with users in both VLAN 2 and VLAN 3. When the user in VLAN 2 needs to communicate with the user in VLAN 3, her traffic is sent to the switch. The multilayer switch is the default gateway for the users, not an external router. The switch can examine the Layer 3 destination address and route the traffic out its interface for the user in VLAN 3. This traffic is switched across the backplane, which is usually much faster than the uplink to a router on a stick.

Figure 6-2   Multilayer Switching

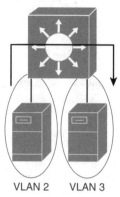

VLAN 2   VLAN 3

Putting the Layer 3 boundary as close to users as possible, such as in the access switch, is generally good practice. This minimizes the size of broadcast and failure domains and reduces traffic within the network. Most multilayer switches can run routing protocols, although the exact routing functionality available depends on the switch's feature license. The commands to configure routing protocols are the same as those used on a router.

Multilayer Switch Interfaces

A multilayer switch can have the following types of interfaces:

- **Layer 2 Interface:** Either an access port assigned to a VLAN or a trunk port.

- **Switch Virtual Interface (SVI):** A virtual software interface that represents a VLAN. Can be either a Layer 2 interface or a Layer 3 interface.

- **Routed Interface:** A physical interface that is not associated with a VLAN and acts like a router port.

SVI Configuration

Switches automatically create an SVI for VLAN 1 by default, and all switch ports are assigned to this VLAN. To create an SVI for any other VLAN, use the configuration mode command **interface vlan** *vlan_no*. SVIs can do the following:

- Route between VLANs

- Provide a default gateway for users in that VLAN

Part II: SWITCH

- Route traffic into or out of its associated VLAN

- Provide an IP address for connectivity to the switch itself

- Provide an interface for routing protocols

Configure an IP address on the SVI to make it a Layer 3 interface. Use an SVI, rather than a routed port, to provide a Layer 3 interface when multiple switch ports are in the VLAN associated with that SVI.

An SVI is considered up as long as at least one port in its associated VLAN is active and forwarding. If all ports in the VLAN are down, the interface goes down to avoid creating a routing black hole. You might not want the status of a particular port (one not connected to a host) to affect the SVI's status. Some Cisco switches enable you to use the following command on that interface to accomplish this:

```
Switch(config-if)# switchport autostate exclude
```

To configure InterVLAN routing using a Layer 3 SVI, you need to perform the following steps:

Step 1.   Enable IP routing.

Step 2.   Create the VLANs.

Step 3.   Create the SVIs.

Step 4.   Associate an IP address with each SVI.

Step 5.   Configure a dynamic routing protocol if needed.

Example 6-2 shows a multilayer switch configured for two VLANs—VLAN 2 and VLAN 3. Each VLAN has an SVI with an assigned IP address. This IP address is the default gateway for hosts in that VLAN. The **ip routing** command enables the switch to begin routing processes. The **show ip interface brief** command verifies that the interfaces are active.

Example 6-2   Configuring Routing with Layer 3 SVIs

```
Switch(config)# ip routing
!
Switch(config)# vlan 2
Switch(config-vlan)# name Data VLAN
!
Switch(config)# vlan 3
Switch(config-vlan)# name Voice VLAN
!
```

```
Switch(config)# interface vlan 2
Switch(config-if)# ip address 10.2.2.2 255.255.255.0
Switch(config-if)# no shut
Switch(config-if)#
Switch(config-if)# interface vlan 3
Switch(config-if)# ip address 10.3.3.3 255.255.255.0
Switch(config-if)# no shut
!
Switch# show ip interface brief
<output omitted>
Vlan2                 10.2.2.2      YES manual up          up
Vlan3                 10.3.3.3      YES manual up          up
```

Another way to use SVIs is with a point-to-point VLAN. Suppose you had two multilayer switches, as shown in Figure 6-3. You could configure the interface connecting them as a routed port. Another option is to create a VLAN that is used only to connect the two switches. Then create a Layer 3 SVI for that VLAN, with a /30 subnet mask.

Figure 6-3   Point-to-Point VLANs

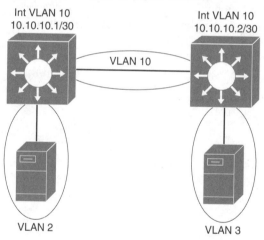

Int VLAN 10
10.10.10.1/30

Int VLAN 10
10.10.10.2/30

VLAN 10

VLAN 2

VLAN 3

Example 6-3 shows the configuration on one of the multilayer switches. Routing is first enabled with the **ip routing** command, and then VLAN 10 is created along with its SVI. The SVI is given an IP address with a 30-bit subnet mask. Interface e0/3, which connects to the peer switch, is placed in VLAN 10, the point-to-point VLAN. The SVI configuration on the other switch mirrors this one, with its own IP address.

Part II: SWITCH

Example 6-3   Configuring a Point-to-Point VLAN

```
Switch(config)# ip routing
!
Switch(config)# vlan 10
Switch(config-vlan)# name P2P VLAN
!
Switch(config-vlan)# interface vlan 10
Switch(config-if)# ip address 10.10.10.1 255.255.255.252
Switch(config-if)# no shut
!
Switch(config-if)# int e0/3
Switch(config-if)# switchport access vlan 10
```

Routed Switch Port Configuration

To configure an interface as a routed port, you must first remove the Layer 2 functionality with the **no switchport** interface command. Then add an IP address to the interface and configure routing as needed. Use a routed port when the link connects to another Layer 3 device because it is not associated with any VLAN. For example, you might use it to connect to a router—as shown in Figure 6-4—or a firewall or uplink to another Layer 3 switch.

Figure 6-4   Routed Switch Port

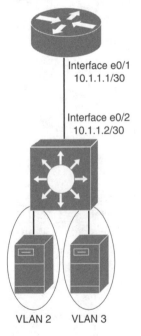

Interface e0/1
10.1.1.1/30

Interface e0/2
10.1.1.2/30

VLAN 2   VLAN 3

Example 6-4 shows an interface e0/2 on a multilayer switch configured as a routed port. Routing is first enabled with the **ip routing** command, and then the port is taken out of Layer 2 mode with the **no switchport** command. Next, an IP address is configured on the interface. EIGRP routing is enabled for the subnet associated with that interface. Similarly, interface e0/1 of the router is configured to connect to the switch. This time there are no sub-interfaces or dot1q commands. The router interface is configured as a normal Layer 3 interface.

Example 6-4   Configuring a Routed Switch Port

```
Layer 3 Switch Configuration
Switch(config)# ip routing
!
Switch(config)# int e0/2
Switch(config-if)# no switchport
Switch(config-if)# ip address 10.1.1.2 255.255.255.252
!
Switch(config)# router eigrp 10
Switch(config-router)# network 10.1.1.0 0.0.0.255
!
Switch# show ip interface brief
Interface          IP-Address      OK? Method Status      Protocol
Ethernet0/0        unassigned      YES unset  up          up
Ethernet0/1        unassigned      YES unset  up          up
Ethernet0/2        10.1.1.2        YES manual up          up


Router Configuration
Router(config)# int e0/1
Router(config-if)# ip address 10.1.1.1 255.255.255.252
!
Router# show ip interface brief
Interface          IP-Address      OK? Method Status      Protocol
Ethernet0/0        unassigned      YES unset  up          up
Ethernet0/1        10.1.1.1        YES manual up          up
```

To verify your configuration, use the commands **show ip interface brief**, **show interface, show {ip / ipv6} route**, or **show running-config interface** *int_no*.

The Layer 2 and Layer 3 Forwarding Process

This section walks you through the switching process and focuses on order of operations. The sequence in which things happen is extremely important for two reasons. First, the series of events is good test material. Second, understanding the processing order enables you to evaluate how the various filtering and forwarding mechanisms interact and troubleshoot problems. (Examples include error checking, access-lists, VLAN access-lists, routing, and QoS.)

Layer 2 Forwarding

A multilayer switch performs Layer 2 forwarding when the destination MAC address is mapped to one of its interfaces. The steps involved in Layer 2 forwarding are as follows:

Input:

Step 1. Receive frame.

Step 2. Verify frame integrity.

Step 3. Apply inbound VLAN ACL (VLAN Access Control List).

Step 4. Look up destination MAC (Media Address Code).

Output:

Step 1. Apply outbound VLAN ACL.

Step 2. Apply outbound QoS ACL.

Step 3. Select output port.

Step 4. Place in port queue.

Step 5. Rewrite source and destination MAC, and frame check sequence.

Step 6. Forward.

Layer 3 Forwarding

A multilayer switch performs Layer 3 forwarding when the destination MAC address is one of the switch's own addresses. The steps involved in Layer 3 forwarding are as follows:

Input:

Step 1. Receive frame.

Step 2. Verify frame integrity.

Step 3. Apply inbound VLAN ACL.

Step 4. Look up destination MAC.

Routing:

Step 1. Apply input Layer 3 ACL.

Step 2. Switch if entry is in CEF cache; otherwise, examine Layer 3 routing table to determine outbound interface.

Step 3. Apply output Layer 3 ACL.

Output:

Step 1. Apply outbound VLAN ACL.

Step 2. Apply outbound QoS ACL.

Step 3. Select output port.

Step 4. Place in interface queue.

Step 5. Rewrite source and destination MAC, IP checksum, and frame check sequence, and decrement TTL (Time to Live field in the IP header).

Step 6. Forward.

Understanding the Switching Table

Multilayer switches use Application-Specific Integrated Circuits (ASIC) to forward packets at wire speed. The Content Addressable Memory (CAM) table, used for Layer 2 switching, is created by recording the source MAC address and ingress port of each frame. It contains binary values (0 or 1) and must find an exact match to have a hit.

In comparison, multilayer switching (MLS) uses a ternary content addressable memory (TCAM) table to store information needed by Layer 3 and higher processing. This might include QoS settings and ACLs. Values in the TCAM table include ternary values (0, 1, or wildcard). An exact match is not required—the longest match is considered a hit.

Understanding Switch Forwarding Architectures

Packets entering a router or multilayer switch are handled by one of three types of switching:

- **Process switching:** Each packet must be examined by the CPU and handled in software. This is the slowest method, used in routers only.

Part II: SWITCH

- **Fast switching:** The CPU process switches the first packet in each flow and then caches that information and switches subsequent packets in hardware. It is faster than process switching and is used in routers and multilayer switches. Fast switching is also called *route caching*.

- **Cisco Express Forwarding (CEF):** A table is prebuilt with adjacency information for all destinations in the routing table. CEF is the fastest switching method and the default for Cisco routers and multilayer switches. It is also called *topology-based switching*.

CEF Switching

Multilayer switching (MLS) is a switch feature that enables the switch to route traffic between VLANs and routed interfaces in a highly optimized and efficient manner. CEF is used to facilitate MLS (see Figure 4-1). CEF performs the following:

- Separates control plane hardware from data plane hardware.

- The control plane runs in software and builds Forwarding Information Base (FIB) and adjacency table.

- The data plane uses hardware to forward most IP unicast traffic.

- Uses TCAM table.

- Can be centralized or distributed.

Not all types of traffic can be handled by CEF. Some types that are punted (sent to the processor for handling) are

- Packets with IP header options

- Tunneled traffic

- 802.3 (IPX) or other unsupported encapsulation types

- Packets with an expiring TTL

- Packets that must be fragmented

By default, CEF is on and supports per-destination load sharing. You can use several commands to view CEF information, to gain a greater understanding of the switching, and to assist in troubleshooting problems.

View the CEF FIB with the **show ip cef** command, as demonstrated in Example 6-5.

Example 6-5   The show ip cef Command

```
Switch# show ip cef
Prefix                  Next Hop           Interface
0.0.0.0/0               no route
0.0.0.0/8               drop
0.0.0.0/32              receive
10.1.1.0/30             attached           Ethernet0/2
10.1.1.0/32             receive            Ethernet0/2
10.1.1.1/32             receive            Ethernet0/2
10.1.1.3/32             receive            Ethernet0/2
10.2.2.0/24             attached           Vlan2
10.2.2.0/32             receive            Vlan2
10.2.2.2/32             receive            Vlan2
10.2.2.255/32           receive            Vlan2
10.3.3.0/24             attached           Vlan3
10.3.3.0/32             receive            Vlan3
10.3.3.3/32             receive            Vlan3
10.3.3.255/32           receive            Vlan3
10.10.10.0/30           attached           Vlan10
10.10.10.0/32           receive            Vlan10
10.10.10.1/32           receive            Vlan10
10.10.10.3/32           receive            Vlan10
127.0.0.0/8             drop
224.0.0.0/4             drop
Prefix                  Next Hop           Interface
224.0.0.0/24            receive
240.0.0.0/4             drop
255.255.255.255/32      receive
```

View the detailed CEF FIB entry for an interface with the command
show ip cef {*interface*} **detail**. The output from this command is shown
in Example 6-6.

Example 6-6   The show ip cef detail Command

```
Switch# show ip cef ethernet 0/2 detail
IPv4 CEF is enabled and running
VRF Default
 24 prefixes (24/0 fwd/non-fwd)
 Table id 0x0
 Database epoch:        0 (24 entries at this epoch)


10.1.1.0/30, epoch 0, flags attached, connected, cover dependents,
 need deagg
```

Example 6-6 Continued

```
Interest List:
  - ipv4fib connected receive
Covered dependent prefixes: 2
  need deagg: 2
attached to Ethernet0/2
```

Troubleshoot CEF drops with the command **show cef drop**.

Troubleshoot CEF adjacencies with the command **show adjacency**.

CHAPTER 7

Switch Security Features

Traditional security focuses on the network perimeter, such as firewalls, and on mitigating Layer 3 attacks. However, networks must be protected against Layer 2 attacks, too. These are typically launched from devices inside the network by either a rogue device or a legitimate device that has been compromised. Rogue devices might be placed maliciously or innocently connected by a well-intentioned employee. For instance, someone wanting more connections might add an access switch or wireless access point to a port in their office. The switch might then become the Spanning Tree root bridge and disrupt user traffic.

The following are four common types of attacks against a switched network:

- **MAC address-based attacks:** MAC address flooding

- **VLAN-based attacks:** Attacks against devices in the same or different VLAN

- **Spoofing attacks:** DHCP spoofing, MAC spoofing, Address Resolution Protocol (ARP) spoofing, and Spanning Tree attacks

- **Attacks against the switch:** Cisco Discovery Protocol (CDP) manipulation, Telnet attacks, and Secure Shell (SSH) attacks

MAC Address-Based Attacks

Common MAC address-based attacks rely on overloading the switch's CAM table and can be mitigated by using port security and port-based access control lists. 802.1x authentication also helps prevent attacks from unauthorized devices connected to switch ports and is covered later in this chapter.

MAC Address Flooding

In a MAC address flooding attack, the attacker fills the switch's Content Addressable Memory (CAM) table with invalid MAC addresses. After the table is full, all traffic with an address not in the table is flooded out all interfaces. This has two bad effects: more traffic on the LAN and more work for the switch. This can also cause the CAM tables of adjacent switches to overflow. Additionally, the intruder's traffic is also flooded, so he has access to more ports than he would normally have. After the attack stops, CAM entries age out and life returns to normal. Meanwhile, the attacker might have captured a significant amount of data.

The following two sections examine how port security and port-based access control lists help mitigate MAC address attacks.

Port Security

Port security limits the number of MAC addresses allowed per port and also which MAC addresses are permitted. Allowed MAC addresses can be manually configured or the switch can sticky learn them. A *sticky learned* address is one that the switch learns dynamically, and then adds to the configuration as a statically mapped address. Table 7-1 lists port security commands; these are given at the interface.

Table 7-1   Port Security Commands

Command	Description
switchport port-security	Enables port security on that interface.
switchport port-security *maximum value*	Specifies the max MAC addresses allowed on this port. Default is 1.
switchport port-security violation {**shutdown** I **restrict** I **protect**}	Configures the action to be taken upon a port security violation. Default is shutdown.
switchport port-security mac-address	Statically associates a specific MAC address with a port.
switchport port-security mac-address sticky	Enables the switch port to dynamically learn secure MAC addresses. MAC addresses learned through that port, up to the maximum number if a maximum is configured, are treated as secure MAC addresses.
show port security [interface *interface I address*]	Verifies port security actions.

A port security violation occurs when the maximum number of MAC addresses is reached and a MAC address not associated with the port attempts to use the port. It can also occur when a station whose MAC address is associated with a different port attempts to access this port. As you can see from Table 7-1, port security has three ways to respond to a violation: shutdown, restrict, and protect:

- **Shutdown** puts the port into error disable mode, generates Syslog messages, and increases the security violation count (shown in the last line of the output in Example 7-1).

- **Restrict** transmits traffic from "legal" MAC addresses but blocks traffic from all other devices. Generates Syslog messages and increases the security violation count, but does not error disable the port. This is the recommended mode.

- **Protect** allows "legal" traffic and blocks all other MAC addresses, just as Restrict mode does. However, it does not generate Syslog messages or increase the security violation count.

Configuring Port Security

Example 7-1 shows how to configure and verify port security. In this example, the port security mode is set to Restrict, and a maximum of two MAC addresses are allowed. The MAC addresses are sticky learned— the first two devices to access the port have their MAC addresses associated with the port. The configuration is verified in two ways: by the **show port security** command and by displaying the interface configuration. Note that a MAC address has been added to the interface configuration; this is the sticky MAC address the switch learned automatically.

Example 7-1   Using Port Security

```
Switch(config)# interface e0/0
Switch(config-if)# switchport port-security maximum 2
Switch(config-if)# switchport port-security violation restrict
Switch(config-if)# switchport port-security mac-address sticky
Switch(config-if)# switchport port-security
!
Switch# show port-security interface e0/0
Port Security              : Enabled
Port Status                : Secure-Up
Violation Mode             : Restrict
Aging Time                 : 0 mins
Aging Type                 : Absolute
SecureStatic Address Aging : Disabled
Maximum MAC Addresses      : 2
Total MAC Addresses        : 1
Configured MAC Addresses   : 0
Sticky MAC Addresses       : 1
Last Source Address:Vlan   : aabb.cc00.5600:1
Security Violation Count   : 0
!
```

Part II: SWITCH

Example 7-1 Continued

```
Switch# show run int e0/0
interface Ethernet0/0
 switchport mode access
 switchport port-security maximum 2
 switchport port-security
 switchport port-security violation restrict
 switchport port-security mac-address sticky
 switchport port-security mac-address sticky aabb.cc00.5600
 duplex auto
```

Error-Disabled Ports

Ports are placed into error disable state for many reasons in addition to port security violations. To view these reasons, use the global configuration command **errdisable detect cause ?**. To change which actions trigger an error disable, use the same command but add the desired causes. Normally you must shut and then reenable a port to recover from an error state. To automate recovery from a specific cause, use the global commands **errdisable recovery cause** *cause* and **errdisable recovery interval** *seconds*.

Port Access Lists

Port access lists (PACL) are applied to Layer 2 interfaces. They can only be applied inbound and do not have any effect upon the traffic from Layer 2 control protocols, such as Cisco Discovery Protocol (CDP) or Spanning Tree Protocol (STP). PACLs filter based on MAC address or IP address. An IP address PACL is configured exactly the same as a regular IPv4 or IPv6 access list. The difference is that it is applied to a Layer 2 interface rather than a Layer 3 one.

A MAC PACL is configured a little differently. Only extended, named ACLs are supported. They do not filter IP, ARP, or MPLS traffic. Configure a MAC PACL with the command **mac access-list extended** *name*, and apply it to the interface with the command **mac access-group** *name* **in**. Example 7-2 shows a PACL that enables traffic with a source MAC address of aabb.cc00.5600 bound for any destination. It is applied to interface e0/0.

Example 7-2 Configuring PACLs

```
Switch(config)# mac access-list extended MAC-ACL
Switch(config-ext-macl)# permit host aabb.cc00.5600 any
!
Switch(config)# int e0/0
Switch(config-if)# mac access-group MAC-ACL in
```

VLAN-Based Attacks

VLAN-based attacks disrupt traffic within a VLAN or allow a station to access a VLAN other than its own. This is accomplished with switch spoofing or with 802.1Q double-tagging.

Storm Control

An Internet denial-of-service attack attempts to send so much traffic to a device that the bandwidth is consumed and the device processes cannot keep up. This can happen on a LAN also, where it is called a *traffic storm*. A traffic storm results from malicious actions, such as a denial-of-service attack, or more innocent causes, such as a malfunctioning host or an STP misconfiguration. They are composed of unicast, multicast, or broadcast traffic. The Storm Control feature monitors ingress traffic on a port over 1-second intervals and blocks traffic if it becomes excessive. It can optionally error-disable the port and/or send an SNMP trap.

Configure an upper threshold and an optional lower threshold for each type of traffic (unicast, multicast, and broadcast). Storm Control blocks traffic when it exceeds the upper threshold and then reenables the interface when traffic falls below the lower threshold. The rate of traffic is measured in different ways depending on the exact hardware and IOS version. Options include percentage of traffic, bits per second, and packets per second. Storm Control is configured on a per-interface basis. If you want to use this feature with an EtherChannel, enable it only on the Port-Channel interface, not the physical channel members. The interface commands to configure and verify Storm Control are shown in Example 7-3.

Example 7-3 Storm Control Configuration and Verification Commands

```
storm-control {broadcast | multicast | unicast} level {level
  [level-low] | bps bps [bps-low] | pps pps [pps-low]}
storm-control action {shutdown | trap}
show storm-control [interface-id] [broadcast | multicast |
  unicast]
```

Switch Spoofing

Switch spoofing involves a station configured to negotiate a trunk link between itself and the switch. By default, switches dynamically negotiate trunking status using Dynamic Trunking Protocol (DTP). If a computer uses DTP to establish a trunk link to the switch, it receives all traffic bound for every VLAN allowed on that trunk. By default, all VLANs are allowed on a trunk.

Part II: SWITCH

Mitigate switch spoofing by turning off DTP on all ports that should not become trunks, such as most access ports, using the interface command **switchport nonegotiate**. If the port should be an access port, configure it as such with the interface command **switchport mode access** and turn off CDP on that port. Additionally, shut down all unused ports and assign them to an unused VLAN. The commands to accomplish this are shown in Example 7-4.

Example 7-4   Securing an Unused Port

```
Switch(config)# interface interface
Switch(config-if)# switchport mode access
Switch(config-if)# switchport access vlan vlan
Switch(config-if)# shutdown
```

802.1Q Double-Tagging

A double-tagging—or *VLAN Hopping*—attack is possible because 802.1Q trunking does not tag frames from the native VLAN. In this assault, the attacking computer negotiates a trunk port between itself and the switch and then generates frames with two 802.1Q tags. The first tag matches the native VLAN of the trunk port, and the second matches the VLAN of a host it wants to attack, as shown in Figure 7-1. The first switch in the path strips off the first 802.1Q tag and forwards it to adjacent switches. The next switch forwards the frame based on the VLAN listed in the second tag.

Figure 7-1   VLAN Hopping by 802.1Q Double-Tagging

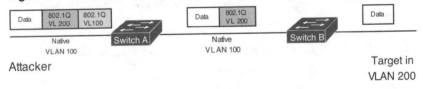

The double-tagging method of a VLAN hopping attack works even if trunk ports are set to DTP Off mode if the trunk has the same native VLAN as the attacker's access VLAN.

Switch A removes the first tag for VLAN 100 because it matches the native VLAN for that link. It forwards the frame out all links with the same native VLAN, including its link to Switch B. Switch B sees the frame come in with an 802.1Q tag for VLAN 200, so it forwards it out the VLAN 200 link to the victim computer.

To mitigate this type of attack, use the same strategies used for switch spoofing. Set the native VLAN to one not used for any access traffic. Configure the switch to tag native VLAN frames with the global command **vlan dot1q tag native**. You can also use VLAN access control lists, called *VACLs*, or implement private VLANs. Layer 3 access switches make this type of attack impossible because there are no trunk links between switches. These types of attacks are rare because the prevention is so well known and the attack is difficult to implement. An attacker must know native VLAN and user VLAN information. The network topology must support this type of attack also.

VLAN Access Control Lists

VLAN access control lists (VACL) filter traffic within the same VLAN. They are similar to route-maps in that they are composed of statements that contain match and set conditions. In a VACL, the "set" conditions are called *actions*. Actions vary by hardware and IOS version but may include **forward**, **drop**, **capture**, and **redirect**. Like route maps, VACL statements are numbered for ordering. After configuration, VACLs are applied to traffic in specified VLANs.

Similar to PACLs, there are both IP and MAC address VACLs. IP address VACLS filter IP traffic, of course, and MAC address VACLs filter all traffic *except* IP and certain control traffic.

Example 7-5 shows a sample VACL that instructs the switch to drop traffic matching ACL 101 (not shown) and forward all other traffic. The VACL is applied to VLAN 100 in the final command.

Example 7-5   Configuring a VACL

```
Switch(config)# vlan access-map Drop101 10
Switch(config-access-map)# match ip address 101
Switch(config-access-map)# action drop
!
Switch(config-access-map)# vlan access-map Drop101 20
Switch(config-access-map)# action forward
!
Switch(config)# vlan filter Drop101 vlan-list 100
```

Part II: SWITCH

To view VACL settings, use the commands **show vlan access-map**
vacl_name or **show vlan filter access-map** *vacl_name*.

Private VLANs

Private VLANs (PVLAN) enable large companies or service providers to
isolate users into separate broadcast domains. Using a VLAN for each group
is not scalable. For example, the switch's maximum number of VLANs
limits the number of customers an ISP can have. Each VLAN requires a
separate IP subnet, which is also a limiting factor.

PVLANs divide a primary VLAN into secondary VLANs, letting you isolate
a set of ports from other ports within the same primary VLAN. An IP subnet
is assigned to the primary VLAN. Devices in different secondary VLANs
cannot communicate, even though they are in the same primary VLAN.
There are two types of secondary VLANs:

- **Community VLANs:** Ports can communicate with other ports in the
  same community VLAN.

- **Isolated VLANs:** Ports cannot communicate with each other.

Ports within a private VLAN can be one of three types:

- **Community:** Communicates with other community ports and with
  promiscuous ports.

- **Isolated:** Communicates only with promiscuous ports.

- **Promiscuous:** Communicates with all ports. Mapped to one primary
  VLAN.

Table 7-2 shows the commands to configure a primary private VLAN,
secondary PVLANs, and their associated ports.

Table 7-2   Configuring Private VLANs

Command	Description
vlan *vlan-id*	Enters VLAN configuration mode.
private-vlan {community | isolated | primary}	Configures the VLAN as a private VLAN and specifies the type. Repeat this command to configure all primary and secondary VLANs.
vlan *primary-vlan-id*	Enters VLAN configuration mode.

Command	Description
private-vlan association *secondary_vlan_list*	Associates secondary VLANs with the primary one. Separate the secondary VLAN numbers with a comma, no spaces.
switchport mode private-vlan {host | promiscuous}	Configures a port as either a host port (for community or isolated) or a promiscuous port.
switchport private-vlan host-association *primary_vlan ID secondary_vlan_ID*	Associates a host port with its primary and secondary PVLANs.
private-vlan mapping *primary vlan_ID secondary_vlan_list*	Associates a promiscuous port with its primary and secondary PVLANs.
show interfaces *interface* **switchport**	Verifies the VLAN configuration.
show interfaces private-vlan mapping	Verifies the private VLAN configuration.

Protected Ports

On some lower-end switches, protected ports provide a simple version of private VLANs. This is also known as *Private VLAN Edge*. Traffic from a protected port can access only an unprotected port. Traffic between protected ports is blocked. Configure port protection at the interface:

```
Switch(config-if)# switchport protected
```

Spoof Attacks

Spoof attacks include DHCP spoofing, MAC address spoofing, and ARP spoofing.

DHCP Spoofing

A DHCP spoofing attacker listens for DHCP requests and answers them, giving its IP address as the client default gateway. The attacker then becomes a "man-in-the-middle" because all off-net traffic flows through it.

DHCP snooping prevents DHCP spoofing attacks.

DHCP snooping defines trusted and untrusted ports. When DHCP snooping is enabled, only ports that uplink to an authorized DHCP server should be configured as trusted. Trusted ports are allowed to send all types of DHCP

Part II: SWITCH

messages. All other ports on the switch are untrusted by default and can send only DHCP requests. If a DHCP response (or "offer") is seen on an untrusted port, the port is shut down.

Note

DHCP snooping configuration is user impacting because the switch drops all DHCP requests until the ports are configured. You should perform this during off hours or during a maintenance window.

Configure DHCP snooping with the following commands, either globally or for a particular VLAN. Configure only individual ports that uplink to DHCP servers as trusted ports. Example 7-6 shows the commands to configure DHCP snooping. In the example, DHCP snooping is first enabled globally on the switch. The **ip dhcp snooping information option** command configures the switch to send the client's switch port identification using DHCP option 82. DHCP snooping is then enabled specifically on VLAN 100. Interface e0/1 is the uplink toward the DHCP server, so it is configured as a trusted port. All other ports on the switch are untrusted by default.

Example 7-6   Configuring DHCP Snooping

```
Switch(config)# ip dhcp snooping
Switch(config)# ip dhcp snooping information option
Switch(config)# ip dhcp snooping vlan 100
!
Switch(config-if)# ip dhcp snooping trust
```

Verify DHCP snooping with the commands **show ip dhcp snooping** and **show ip dhcp snooping binding**.

IP Source Guard

To protect against IP address spoofing, the IP Source Guard feature tracks the IP addresses of the hosts connected to each port and prevents traffic sourced from another IP address from entering that port. The tracking can be done based on just an IP address or on both IP and MAC addresses.

IP Source Guard leverages DHCP Snooping to create a binding between port and source host IP and MAC addresses. It creates a dynamic VACL for each port where it is enabled, permitting only the source addresses in its binding for that port.

Enable IP Source Guard for just IP addresses on host access interfaces with the interface command **ip verify source**. Enable IP Source Guard for both IP and MAC addresses on host access interfaces with the **ip verify source port-security** command. Verify your configuration with the **show ip verify source** command.

ARP Spoofing and DAI

In an ARP spoofing attack, the attacker sends out gratuitous (unsolicited) ARP messages giving the IP address of the local default gateway, with its own MAC address as the Layer 2 address. Local devices overwrite their existing correct ARP information with the incorrect one, and, thus, they forward off-net traffic to the attacker (it becomes a man in the middle). If the attacker then forwards it on to the legitimate router, this type of attack might go undetected by the users.

Dynamic ARP Inspection (DAI) works with DHCP Snooping to stop ARP spoofing. DAI defines trusted and untrusted interfaces. It intercepts ARP messages on untrusted ports and checks them against the IP address/MAC address bindings in the DHCP Snooping database. They must match for the switch to forward the traffic. Access ports should be configured as untrusted, and ports that connect to other switches or to a router should be trusted.

Enable DAI on a VLAN or multiple VLANs, and configure trusted interfaces. Remember to also enable DHCP Snooping on the same VLANs and interfaces. You can optionally configure a rate limit or configure which addresses DAI matches against. (The default is IP and MAC address.) The basic commands are

```
Switch(config)# ip arp inspection vlan vlan_id
!
Switch(config-if)# ip arp inspection trust
```

Securing Your Switch

The following are some recommendations for limiting the effect of attacks against the switch itself:

■ Physically secure access to the device.

■ Use passwords that are not susceptible to a dictionary attack. Add numbers or substitute numbers and symbols for letters.

Part II: SWITCH

- Limit VTY access using an access list and strong passwords.

- Use SSH instead of Telnet.

- Use banners that warn against unauthorized access.

- Remove unused services, such as finger, the TCP and UDP small servers, service config, and HTTP server.

- Set up and monitor Syslog.

- Disable automatic trunking on all nontrunk ports.

- Use a unique VLAN for the native VLAN, and manually configure the native VLAN on trunk ports.

- Disable CDP on ports where it is not needed.

- Shut down unused ports and put them in a separate, untrunked VLAN.

- Use Spanning Tree protection mechanisms, such as BPDU Guard and Root Guard.

- Use AAA authentication when possible.

Using AAA

AAA stands for authentication, authorization, and accounting. It helps protect both the network and network devices by ensuring that only authorized users and devices connect to network resources, and by tracking and controlling their actions once they are connected.

- **Authentication** proves the identity of the person logging in to the device via a username and password, token card, biometrics, or other method.

- **Authorization** determines what actions that person is allowed to perform, such as accessing privileged mode, running certain commands, or access network resources.

- **Accounting** maintains records of what the person did while they were logged in, such as commands executed and login/logout times.

Cisco devices support AAA either through a local database (using the **username/password** command) or through external security servers. External servers use either RADIUS or TACACS+.

RADIUS

The Remote Authentication Dial-In User Service (RADIUS) was, as its name implies, originally created for dial-up networks. It enabled a centralized server to communicate with remote access servers and authenticate dial-in users. RADIUS is a standard protocol described in RFCs 2865 and 2866. It runs over UDP. RADIUS provides only one-way authentication— a holdover from its creation as a client/server protocol—so it is useful for user authentication to a central authority but not for mutual authentication between devices. It encrypts passwords, but the rest of its messages are sent in clear text. RADIUS combines authentication and authorization in one user profile and accounting in another.

TACACS+

The Terminal Access Controller Access System (TACACS) is a Cisco proprietary AAA protocol. The current version is TACACS+. It runs over TCP, which makes it more reliable but also a bit slower on startup due to the TCP handshake. It provides two-way authentication and encrypts its entire message body. TACACS+ separates authentication, authorization, and accounting, enabling administrators to mix and match among the three.

Configuring AAA

The first step in configuring AAA is to enable its operation on the switch with the command **aaa new-model**. You then configure the desired settings, as discussed in the following sections.

Local Authentication

Configure a local username and password database as a backup in case the AAA server is not reachable. For the switch to check this database, you must use the **local** keyword when configuring AAA authentication. In the following commands, AAA is first enabled on the switch and then a username of CCNP is configured with a password of Certified:

```
Switch(config)# aaa new-model
Switch(config)# username CCNP secret Certified
Switch(config)# aaa authentication login default local
```

RADIUS Authentication

Example 7-7 shows the commands to enable RADIUS login authentication on a switch (these same commands are used by most Cisco devices).

This example assumes that an external RADIUS server has already been set up, and its IP address is 10.1.1.1. The switch is configured with the server address and a key to be used for authentication and encryption. Next, that server is linked to a RADIUS group named *CCNP_RAD*. The switch is then configured with a default login authentication process of first trying the RADIUS server and then checking the local database. Finally, users logging in to the console port are required to implement this default authentication process.

Example 7-7   Configuring RADIUS Authentication

```
Switch(config)# aaa new-model
!
Switch(config)# radius server CCNP1
Switch(config-radius-server)# address ipv4 10.1.1.1
Switch(config-radius-server)# key cisco123
!
Switch(config)# aaa group server radius CCNP_RAD
Switch(config-sg-radius)# server name CCNP1
!
Switch(config)# aaa authentication login default group CCNP_RAD
  local
!
Switch(config)# line con 0
Switch(config-line)# login authentication default
```

TACACS+ Authentication

Example 7-8 shows the commands to enable TACACS+ login authentication on a switch. These commands echo the ones in Example 7-7, with the keyword **radius** replaced by the keyword **tacacs**.

Example 7-8 assumes that an external TACACS+ server has already been set up and its IP address is 10.2.2.2. The switch is configured with the server address and a key to be used for authentication and encryption. Next, that server is linked to a TACACS+ group named *CCNP_TAC*. The switch is then configured with a default login authentication process of first trying the TACACS+ server and then checking the local database. Finally, users logging in to the console port are required to employ this default authentication process. Note that this could have been applied to the VTY ports also.

Example 7-8   Configuring TACACS+ Authentication

```
Switch(config)# aaa new-model
!
Switch(config)# tacacs server CCNP2
```

```
Switch(config-server-tacacs)# address ipv4 10.2.2.2
Switch(config-server-tacacs)# key 123cisco
!
Switch(config)# aaa group server tacacs+ CCNP_TAC
Switch(config-sg-tacacs+)# server name CCNP2
!
Switch(config)# aaa authentication login default group CCNP_TAC
 local
!
Switch(config)# line con 0
Switch(config-line)# login authentication default
```

Configuring Authorization

Example 7-9 shows how to configure basic command authorization using a
TACACS+ server. The same commands can be used with a RADIUS server,
substituting the keyword **radius** instead of **tacacs+**. This example uses
TACACS+ to authorize access to the EXEC shell and to commands at privilege levels 1 and 15. Authorization is performed by the TACACS+ server if
it is available, and by the local database if not. The example uses the server
group configured in Example 7-8. Note that authentication must be enabled
for authorization to work.

Example 7-9   Configuring AAA Authorization

```
Switch(config)# aaa new-model
!
Switch(config)# aaa authorization exec default group CCNP_TAC
 local
Switch(config)# aaa authorization commands 1 default group CCNP_
 TAC local
Switch(config)# aaa authorization commands 15 default group CCNP_
 TAC local
```

Configuring Accounting

The following configuration illustrates basic accounting using a TACACS+
server. As with authorization, this requires that authentication be enabled.
Here, the start and stop times of an EXEC session are recorded:

```
Switch(config)# aaa new-model
!
Switch(config)# aaa accounting exec default start-stop group
 CCNP_TAC
```

Part II: SWITCH

Verifying AAA Operation

The **show aaa servers** command ensures that the configured servers are reachable and active. This also provides statistics about the operation of all three types of AAA services, as shown in Example 7-10. To view AAA client statistics, use the **show aaa clients** command. Troubleshoot AAA by the debugging command **debug aaa {authentication | authorization | accounting}**.

Example 7-10   Using the show aaa servers Command

```
Switch# show aaa servers

RADIUS: id 1, priority 1, host 10.1.1.1, auth-port 1645, acct-port
  1646
      State: current UP, duration 1065s, previous duration 0s
      Dead: total time 0s, count 0
      Quarantined: No
      Authen: request 0, timeouts 0, failover 0, retransmission 0
              Response: accept 0, reject 0, challenge 0
              Response: unexpected 0, server error 0, incorrect 0,
                time 0ms
              Transaction: success 0, failure 0
              Throttled: transaction 0, timeout 0, failure 0
      Author: request 0, timeouts 0, failover 0, retransmission 0
              Response: accept 0, reject 0, challenge 0
              Response: unexpected 0, server error 0, incorrect 0,
                time 0ms
              Transaction: success 0, failure 0
              Throttled: transaction 0, timeout 0, failure 0
      Account: request 0, timeouts 0, failover 0, retransmission 0
              Request: start 0, interim 0, stop 0
              Response: start 0, interim 0, stop 0
              Response: unexpected 0, server error 0, incorrect 0,
                time 0ms
              Transaction: success 0, failure 0
              Throttled: transaction 0, timeout 0, failure 0
      Elapsed time since counters last cleared: 17m
      Estimated Outstanding Access Transactions: 0
      Estimated Outstanding Accounting Transactions: 0
      Estimated Throttled Access Transactions: 0
      Estimated Throttled Accounting Transactions: 0
      Maximum Throttled Transactions: access 0, accounting 0
      Requests per minute past 24 hours:
              high - 0 hours, 18 minutes ago: 0
              low  - 0 hours, 18 minutes ago: 0
              average: 0
```

Port-Based Authentication

802.1x authentication requires an end-user device, called a *client*, to be authenticated before it is allowed access to the LAN. This can be combined with port security to enable only authenticated clients with specified MAC addresses to access a port. Currently, RADIUS is the only 802.1x authentication server supported.

When a computer connects to a switch port configured for 802.1x authentication, it follows these steps:

Step 1. The port is in the unauthorized state, allowing only 802.1x EAP over LAN (EAPOL), CDP, and STP traffic.

Step 2. The client connects to the port. The switch either requests authentication or the client sends an Extensible Authentication Protocol over LAN (EAPOL) frame to begin authentication.

Step 3. The switch relays authentication information between the client and a RADIUS server that acts in proxy for the client.

Step 4. If authentication succeeds, the port transitions to the authorized state, and normal LAN traffic is allowed through it.

Table 7-3 shows the commands to configure 802.1x authentication on a switch. You must additionally specify the RADIUS server IP address as shown in Example 7-7. You might also want to configure a AAA group as shown in that same example.

Table 7-3   Configuring 802.1x Port Authentication

Command	Description
(config)# **aaa new-model**	Enables AAA on the switch
config)# **aaa authentication dot1x default group radius**	Creates a AAA method list that says to use 802.1x authentication by default, using a RADIUS server (configured separately)
(config)# **dot1x system-auth-control**	Globally enables 802.1x authentication on the switch
(config-if)# **dot1x port-control [auto	force-authorized	force-unauthorized]**	Enables 802.1x authentication on an interface of the switch and sets default port state

Use **show authentication sessions** to view the devices authenticated by interface. Verify 802.1x authentication with the command **show dot1x**.

Part II: SWITCH

CHAPTER 8

Campus Network Design

An *enterprise campus* generally refers to a network in a specific geographic location. It can be within one building or span multiple buildings near each other. Large enterprises might have multiple campuses connected by a WAN. For the purposes of the CCNP Switch exam, a campus network includes the Ethernet LAN portions of a network outside the data center. Using models to describe the network architecture divides the campus into several internetworking functional areas, thus simplifying design, implementation, and troubleshooting.

The Hierarchical Design Model

Cisco has used the three-level hierarchical design model for years, but it is still relevant. The hierarchical design model divides a network into three layers: access, distribution, and core.

The access layer provides end-user access to the network. Local devices, such as phones and computers, access the local network. Remote users or sites access the corporate network across the WAN or Internet. Access layer design should provide

- High availability within the hardware itself, such as redundant power supplies and redundant supervisor engines. Software redundancy via access to redundant default gateways using a first-hop redundancy protocol (FHRP).

- Converged network support by providing access to IP phones, computers, and wireless access points. Support for QoS and multicast.

- Security through switching tools, such as Dynamic ARP Inspection, DHCP snooping, BPDU Guard, port-security, and IP source guard.

- Network access control.

The distribution layer is the aggregation point for access switches. It provides highly available network access, QoS, fast path recovery, and load balancing. Design considerations for the distribution layer include

- Obtain high availability through redundant distribution layer switches providing dual paths to the access switches and to core switches. Use FHRP protocols to ensure connectivity if one distribution switch is removed.

- Apply routing policies, such as route selection, filtering, and summarization, at this layer.

- If a Layer 2 access is used, then this layer is the default gateway for access devices.

- Segment and isolate workgroups (and workgroup problems) from the core, traditionally by using a combination of Layer 2 and Layer 3 switching.

The core layer is the backbone that provides a high-speed, Layer 3 path between distribution layers and other network segments. It offers reliability and scalability in the following ways:

- Reliability through redundant devices, device components, and paths.

- Scalability through scalable routing protocols. Having a core layer in general aids network scalability by providing 10 gigabit (and faster) connectivity; data and voice integration; and convergence of the LAN, WAN, and MAN.

- Minimal policies that would slow traffic down.

A set of distribution devices and their accompanying access layer switches are termed a *switch block*.

Core Layer

Is a core layer always needed? Without it, the distribution switches must be fully meshed. This becomes more of a problem as a campus network grows larger. A general rule is to add a core when connecting three or more buildings, or four or more pairs of building distribution switches. The following are some benefits of a campus core:

- Adds a hierarchy to distribution switch connectivity

- Simplifies cabling because a full mesh between distribution switches is not required

- Reduces routing complexity by summarizing distribution networks

Part II: SWITCH

Small Network Design

In a small network located within one building, the core and distribution can be combined into one layer. *Small* is defined as fewer than 200 end devices. In very small networks with very few users, one multilayer switch might provide the functions of all three layers. Figure 8-1 shows a sample small network with a collapsed core.

Figure 8-1   Small Network Example

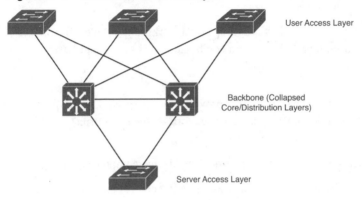

Campus Network Design

A campus network, with users located in multiple buildings, is more likely to have several distribution switches and thus require a core layer. Each building is a campus block with access switches uplinked to redundant multilayer distribution switches, which are uplinked to redundant core switches, as shown in Figure 8-2.

Figure 8-2   Campus Network Example

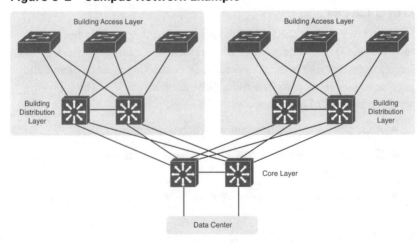

Network Traffic Flow

The need for a core layer and the specific devices chosen for the core also depend on the type of network traffic and traffic flow patterns. Modern converged networks include different traffic types, each with unique requirements for security, QoS, transmission capacity, and delay. These include

- IP telephony signaling and media

- Core application traffic, such as enterprise resource programming (ERP) and customer relationship management (CRM)

- Multicast media

- Network management

- Application data traffic, such as web pages, email, file transfer, and database transactions

- Scavenger class traffic that requires less-than-best-effort treatment

The different types of applications also have different traffic flow patterns. These might include the following:

- Peer-to-peer applications, such as IP phone calls, videoconferencing, file sharing, and instant messaging, provide real-time interaction. This traffic might not traverse the core at all if the users are local to each other. The network requirements vary, with voice having strict jitter needs and videoconferencing using high bandwidth.

- Client/server applications require access to servers such as email, file storage, and database servers. These servers are typically centralized in a data center, and users require fast, reliable access to them. Server farm access must also be securely controlled to deny unauthorized users.

- Client-enterprise edge applications are located on servers at the WAN edge, reachable from outside the company. These can include email and web servers, or e-commerce servers, for example. Access to these servers must be secure and highly available.

- Cloud applications can encompass any of the preceding types of traffic. They require the appropriate treatment as they traverse the network to and from the Internet access point.

Planning a Network Implementation

Using a structured approach to planning and implementing any network changes or new network components is important. A comprehensive life-cycle approach lowers the total cost of ownership, increases network availability and business agility, and provides faster access to applications and services.

The Prepare, Plan, Design, Implement, Operate, and Optimize (PPDIOO) lifecycle approach is one structure that can be used. The components are

- **Prepare:** Organizational requirements gathering, high-level architecture, network strategy, business case strategy

- **Plan:** Network requirements gathering, network examination, gap analysis, project plan

- **Design:** Comprehensive, detailed design

- **Implement:** Detailed implementation plan, and implementation following its steps

- **Operate:** Day-to-day network operation and monitoring

- **Optimize:** Proactive network management and fault correction

Network engineers at the CCNP level are most likely involved in the Implement and Operate phases. They might also participate in the Design and Optimize phases. Creating a detailed implementation plan that includes test and verification procedures and a rollback strategy is important. Each step in this plan should consist of the following:

- Description

- Reference to the design document

- Detailed implementation and verification instructions

- Detailed rollback instructions

- Estimated time needed for completion

A complex implementation should be done in sections, with testing at each incremental section.

Resiliency and High Availability

One goal for almost every designer is to create a highly available network—one where failures are rare and self-healing. A highly available network is a resilient network that employs various methods to enable it to recover and continue operating in the event of a failure. Resiliency leads to high availability through the following components:

- **Network-level resiliency:** This includes redundant links and redundant devices, but it doesn't stop there. Those devices must be configured so they fail between devices, or links, quickly.

- **System-level resiliency:** This includes redundancy within the hardware, such as dual power supplies, and cold-standby parts, such as extra stackable switches or switch modules. It also has features within the hardware that enable fast failover.

- **Network management and monitoring:** You must detect a failure immediately and be informed of the actions taken automatically to remediate it. For accurate monitoring statistics, it is important that network clocks be synchronized. Use Network Time Protocol (NTP) for this purpose. Syslog, Simple Network Management Protocol (SNMP), and Internet Protocol Service Level Agreement (IP SLA) are some tools that help you monitor and track your network's resiliency.

Fast Failover and Convergence

Recall that in a Layer 2 network, Spanning Tree Protocol blocks redundant links by default so that they are in an active/backup configuration. Layer 2 EtherChannels change that dynamic and enable multiple links to be active. If a failure occurs, they distribute traffic across the remaining links. Layer 3 links between all switches contain STP within the switch, minimizing STP issues. Use Layer 3 EtherChannels to increase the bandwidth between switches, or switch and hosts.

Configure your devices for fast convergence to avoid traffic drops when a link fails. RSTP is preferred over 802.1D STP because it provides faster failover. Use routing protocols, such as EIGRP, that have fast convergence times. You might need to tune the Layer 2 and Layer 3 protocol timers.

When measuring network resiliency, consider how long it takes for failover and convergence at all layers of the OSI stack, not just Layers 1–3. Table 8-1 outlines some of the typical convergence times.

Table 8-1   Convergence Times for Network Components

Network Component	Convergence Time
Rapid Spanning Tree	Subsecond for minor failures, 1–2 seconds for major failures.
EtherChannel	Approximately 1 second to redirect traffic to a different link in the channel.
First-hop redundancy protocols, such as HSRP, VRRP, or GLBP	Default of 10 seconds. Recommended tuning of hello time to 1 second and hold time to 3 second yields a 3-second convergence time
Routing protocols	Subsecond for OSPF and EIGRP with recommended tuning of timers.

Redundancy

Redundancy increases network availability because it eliminates single points of failure by providing duplicate devices and links. This costs more, so the added price must be balanced against the added benefit. Add redundancy where it has the most impact on availability, in the core of your network, data center, or e-commerce module. Critical WAN or ISP connections are another typical location.

A redundant network has path diversity with multiple links between multiple devices. It can have geographic diversity, with data centers in multiple sites. Networks frequently have dual core and distribution switches, with dual uplinks to each. Dual WAN providers, with dual WAN edge routers, are commonly used. Companies can design their networks with connections to dual Telco central offices and power substations to achieve additional redundancy.

Be aware that redundancy does not always equal resiliency. Too much redundancy can increase the network complexity to a point that it becomes harder to troubleshoot and actually leads to a less-available network. Too many paths exist for the data to follow, so it becomes less deterministic. The cost is much higher as well.

Figure 8-3 shows where you would typically use redundancy within a campus network. Access switches are either chassis based—with dual Supervisor engines and dual power supplies—or are stackable switches. They have redundant, fully meshed links to redundant distribution switches, which, in turn, have redundant links to redundant core switches. Distribution and core switch pairs are connected via a Layer 3 link. This design minimizes single points of failure and enables the network to recover from a link or switch failure.

Figure 8-3   Designing for Redundancy

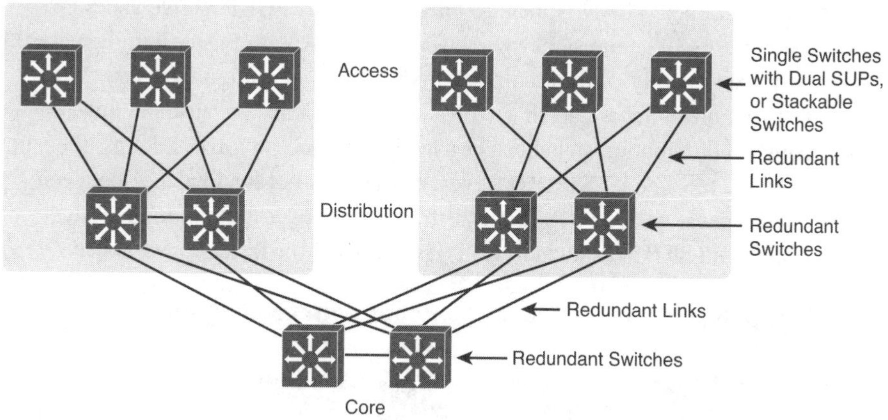

Layer 2 versus Layer 3 Access Design

You can use a Layer 2 or a Layer 3 access layer. When using Layer 2 access switches, VLANs can either be distributed across multiple switches or local to each switch. Figure 8-4 shows Layer 2 access switches with VLAN 10 on both of them. This design is not recommended. The FHRP Active switch and the STP Root must be statically configured as the same switch. STP blocks one uplink per access switch. RSTP helps speed convergence.

Figure 8-4   Layer 2 Access Switches with Distributed VLANs

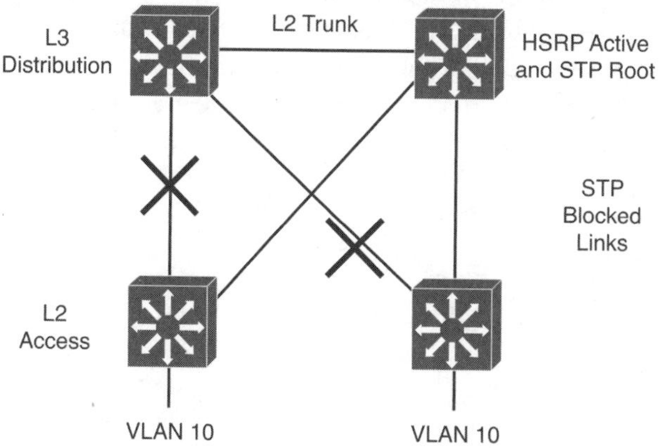

There must be a physical link between distribution switches, and it should be a Layer 2 trunk. Without that link, any traffic between switches must go through an access switch. Additionally, failure of one of the access-to-distribution uplinks causes packets to be dropped until the FHRP dead timer expires.

Figure 8-5 shows the recommended design when using Layer 2 access switches. Each VLAN is local to one switch. The FHRP Active and STP Root must still be the same switch for each VLAN. In this design, however, they are statically configured per VLAN as shown in Figure 8-5, so the distribution switches can share roles and traffic load. Because the link between distribution switches is Layer 3, there are no Layer 2 loops; thus, no links are blocked by STP. However, traffic does not load balance between links because each switch forwards traffic only over the link to its HSRP Active and STP Root switch. RSTP is still used for faster convergence.

Figure 8-5   Layer 2 Access Switches with Local VLANs

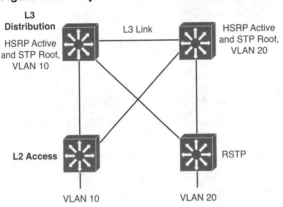

In Figure 8-6 the access switches are Layer 3. This gives the faster convergence and is easiest to implement. All links between switches are Layer 3. There is no need for HSRP, although STP should still be enabled in case of a misconfiguration. Access switches can load balance traffic across both uplinks. The access switches either run a routing protocol or use static routes. The distribution switches summarize routes for the access VLANs.

Figure 8-6   Layer 3 Access Switches

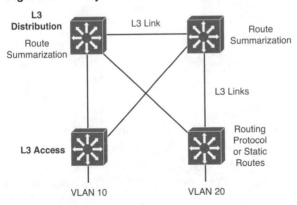

Part II: SWITCH

SSO, NSF, and ISSU

Stateful switchover (SSO) along with non-stop forwarding (NSF) enhances Layers 2–4 convergence time in Cisco devices having redundant route processors (RP). In Cisco chassis-based switches, the route processor is the Supervisor engine. SSO provides smooth transition between redundant Supervisor engines. NSF enables the data plane to continue forwarding traffic while the control plane converges. Supervisor upgrades can be accomplished without rebooting the switch by using In-Service Software Upgrade (ISSU).

When using SSO, only one RP is active. The standby RP synchronizes its configuration and dynamic state information (such as CEF, MAC, and FIB tables) with the active RP. When the active RP fails, SSO enables the standby RP to take over immediately. NSF keeps the switch forwarding traffic during the switchover, using the existing route and CEF tables. The goal of using NSF with SSO is to prevent routing adjacencies from reset- ting, which prevents a routing flap. The switchover to the new RP must be completed before routing timers expire, or the router's neighbors tear down their adjacency and routing is disrupted. When the new RP is up, the old routes are marked as stale and the RP asks its routing peers to refresh them. When routing is converged, it updates the routing and CEF tables on the switch and the line cards.

NSF is supported with EIGRP, OSPF, ISIS, and BGP. An NSF-capable router supports NSF; an NSF-aware router does not support NSF but acknowledges it and continues forwarding traffic during SSO.

Use NSF with SSO in locations where you do not have a duplicate switch for failover, such as at the user access or Enterprise network edge; otherwise, it can actually cause longer convergence. Routing protocol timers can be tuned very short to provide fast convergence. With SSO, the switchover to the standby RP might not occur before the tuned routing Dead timer expires and the adjacency is reset.

ISSU is a process that takes advantage of SSO and NSF to keep the switch operating during a software upgrade or downgrade. Basically, it involves the following steps:

Step 1. Load the new software on the standby route processor/Supervisor engine.

Step 2. Designate the standby RP as the active one.

Step 3. Test the upgrade.

Step 4. Commit the changes, which resets the (previously active) standby RP and boots it with the new software.

Virtual Switching System

Virtual Switch System (VSS) technology creates one logical switch from two physical switches. The two switches are managed as one and remain synchronized using an interchassis version of SSO and HSF. The data plane and switch fabric are active and forward traffic on both switches, but only one of the switches handles the control plane. A 10 Gb Virtual Switch Link (VSL) is required between the switches; configuring multiple VSL links for redundancy is good practice. The two switches are not required to reside physically in the same location as long as the VSL links are operational.

As of this writing, VSS is available on Cisco Catalyst 6800, 6500, 4500, and 4500X switches with VSS-compatible Supervisor engines and software.

Using Standalone Access Switches

Using more than one standalone switch, such as the Cisco 2960X, 3650, or 3850, in the same access closet requires special design consideration. Consider either daisy-chaining the switches or using the Cisco Stackwise technology. When you daisy-chain switches, they connect with regular Ethernet links that are usually configured as trunks. Two members of the chain typically uplink to one distribution switch each. You must add a link between the top and bottom switch; otherwise, a failure in the link between two access switches might cause return traffic to be blackholed. Alternatively, you can configure the link between the distribution switches as a Layer 2 trunk. Each daisy-chained switch must be managed separately.

Stackwise technology enables you to manage a group of access switches as one. Special Stackwise cables connect the switches and extend the backplane between peer switches. You should still connect the top and bottom members of the stack, but this is accomplished using a Stackwise cable. Two or more stack member switches then uplink to the distribution switches. The connection between distribution switches can then be a Layer 3 link without the worry of blackholing return traffic.

PART III

TSHOOT

CHAPTER 1

Tools and Methodologies of Troubleshooting

Troubleshooting Methodology

The responsibilities of a network administrator boil down to these essential goals: maximize performance and availability while minimizing cost and time to repair.

This chapter focuses on minimizing time to repair. The time needed to restore functionality is predicated on two things: preparation and technique. This chapter concentrates on both the techniques that you can apply to minimize downtime and the elements of preparation, such as documentation and scheduled preventative maintenance.

Note

The TSHOOT test doesn't assume a specific troubleshooting process. You might find that various troubleshooting techniques are useful in different situations. The test advocates a structured approach to troubleshooting, based on the scientific method.

One framework for troubleshooting, based on the scientific method, is described as a six-step process:

Step 1. Define the problem.

Step 2. Gather information.

Step 3. Analyze information and eliminate possibilities.

Step 4. Hypothesize.

Step 5. Test hypothesis.

Step 6. Interpret results and, if necessary, generate a new hypothesis.

The first step—problem description—is accomplished when a user reports a problem. The initial problem description tends to be overly general; for example, "The Internet is down!"

A troubleshooter's initial response should therefore be to (Step 2) gather more information and use this to (Step 3) eliminate possibilities. Determine symptoms by talking to the user, personal observation, or referring to management systems such as NetFlow, Syslog, and SNMP monitors. Eliminating possibilities depends on experience and understanding the technology and topology.

When you have an adequate description of the problem, form a hypothesis (Step 4). An hypothesis is a possible explanation whose symptoms would be similar to observations. It should suggest a way to prove or disprove itself (Step 5). For example, if you suspect that the WAN connection is down, looking at the interface status or pinging a remote device can test that thought.

Test results either support or refute a theory (Step 6). A single test result can't prove a theory—just support it. For example, **ping** might be used to test a WAN connection. A ping timeout cannot, by itself, be considered definitive. The target might be shut down or have a firewall that drops ICMP. Test results should be confirmed through several different lines of evidence. If the tests contradict the hypothesis, start over with a new theory.

After an hypothesis is accepted as a reasonable explanation, take action to fix the problem. Of course, any action is another type of test. If it doesn't fix the problem, simply develop a new hypothesis and repeat the process.

Structured Troubleshooting

The term *structured troubleshooting* describes any systematic way of collecting information, forming a hypothesis, and testing it. In a structured approach, each unsuccessful test rules out an entire class of possibilities and hopefully suggests the next hypothesis. An unstructured (random) approach usually takes much longer and is less likely to be successful.

A number of techniques have been used successfully, their common feature being a rigorous and thoughtful approach that collects and analyzes data. Some of these are described with the first three techniques focusing on the venerable OSI model as shown in Figure 1-1:

- **Bottom up:** Start with the OSI physical layer and work up.

- **Top down:** Start at the OSI application layer and drill down.

- **Divide and conquer:** Start at the network layer and follow the evidence, developing specific tests of each hypothesis.

Figure 1-1   OSI Model

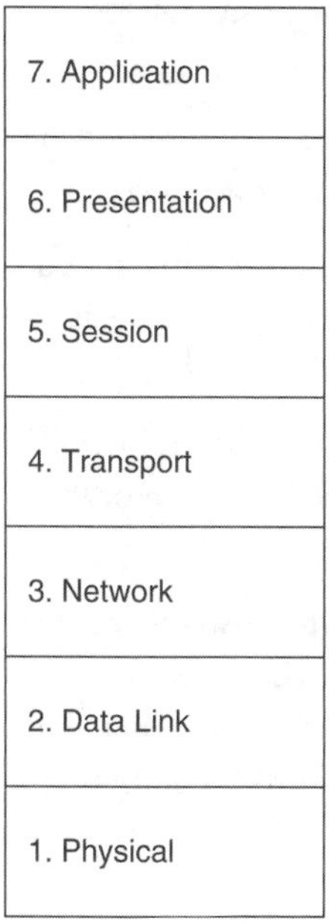

7. Application
6. Presentation
5. Session
4. Transport
3. Network
2. Data Link
1. Physical

Table 1-1 describes how some readily available IOS or PC commands can be used to support an OSI-driven troubleshooting approach.

Table 1-1   Tools Corresponding to OSI Levels

OSI Layer	Tool
Application	Nslookup (from PC; tests DNS)
Transport	Telnet (tests TCP ports)
	Ttcp (can test UDP ports)
Network	**show ip interface**
	show ip route
	ping and traceroute
Data Link	**show interface**
	show ip arp
Physical	**show inventory**
	show environment
	show memory
	show process
	Visually inspect cable and connections

A second set of troubleshooting techniques focuses more on the environment in which the device exists. These approaches consider hardware, interconnectivity, and standards:

- **Follow the path:** Consider the "packets perspective" and examine the devices and processes encountered moving through the network.

- **Spot differences:** Compare the configuration to an older version or a similar device. Tools such as Diff and WinDiff make this comparison easy.

- **Move the problem:** Swap components to see whether the problem stays with the device or moves with the component. A version of this is a strategic reboot to see whether that resolves the issue.

- **What changed** (*post hoc ergo proptor hoc*)**:** Determine whether something changed right before the problem developed. The theory here is that timing implies causation. Sometimes this does provide a clue, but many things happen contemporaneously in networks every second. *Use cautiously—this troubleshooting method can easily provide a false lead.*

- **Shoot from the Hip:** Finally, all troubleshooters engage in guessing occasionally. Although rarely acknowledged as a rigorous approach, sometimes experience and intuition lead to very quick solutions. This can be incredibly impressive when it works; the trick is to not let this become a series of random stabs when it doesn't work.

There isn't a single "best method," although a technician might find one more suitable for a given problem. Being familiar with each technique and changing approaches as necessary is a good idea.

What to Do When Nothing Works!

Occasionally, problems seem to defy explanation. Here are some ideas, in no particular order, that enable you to continue to work on the problem and get past a block:

- **Test assumptions:** Usually, issues appear to be "weird" because the symptoms are inadequately understood. If you reach a dead end, one way to restart is to go back to your original description and test assumptions to make sure the description is accurate.

- **Clean up:** As a child, when I lost a favorite toy and couldn't find it my mother would say, "I bet you'll find it if you clean your room." She was right more often than not, and the same principle applies to networks. Configurations accumulate dross—ACLs no longer used, abandoned routing protocols or neighbors, unplugged interfaces. The physical network also collects trash, like messy wiring closets. When stumped, clean up! Sometimes the solution emerges as you work.

- **Take a break:** Troubleshooting is a creative process. As the pressure builds and you cover the same ground again and again, troubleshooters lose perspective and become willing to try anything to *just make the pain go away.* If you find yourself getting to the point of frustration, ask a teammate to take over for a bit and walk away. As you let your mind wander, sometimes the answer pops into your head!

- **Get help:** Troubleshooters can easily develop a fighter pilot mentality and lose perspective! Ask another networker to brainstorm, ask the server or application people what they see, ask your service provider to take a look if it's a WAN connection—and better yet, your organization probably pays Cisco a lot of money for a SmartNet contract, so call TAC!

Best Practices for Routine Maintenance

Each of the troubleshooting practices described in this chapter assumes that good documentation exists and that appropriate tools are available. Troubleshooting is much more frustrating and time consuming when the necessary preparation isn't accomplished.

Maintenance might seem separate from the process of troubleshooting, but imagine it as the other side of the same coin. Any device that is well maintained is more reliable, suffers fewer problems, and is easier and quicker to repair. Network owners, such as businesses and governments, want computer systems that are consistently available. Good troubleshooting technique minimizes the length of time of an outage, but good maintenance technique reduces outages.

You must select the appropriate tools and techniques for the network you maintain, based on law, company policy, and your experience. You must understand that whichever elements you incorporate into your strategy, a structured approach to maintenance is a key part of reducing unplanned outages.

Part III: TSHOOT

Note

The TSHOOT test doesn't assume a specific approach to maintenance. Organizations might produce documentation and monitor their networks in unique ways. TSHOOT focuses on understanding the general practices that are used to successfully maintain a network.

Methodology

Many activities are reactive, and interrupt-driven issues can easily monopolize your time. Defining a preventative maintenance schedule helps avoid "firefighting." Taking a more structured approach—as opposed to waiting for the phone to ring—also helps to recognize problems earlier and respond to them more efficiently. A broader perspective toward the network also provides an opportunity to align costs with the organization's goals and budget effectively.

Several generic maintenance frameworks are available. Some organizations embrace a specific methodology, but many organizations pick and choose pieces that fit their environment. The important point is to have a documented approach to maintenance. If your organization doesn't have a documented strategy, you might want to research some of these models:

- IT Infrastructure Library (ITIL)

- FCAPS

- Telecommunications Management Network (TMN)

- Cisco Lifecycle Services/PPDIOO

- Microsoft Operations Framework

After you choose a specific model, map the model onto processes you can implement to maintain the network, and then select the tools that you will use.

Common Tasks

Although organizations have different expectations, the management of every network includes some basic components. Planning and accomplishing these tasks repetitively and competently is a key to successful network management.

Some common tasks include

- Getting additions, moves, and changes approved through change control

- Compiling documentation

- Preparing for disaster

- Capacity planning/utilization monitoring

- Troubleshooting

- Proactive scheduled maintenance

Preventative maintenance is the process of anticipating potential sources of failure and dealing with the problem before it occurs. Anticipating every source of failure is not possible, but careful thought can help identify candidates. One technique to recognize issues is to look at prior records of error, such as trouble tickets, ISP records, network monitoring systems, or purchase records. Use this information to categorize and rank the experience of your network.

Organizations are typically willing to accept small periods of scheduled downtime to offset the probability of long periods of unscheduled downtime. Using the data collected from your experience, consider the steps that can be taken during this window of time. Operating systems can be patched or upgraded to more stable and secure versions. Redundancy can be tested to ensure smooth failover, and disaster recovery plans can be exercised. Additionally, normal business changes (such as new circuits) can be accomplished during this period to minimize disruption.

Most large organizations use a system of change controls to enforce a thought-out approach to configuration modifications. Change control involves producing a document that describes the alteration to be made, who will make it, when the change will be made, and who will be affected. A well-written change control document also includes some notes about how the new configuration can be "backed out" if something goes wrong. This change control is then approved by management.

Change control systems help the business balance the need to update network components and configurations against the risk of changes. Change control systems also protect the network administrator—if each change is well thought out and thoroughly communicated, the business has the opportunity to accept the risks inherent in change.

Documentation reduces troubleshooting time and increases efficiency in project communication as networks are changed and upgraded. Although the task is time consuming, the importance of keeping accurate and up-to-date documentation cannot be overemphasized. Well-maintained documentation includes details such as

- Configuration templates or standards
- Configuration history
- Equipment inventory (including serial number and support contract information)
- Circuit inventory (including circuit ID and service provider contact)
- IP address assignment

- Network drawings

- Communication plan

- Out-of-band communication details

- Expected traffic patterns

Templates can be fill-in-the-blank versions of a complete configuration or can be snippets that show how your organization handles specific issues, such as IPsec tunnels. Either way, templates provide an opportunity for consistency and enable technicians to more quickly move from interpreting to troubleshooting. Consider, for instance, access lists and how easily they might be confused. Access list 100 might typically be related to permitting SNMP to certain destinations but on some devices is used to filtering traffic on the public interface. Understanding the ramifications of confusion in this situation, one can easily see the benefit of standardizing things such as labels. (And in this case, using named access lists, not numbered, is probably best.)

The documentation for the communication plan should include contact information for internal IT and management contacts and vendor and service provider information. The plan should also specify who should be contacted, in what circumstances, and how often. For example, should a technician update the business contact or the network operations center? Is there a prescribed after-action review?

Often, the individual documentation elements are combined, such as IP addresses and circuit IDs on the network diagram, or simplified, such as using a TFTP server directory to keep configuration history.

Documentation should also include a disaster recovery plan. Disasters come in many sizes, so it pays to consider several cases. If the problem is related to a single piece of equipment, consider Cisco SmartNet maintenance as a way to guarantee backup hardware is onsite quickly. Even where a spare is procured, you need a backup of the configuration and IOS. If getting a spare involves a service contract, the serial number might also be required. Someone onsite needs a console cable and a laptop with a serial port. Larger disasters, such as a fire, might require failing over to another location. This failover plan should be tested periodically to ensure it is complete and accurate, and that the participants are familiar with their responsibilities.

A final common piece to managing the network is to have some form of network monitoring. Network monitors take many forms, from simple no-frills systems to complex central management. These systems are available from a variety of vendors and through open source. Regardless of which system you choose, you need to pull data showing utilization, availability, performance, and errors. The system should alert the staff through emails or SMS messages so that you are aware of problems before the phone rings.

After the monitoring system is in place, periodically characterize performance as a snapshot. A snapshot describes the expected performance of a system and enables you to compare later performance and recognize change. For instance, changes in jitter or in dropped packets might indicate that a WAN link is oversubscribed. In addition, a functional baseline for performance metrics serves as a critical diagnostic tool for security breaches and zero-day attacks and worms. Without thorough knowledge of typical behavior on a given network, aberrant traffic analyses become a subjective art.

Troubleshooting Tools

Most network administrators have a variety of tools in their tool bag. Some of the basic tools include a configuration history, device logs, and documentation. As the number of devices maintained grows, tools that collect data about the performance of the network and tools that collect user issues become increasingly important.

Two of the most basic tools are ping and traceroute.

Ping tests connectivity and is so commonly used that even end users are passingly familiar with it. A ping response shows that a working path between two end points exists. End systems sometimes have firewalls that prevent response, but generally ping is a reasonable first test of network connectivity, as shown in Example 1-1.

Example 1-1   Ping

```
R1# ping 10.186.1.1

Type escape sequence to abort.
Sending 5, 100-byte ICMP Echos to 10.186.1.1, timeout is 2 seconds:
!!!!!
Success rate is 100 percent (5/5), round-trip min/avg/max = 8/9/12
ms
```

Exclamation marks show a response, but there is a lot of information besides the most obvious part. First, pay attention to the pattern of the response. Alternating success and failure (!.!.!) is a classic sign of a load balancing problem, where one path succeeds and the other fails. Second, consider the response time. Many applications depend on quick response. Voice, for example, assumes a round-trip time of less than 150 ms. The response time can also clue the troubleshooter to utilization issues. If the response time is much larger than usual that might indicate a heavy traffic load and queuing. If you notice that the minimum and maximum times vary widely, this could also be a sign of queuing because of a heavy load.

Ping can do a lot more than that simple test, however. Privileged mode supports an extended ping that enables every aspect of ping to be controlled. This opens up many more tests that can be accomplished with the humble command.

Example 1-2 is an extended ping. Notice that the command **ping**—without a specified destination—is entered in privileged mode. It sends five pings of 100 bytes, then five of 200 bytes, continuing to 1500-byte pings. The DF bit (do not fragment) is set. A similar ping might be used if you suspect that an intermediate link didn't support the same size MTU as the source and destination. A more detailed explanation of the command is found after Example 1-2.

Example 1-2   Extended ping

```
R1# ping
Protocol [ip]:
Target IP address: 10.186.1.1
Repeat count [5]:
Datagram size [100]:
Timeout in seconds [2]:
Extended commands [n]: y
Source address or interface: loopback0
Type of service [0]:
Set DF bit in IP header? [no]: y
Validate reply data? [no]:
Data pattern [0xABCD]:
Loose, Strict, Record, Timestamp, Verbose[none]:
Sweep range of sizes [n]: y
Sweep min size [36]: 100
Sweep max size [18024]: 1500
Sweep interval [1]: 100
Type escape sequence to abort.
Sending 75, [100..1500]-byte ICMP Echos to 10.186.1.1, timeout is 2
  seconds:
Packet sent with a source address of 10.1.1.1
Packet sent with the DF bit set
!!!!!!!!!!!!!!!!!!!!!!!!!!!!!!!!!!!!!!!!!!!!!!!!!!!!!!!!!!!!!!!!!!!!!!!!!!!!!
  !!!
!!!!!
Success rate is 100 percent (75/75), round-trip min/avg/max =
8/10/12 ms
```

Remember that defaults are shown in square brackets. Selecting all the defaults is similar to a normal ping.

Sometimes, testing involves repeatedly pinging (for instance, when you believe that an interface is flapping up and down). An extended ping with a repeat count of 99999 can be used to interactively test the network over a period of time.

Pings can be set to different packet sizes through the Datagram Size variable. The router can automate testing a range of sizes. To do so, use the extended commands and choose to sweep a range of sizes.

If a router is asked to forward a packet that is larger than the MTU of the transmitting link, it normally breaks the packet into smaller pieces. Setting the DF bit instructs receiving routers to discard the traffic rather than fragment it.

Using different size packets and setting the DF bit allows testing MTU. When the MTU limit is reached, all subsequent pings are dropped.

Another beneficial testing technique is to change the source interface. Pings are normally sourced from the transmitting interface. Using an internal interface as the source shows that the receiving device and the intermediate routers understand how to route back to that prefix.

A final idea is to try different Type of Service settings. Many networks now carry voice, video, and prioritized data. Voice is commonly set to ToS 5, so pinging using ToS 5 enables a peek into how the QoS settings are functioning.

Like ping, there is an extended version of traceroute. It has a few of the same capabilities, with one other significant testing capability. Traceroute in IOS uses UDP, and extended traceroute enables setting the UDP port. This can be employed to test performance for applications that use UDP, such as voice. This is important when trying to diagnose the effects of firewalls and access lists.

Example 1-3 shows extended traceroute. The only choice specified in Example 1-3 is to use UDP port 16000.

Example 1-3   Extended traceroute

```
R1# traceroute
Protocol [ip]:
Target IP address: 10.200.1.1
Source address:
Numeric display [n]:
Timeout in seconds [3]:
```

Part III: TSHOOT

Example 1-3   Continued

```
Probe count [3]:
Minimum Time to Live [1]:
Maximum Time to Live [30]:
Port Number [33434]: 16000
Loose, Strict, Record, Timestamp, Verbose[none]:
Type escape sequence to abort.
Tracing the route to 10.200.1.1
```

In the same way the UDP port connectivity can be probed with traceroute, telnet can be used to test TCP ports. Telnet does not offer many options, but by changing the target port, different network services can be tested. Example 1-4 shows that email and the web server respond on the appropriate ports.

Example 1-4   Telnet to a Service

```
R1# telnet www.example.com 25
Translating "www.example.com"...domain server (10.1.2.2) [OK]
Trying www.example.com (172.16.0.25, 25)... Open
220 www.example.com ESMTP Postfix

R1# telnet www.example.com 80
<ctrl-c>
HTTP/1.1 400 Bad Request
```

Configurations

A configuration history is built by saving the device configuration to a central point periodically or after each change. IOS supports a variety of remote targets, including HTTP/S and SCP. FTP and TFTP are commonly used because implementations are bundled with many operating systems, and free open-source versions are readily available.

One way to build a configuration history is to save your configuration after each change. Saving the file with the date attached makes it easy to sort later, and adding a .txt file makes it easy for Windows-based machines to open the file. In Example 1-5, the TFTP server has a directory for each site and the configuration is saved with the date.

Example 1-5   Saving a Configuration

```
R1# copy run tftp
Address or name of remote host []? 192.168.255.10
```

```
Destination filename [R1-confg]? R1/R1-14-06-03.txt
!!
820 bytes copied in 2.628 secs (312 bytes/sec)
```

Logging events and alerts to Syslog is another important tool. Syslog is a facility that receives alerts from network equipment and stores them in a common log. Again, many versions of Syslog are available. Events are logged based on a severity scale, from zero to seven. Choosing a logging level tells the router to transmit events at that level and lower. To set up Syslog support on an IOS device, the **logging** keyword is used, as shown in Example 1-6.

Example 1-6   logging

```
R1(config)# logging trap ?
<0-7> Logging severity level
alerts Immediate action needed (severity=1)
critical Critical conditions (severity=2)
debugging Debugging messages (severity=7)
emergencies System is unusable (severity=0)
errors Error conditions (severity=3)
informational Informational messages (severity=6)
notifications Normal but significant conditions (severity=5)
warnings Warning conditions (severity=4)
<cr>
R1(config)# logging on
R1(config)# logging 192.168.255.10
R1(config)# logging trap informational
```

As the rate of log entries grows (because there are more devices or the sensitivity is changed), finding the appropriate information in the logs becomes more cumbersome. One critical way to support tying events together in the log is to have accurate time on each device so that log entries have a consistent time. Timestamps are vital in forensics and post mortems, where sequence and patterns of events evolve into chains of evidence.

Time is synchronized on network devices using the network time protocol (NTP). Setting up NTP is straightforward; specify the NTP server with the command **ntp server** *<ip address>*. Time servers are organized by stratums, where stratum 1 clocks are super-precise atomic clocks, stratum 2 devices get their time from stratum 1, stratum 3 devices ask stratum 2, and so on. Public stratum-1 devices are listed on the Internet; it is considered a courtesy that each organization has a minimal number of connections to a stratum-1 device and that other clocks in the organization pull from these stratum-2 devices.

Part III: TSHOOT

Another time-related logging issue to consider is time zone. Will your organization log using local time zones or the time zone of headquarters, or set all devices to GMT? Example 1-7 demonstrates the time zone set to GMT, logging set, and the router set to use a remote NTP server.

Example 1-7   Time Setup

```
service timestamps debug datetime msec localtime
service timestamps log datetime msec localtime
ntp server 192.168.1.1
clock timezone GMT 0 0
service timestamps debug datetime msec localtime
service timestamps log datetime msec localtime
```

Cisco IOS supports archive and restore features that make maintaining a configuration history and logs easy. The archive function maintains a current copy of the configuration and a set of previous ones. The archive can be maintained within the router or at an accessible URL. The restore function enables the router to smoothly revert to any of the saved configurations.

Setting up the archive function involves going into the archive configuration mode. The **path** command specifies a backup location, and time-period is used to periodically back up the configuration. If write-memory is specified, an archive copy is made whenever the configuration is saved. Archive copies have a version number on the end, such as "-1." This version number is reset with each router reset, so it is difficult to use as a long-term archive. The path can include $h for the hostname and $t for time, so it is possible to timestamp each saved file. Using the timestamp is impractical with a Windows TFTP server, however, because the timestamp includes colons. In Example 1-8, the filename is hostname.txt and results in R1 saving files named R1.txt-1 and R1.txt-2. Example 1-8 is set to back up at the maximum periodic interval, so most backups happen because the administrator saves the configuration.

Example 1-8   Archive Configuration

```
archive
path tftp://192.168.255.10/$h.txt
write-memory
time-period 525600
```

The router uses a standard name structure for all saved files, counting up to 14 and then cycling back to 1. This is difficult to use as a complete configuration history. One possible solution is to save the archive to flash and have administrators save to TFTP periodically (which automatically updates the flash archive) as shown in Example 1-9. The periodic backup could be set to run once a week, just in case someone forgot to **copy run start**.

Example 1-9   Periodic Archive

```
archive
path flash://$h
write-memory
time-period 10080
```

Archive can help troubleshoot in two ways. First, archive can compare differences between numerous versions of the configuration: **archive config differences**. Second, archive can be used to supplement syslog with all commands executed on the router. In archive configuration mode, enter log config mode. **logging enable** turns on command capture; **hidekeys** prevents logging passwords. Normally, the log of commands is kept in memory on the router, but **notify syslog** exports the commands to syslog. This configuration is shown in Example 1-10.

Example 1-10   Archive Logs

```
archive
path flash://$h
write-memory
time-period 10080
log config
logging enable
hidekeys
notify syslog
```

To review the archive files, use the **show archive** command, as follows:

```
R1# show archive
```

Finally, the archiving function adds the capability to restore to a previous configuration. Administrators traditionally replaced an old configuration with **copy tftp run** (which merged into the running configuration) or **copy tftp start** (which replaced the configuration completely but required a restart).

An archive can be restored with the **configure replace** command. The router compares the running configuration against the archive and builds and applies a list of commands necessary to match the archive. This method avoids reapplying existing commands or rebooting to make the migration:

```
R1# configure replace tftp://192.168.255.10/R1-5
```

Part III: TSHOOT

This applies all necessary additions and deletions to replace the current running configuration with the contents of the specified configuration file, which is assumed to be a complete configuration, not a partial configuration.

Troubleshooting often requires changes to the configuration that can potentially break connectivity. One suggestion is to use **reload in 5** to schedule a reload in 5 minutes. If a command inadvertently breaks the connection, the router reboots to the last saved configuration. If everything works, **reload cancel** prevents the reboot. The same functionality is available with **configure replace filename time** but avoids the reboot by simply restoring a working configuration at a specified time. Prevent the rollback by confirming the change with **configure confirm**.

Other Tools

Documentation is a huge part of troubleshooting, and there are many tools you can use to compile the material. One of the key things to understand about documentation is that it must be easy to update or it quickly becomes stale. This type of documentation is explored in the later section "Discovery."

Microsoft Visio is a common way to document connectivity. A database or spreadsheet is frequently used to track inventory. Employ a ticketing system to list issues and gather trending data. Wikis can also enable the network staff to produce and edit documentation.

There isn't a definitive way to produce documentation; having documentation that is useful in the troubleshooting process is critical. Ideally, the material should also feed directly into the disaster recovery process, so it should include part numbers, serial numbers, service contracts, and a variety of information that isn't strictly part of the "network" description.

Cisco has a variety of helpful web-based tools. The Dynamic Configuration tool is useful in planning hardware configurations; it confirms compatibility and builds a parts list to help you plan a project. The Feature Navigator verifies that a specific feature is in a particular version of IOS. The Power Calculator calculates the required power supply for Power over Ethernet (PoE) installations. Many other tools are available through Cisco Connection Online (CCO), so it's worth spending some time understanding the width of the offering.

A final category of tools to consider are the network performance monitoring tools. Typically, monitoring and performance tracking in a small organization is accomplished with a phone—people call when they have problems. As an organization grows, however, recognizing problems before they occur becomes more important. This same information can be used to budget hardware and circuit upgrades.

Monitoring tools typically use SNMP, NetFlow, pings, and Syslog data to compile statistics about the current and historical behavior of the network. Typically, networks are monitored for capacity usage, availability, delay, and CPU and memory utilization. Solarwinds, nGenius, OPNET Net Doctor, SP Guru, and WhatsUpGold each make products that fulfill these functions, and MRTG is a similar open-source project.

Remember to plan a monitoring system around the service level agreements (SLA) in the environment. Service providers typically offer some performance guarantees, such as minimizing unplanned downtime or minimizing jitter. The business might insist that IT also support SLAs internally. The network monitoring system should provide information to back up both types of SLAs. Cisco has built in an SLA monitoring tool that makes availability statistics known and monitored for critical links and servers. This is called *IP SLA* and is customizable for MPLS, link utilization, RTT, and others. It is quite useful for critical traffic real-time monitoring and notification. Frequently, these statistics are run as a continuous background process between Customer Edge nodes between sites, if remote connectivity between critical traffic endpoints is a business driver.

Working with External Tools

The IOS troubleshooting capabilities are supplemented by external network management tools. Cisco IOS devices support these tools and, in many cases, supply detailed information to the management system. This section describes the methods used to coordinate with these tools.

Packet Sniffing

Packet capture from a laptop or specialized device enables low-level vision into the exact traffic flowing over a link. Capturing traffic shows errors and underlying protocol traffic.

Note

Packet capture might be regarded as wiretapping and a violation of privacy rights in some countries. Enterprise Acceptable Use Policies typically try to gain consent for this. Make sure you understand the legality of packet capturing in each country in which you work.

The issue with packet capture is that switches do not forward all traffic out all ports, so finding a port from which to see all traffic is difficult. SPAN

Part III: TSHOOT

(Switched Port Analyzer) is a tool within IOS switches to direct copies of
packets to a capture port. It is configured by identifying a source port or
VLAN from which traffic should be copied. SPAN is then pointed to an
output port, to which a packet capture tool is attached. SPAN captures traffic
on a switch and output to a trunked VLAN. A second switch then captures
the VLAN and outputs it to a port. This configuration is called *remote SPAN*
(RSPAN).

The generic configuration of SPAN is

```
ASW1(config)# Monitor session [session number]
 [source|destination] [interface|vlan]
```

The following configuration shows what is used when a suspicious device is
on port F0/1 and a packet capture tool is plugged into port F0/24:

```
ASW1(config)# Monitor session 1 source interface f0/1
ASW1(config)# Monitor session 1 destination interface f0/24
```

Router IP Traffic Export (RITE) is similar to SPAN but is used by routers
to capture traffic to a monitoring port. Example 1-11 demonstrates capturing
10 percent of the interesting traffic on f0/1 and exporting it to a device with
a given MAC.

Example 1-11   RITE

```
R1(config)# ip traffic-export profile rite
R1(config-rite)# interface FastEthernet 0/1
R1(config-rite)# bidirectional
R1(config-rite)# mac-address c401.1a30.0000
R1(config-rite)# incoming access-list my_acl
R1(config-rite)# outgoing sample one-in-every 10
R1(config)# interface FastEthernet0/0
R1(config-if)# ip traffic-export apply rite
```

RITE can also be used to export the traffic to a file on the router. From
there, it can be copied off for inspection on a PC:

```
traffic-export interface fastethernet0/0 copy tftp:
```

NetFlow

NetFlow collects summaries of traffic information and transmits the
summary to a NetFlow collector. It is enabled on each monitored interface.
NetFlow supports a version 5 and version 9; this should be set to match the
requirements of your network management system. Finally, NetFlow exports

information to a target IP address. The commands to accomplish these actions are as follows:

```
R1(config-if)# ip flow ingress
R1(config)# ip flow-export version [5|9]
R1(config)# ip flow-export destination [ip-address]
```

In addition to implementing a monitoring system to track NetFlow, an administrator can also peek into the current flows using **show ip cache flow**.

SNMP and EEM

SNMP is another monitoring protocol. Where NetFlow tracks traffic, SNMP can monitor any type of event or statistic from the device. SNMP is supported by most network monitoring systems. The router also has a tool to react to events through embedded event manager (EEM).

SNMP is set up by identifying a server and listing the events to be monitored. If **snmp-server enable traps** is used without specifying specific events, all traps are monitored:

```
R1(config)# snmp-server host [ip-address]
R1(config)# snmp-server enable traps
```

EEM enables custom reactions to events and acts as a supplement to SNMP. Incidents can be triggered by any SNMP event and actions can include (among others) SNMP, syslog, IOS commands, and email messages.

Example 1-12 shows a simple example EEM applet. This applet logs a syslog message and outputs a message to the console in reaction to an administrator entering configuration mode.

Example 1-12   EEM

```
Event manager applet CONFIG-STARTED
Event cli pattern "configure terminal" sync on skip no occurs 1
Action 1.0 syslog priority critical msg "Configuration mode was
  entered"
Action 2.0 syslog priority informational msg "Change control poli-
cies apply.  Authorized access only."
```

Hardware Diagnostics

The commands examined so far have dealt with network issues, but sometimes the problem is within the IOS device. Several commands describe the functional state of an IOS device.

If network hardware is suspected, a good place to start troubleshooting is to understand the external environment. The **show environment all** command displays information about the temperature within the device and the state of the power supplies, as shown in Example 1-13. Especially when trouble-shooting is handled remotely, it is easy to forget power and air conditioning, but problems in either area can lead to device malfunction.

Example 1-13   Show Environment

```
R1# show environment all
Power Supplies:
        Power Supply 1 is AC Power Supply. Unit is on.
        Power Supply 2 is AC Power Supply. Unit is on.

Temperature readings:
        NPE Inlet         measured at 25C/77F
        NPE Outlet        measured at 27C/80F
        I/O Cont Inlet    measured at 25C/77F
        I/O Cont Outlet   measured at 28C/82F
        CPU Die           measured at 43C/109F

Voltage readings:
        +3.30 V           measured at +3.30 V
        +1.50 V           measured at +1.49 V
        +2.50 V           measured at +2.50 V
        +1.80 V           measured at +1.79 V
        +1.20 V           measured at +1.20 V
        VDD_CPU           measured at +1.28 V
        VDD_MEM           measured at +2.50 V
        VTT               measured at +1.25 V
        +3.45 V           measured at +3.43 V
        -11.95            measured at -12.17 V
        +5.15 V           measured at +4.96 V
        +12.15 V          measured at +12.18 V

Envm stats saved 0 time(s) since reload
```

A lack of memory can also cause a network issue. The **show memory** command displays the state of memory on a device, as shown in Example 1-14. Focus on the Free column to determine whether enough is available. A sign of memory issues is %SYS-2-MALLOCFAIL messages.

Example 1-14   show memory

```
R1# show memory
                Head  Total(b)   Used(b)    Free(b)  Lowest(b)  Largest(b)
```

```
Processor  6319860 818832732 74864300 743968432 742841100  727580236
    I/O 38000000  67108864 11964260  55144604  55137712   54643068
Transient 37000000  16777216    58244  16718972  16226680   16718696
...
```

Hardware issues also manifest themselves on the interfaces. The **show controllers** command can reveal some information about the interface— serial interfaces in particular report things such as cable information here. The **show interfaces** command (shown in Example 1-15) displays a good deal of information about the state of the interface. In particular, pay attention to four measurements:

- **Input queue drops:** Signify that the router had more traffic than it could process. Some amount of drops is excusable, but drops could be related to CPU oversaturation. Double-check the processor with the **show processes cpu** command.

- **Output queue drops:** Usually mean that the line is congested.

- **Input errors:** Show duplex errors, interface problems, and CRC errors.

- **Output errors:** Usually related to duplex issues.

Example 1-15 show interface

```
R1# show interface
FastEthernet0/0 is up, line protocol is up
  Hardware is i82543 (Livengood), address is 000a.f3f7.9808 (bia
  000a.f3f7.9808)
  Description: enter port #
  Internet address is 10.100.1.1/16
  MTU 1500 bytes, BW 100000 Kbit/sec, DLY 100 usec,
      reliability 255/255, txload 32/255, rxload 14/255
  Encapsulation 802.1Q Virtual LAN, Vlan ID  1., loopback not set
  Keepalive set (10 sec)
  Full-duplex, 100Mb/s, 100BaseTX/FX
  ARP type: ARPA, ARP Timeout 04:00:00
  Last input 00:00:00, output 00:00:00, output hang never
  Last clearing of "show interface" counters never
  Input queue: 0/75/0/0 (size/max/drops/flushes); Total output
  drops: 0
  Queueing strategy: fifo
```

Example 1-15   Continued

```
Output queue: 0/40 (size/max)
5 minute input rate 5517000 bits/sec, 2571 packets/sec
5 minute output rate 12927000 bits/sec, 2550 packets/sec
   1326060749 packets input, 711066620 bytes
   Received 45468700 broadcasts, 0 runts, 0 giants, 0 throttles
   148 input errors, 0 CRC, 0 frame, 0 overrun, 148 ignored
   0 watchdog
   0 input packets with dribble condition detected
   1191821108 packets output, 2981100223 bytes, 0 underruns
   2 output errors, 0 collisions, 4 interface resets
   5634739 unknown protocol drops
   0 babbles, 0 late collision, 0 deferred
   2 lost carrier, 0 no carrier
   0 output buffer failures, 0 output buffers swapped out
```

Discovery

Network documentation is commonly compiled through a process of network discovery. This process starts from a known device and uses IOS tools to discover neighboring devices, recursively repeating this process moving away from the starting point.

The local router or Layer 3 switch is discovered from the PC by reviewing the default gateway setting. In the absence of a gateway, another option is to capture traffic (most devices are chatty to some extent and advertise details about themselves). DHCP advertisements include routers, and CDP or LLDP advertisements can be viewed to determine neighboring network equipment. BPDUs come from switches, whereas routing protocol updates originate from routers.

The evidence gained from reviewing PC settings and from a protocol capture assumes attachment to the network, but further work assumes that there are known authentication credentials. Attempting to "discover" credentials in the environment is usually viewed as nefarious, so simply asking for a valid username and password is a better practice (and if you can't ask, then it IS nefarious).

Access each discovered device using either telnet or SSH. Cisco devices default to supporting telnet; however, telnet transmits in plain text (even the password!) and is deprecated in favor of SSH in well-managed environments.

Using telnet just requires you know an IP address or name:

```
Telnet 172.16.100.1
```

Setting up SSH is straightforward. There are four requirements:

- Hostname

- DNS domain

- Key

- Enabling SSH

First, set up a hostname and DNS domain, and then enable a local username and password, as shown in Example 1-16.

Example 1-16   SSH Setup

```
Router(conf)# hostname R1
R1(conf)# ip domain-name swidget.com
R1(conf)# username tshoot password tshoot
```

Next, generate an RSA key to be used by SSH. Once generated, the key can be reviewed using **show crypto key mypubkey rsa**.

```
R1(conf)# crypto key generate rsa
```

Finally, SSH is enabled by default. If needed, reenable SSH by adding it as an input method under the VTY. The transport input defines the allowed input methods coming in (note that leaving out **telnet** prevents telnet from working).

```
Line vty 0 4
Transport input ssh
```

After configuring it, test access to the device using the SSH client on the local device. From IOS, this command is **ssh**. SSH requires a username, which is specified with the **-l** option.

```
R2# ssh -l tshoot R1.testdomain.com
```

Most network equipment announces itself to its neighbors using a network discovery protocol. Cisco pioneered this idea with the Cisco Discovery Protocol (CDP); a vendor-neutral version has more recently arrived in the Link Layer Discovery Protocol (LLDP).

CDP is enabled by default on Cisco devices. CDP broadcasts are sent out every 60 seconds on all enabled interfaces, and the device caches any received advertisements in the CDP table. It is globally enabled or disabled using **(no) cdp run** in global configuration mode; it can be enabled or disabled on specific interfaces using **(no) cdp enable**.

Part III: TSHOOT

After you gain access to a device, use **show cdp neighbors** to obtain a list of neighbors; **show cdp neighbors detail** includes additional valuable intelligence, including the IP address of the connected interface.

LLDP is disabled by default on Cisco devices. LLDP broadcasts are sent out every 30 seconds on all enabled interfaces, and the device caches any received advertisements in the LLDP table. It can be globally enabled or disabled using **(no) lldp run** in global configuration mode, and it can be enabled or disabled on specific interfaces using **(no) lldp receive | transmit**.

After gaining access to a device, use **show lldp neighbors** to obtain a list of neighbors; **show lldp neighbors detail** includes additional valuable intelligence, including the IP address of the connected interface. Neighboring IP addresses are used to kick off the process again until the entire network is mapped. Non-Cisco devices pass CDP without processing and are invisible to this type of mapping. LLDP is supported on recent equipment from a variety of manufacturers, but again the discovery protocol can't guarantee a complete picture. Both protocols give an excellent starting foundation for the topology.

ARP can also provide topology information. In a LAN, either ping the broadcast address or use a tool like nmap to sweep the network. The result should fill the switch ARP tables with the MACs of all local devices. The ARP table can then be queried to determine where devices are located.

A complete and accurate inventory is another part of troubleshooting. Of course, this information is much more useful if obtained before a problem occurs and connectivity drops! By comparing the inventory to previous inventories, it is possible to recognize differences (caused, presumably, by hardware failure). An inventory can even help avoid problems; for instance, tracking IP addresses prevents assigning the same address twice.

If the organization has a Cisco SmartNet maintenance contract, the serial number and part-number information is necessary to obtain spares, as shown in Example 1-17.

Example 1-17   Inventory

```
R1# show inventory
NAME: "Chassis", DESCR: "Cisco 7206VXR, 6-slot chassis"
PID: CISCO7206VXR     , VID:   , SN: XXXXXXXXXXX

NAME: "NPE-G2 0", DESCR: "Cisco 7200 Series Network Processing
  Engine NPE-G2"
PID: NPE-G2           , VID: V03 , SN: XXXXXXXXXXX
```

```
NAME: "disk2", DESCR: "256MB Compact Flash Disk for NPE-G2"
PID: MEM-NPE-G2-FLD256 , VID:    , SN:


NAME: "module 0", DESCR: "I/O Dual FastEthernet Controller"
PID: C7200-I/O-2FE/E   , VID:   , SN: XXXXXXXXXXX


NAME: "disk0", DESCR: "Cisco 7200 I/O PCMCIA Flash Disk, 48M"
PID: MEM-I/O-FLD48M   , VID:    , SN:


NAME: "disk1", DESCR: "Cisco 7200 I/O PCMCIA Flash Disk, 48M"
PID: MEM-I/O-FLD48M   , VID:    , SN:


NAME: "module 1", DESCR: "Serial"
PID: PA-8T-V35=       , VID:    , SN: XXXXXXXXXXX


NAME: "module 2", DESCR: "4 port, software configurable Multichannel
  T1/E1 with TDM Port Adapter"
PID: PA-MCX-4TE1        , VID:    , SN: XXXXXXXXXXX


NAME: "module 3", DESCR: "Enhanced 2 port T3/E3 clear channel PA"
PID: PA-2T3/E3-EC       , VID: V01 , SN: XXXXXXXXXXX


NAME: "module 4", DESCR: "8 port, software configurable Multichannel
  T1/E1 without TDM Port Adapter"
PID: PA-MC-8TE1+        , VID:    , SN: XXXXXXXXXXX


NAME: "module 6", DESCR: "8 port, software configurable Multichannel
  T1/E1 without TDM Port Adapter"
PID: PA-MC-8TE1+        , VID:    , SN: XXXXXXXXXXX


NAME: "Power Supply 1", DESCR: "Cisco 7200 AC Power Supply"
PID: PWR-7200-AC      , VID:    , SN:


NAME: "Power Supply 2", DESCR: "Cisco 7200 AC Power Supply"
PID: PWR-7200-AC      , VID:    , SN:
```

Aside from using information obtained by crawling the network, tracking some business variables that will aid in troubleshooting is an excellent idea. These must be obtained through discussions. Two examples of business details include site technical contacts and service providers. If you are not co-located with the equipment, who can you call? If a wide-area link is down, who should you call? Each WAN link must be associated with a vendor, capacity, circuit ID, and vendor contact information.

Self-Documenting Networks

Network discovery can be a tedious, time-consuming process, but the information gained is invaluable to troubleshooting. Ideally, this information would be gathered beforehand and used to produce clear documents and diagrams. However, even the best documentation leaves something out, and the normal state of enterprise documentation is to leave a lot out.

First, part of being a professional is to maintain documentation and insist on a high standard for it. Few people enjoy writing documentation, but if accurate and well maintained, it is a clear mark of someone who takes their profession seriously. For the sake of sanity, spelling out important details should be a priority. If too many elements are required, the act of maintaining documentation takes too much effort and things gradually grow stale. The important pieces are the details that allow troubleshooters to understand connectivity, the information required to interact with service providers, and the ability to renew maintenance contracts.

Second, making networks as self-documenting as possible is good practice. As previously asserted, even good documentation leaves something out that must be discovered during troubleshooting. Furthermore, finding details on the router allows troubleshooting to progress in a smoother way. Self-documenting is a set of practices that permit the device configuration to document the setup of the router. Use your imagination, but here are some ideas to start the process:

- Give the router a descriptive name; for example, a city name like "Hickory" instead of "R1" (this also prevents confusion—when routers all have the same starting or ending characters and the same length of name, accidentally entering the right command on the wrong device is easy to do).

- Each interface supports a **description** command. Use the description to enter what is attached (such as "voice VLAN") and supporting troubleshooting information (for example, "Verizon 20M MPLS CID: uqx123-49591 (800) 555-5555").

- Use named access lists instead of numbers whenever possible. Evaluating a configuration file to understand the function of **access-list 101** is difficult compared to **access-list Match-Web-PBR2Proxy**.

- Match numbers where possible. For example, use a subnet like 172.24.**4**.0/24 on VLAN 4 and assign the VLAN to subinterface g0/1.**4**.

- Take advantage of other places that allow text, such as BGP neighbor descriptions and route map names.

- When there isn't a way to be descriptive, be consistent. For example, if access list 21 is always used to match NAT then building some intuition is possible.

CHAPTER 2

Troubleshooting Switching Technologies

This section focuses on switching. It assumes a standard topology of distribution and access switches. This chapter covers the kinds of issues that occur at Layer 2 in a network.

While reading this chapter, remember the structured approach to problem solving. Define the problem and gather information. Hypothesize and test. Because this chapter groups link issues together, it's easy to proceed on some assumptions, but don't let this be your practice in the real world. Take the time to make sure you understand the problem.

Link issues are amenable to a number of troubleshooting approaches. Good documentation makes any approach easier and more productive. Many times, especially when information is lacking, simply "following the path" is the best approach. Start from the source and work through the network to the destination.

The following issues are presented as tickets, but the focus is on quickly recapping an area of technology in each section.

Link issues are important and becoming more so. Ethernet is ubiquitous in campus networks and data centers. Movement to consolidate networks has collapsed storage and virtualization, and telephony has put more traffic on Ethernet. Maintaining this critical infrastructure involves understanding the component pieces:

- Spanning Tree
- VLANs
- InterVLAN routing
- Gateway redundancy

Hardware

The TSHOOT test spends a lot of time testing commands, but it never hurts to remember the easy ways to diagnose an issue. Using switch link lights is a good example. Link lights show that a physical path exists between two Ethernet devices, as shown in Table 2-1. Over copper, green link lights illustrate that the transmit and receive pairs are properly terminated and each is continuous from one device to the next. An unlit link means that something is wrong—one of the devices is off or the cabling is bad. An orange light means there is a software issue.

Table 2-1   Understanding Link Lights

Light	Resolution
Green	Green lights indicate a physical connection. On copper, they indicate that there is a certain resistance (infinite resistance would mean a broken line). If problems persist, check for electrical interference.
Orange	This indicates a software error, such as ■ Native VLAN mismatch ■ BPDU Guard errors ■ Duplex mismatch ■ STP leaving the port disabled This is best troubleshot through the Command Line Interface (CLI).
Off	Unlit status lights could indicate ■ No cable connected ■ No power ■ Bad cable or connector ■ Bad GBIC ■ Burned-out link light! Try moving the problem: Migrate the cable to another port or replace the cable.

Interface status agrees with the lights as illustrated in Table 2-2. Interfaces come "up" when there is a connected device and when the data link protocol can communicate. Use **show interfaces** to review this status.

Part III: TSHOOT

Table 2-2   Understanding Interface Status

Interface	Interpretation
Interface up/line protocol up	Operational.
Interface up/line protocol down	Possibly no keepalives, encapsulation mismatch, or problem with clock rate.
Interface down/line protocol down	No attached cable, connected device powered off.
Disabled or shutdown	Port is not enabled or a software process has been disabled; port security, for example.
errDisable	Check for a configuration issue, such as EtherChannel misconfiguration, Unidirectional Link Detection (UDLD) problem, Port Aggregation Protocol (PAgP) issue, or BPDU port guard. Use **errdisable detect cause** to troubleshoot. The port can be set to automatically recover with **errdisable recovery**.
Inactive	Assigned VLAN not present.

Sometimes a port isn't down, but it isn't performing as expected. Poor forwarding performance on switches is usually associated with cabling and port problems, duplex mismatch, or Ternary Content Addressable Memory (TCAM) issues.

You can see problems at the physical layer with **show interface**, **show interface counters**, and **show interface counters errors**. Look for the following errors:

- **Align-Err, runs:** Alignment errors are usually associated with cabling, NICs, or duplex mismatch.

- **FCS-Err:** Frame check sequence errors are usually associated with a cabling issue.

- **Xmit-Err:** The transmission buffers are full. Commonly associated with switching a faster link to a slower link.

- **Undersize, Giants:** Suspect the transmitting Network Interface Card (NIC).

- **Single-Col, Multi-Col, Late-Col, Excess-Col:** Collisions are a sign of duplex mismatch.

These commands are shown in Example 2-1.

Example 2-1   Show Interfaces

```
ASW3# show interface fastethernet1/1
FastEthernet1/2 is up, line protocol is up (connected)
  Hardware is C6k 100Mb 802.3, address is 001c.58c8.ac92 (bia
  001c.58c8.ac92)
  MTU 1500 bytes, BW 100000 Kbit, DLY 100 usec,
    reliability 255/255, txload 1/255, rxload 1/255
  Encapsulation ARPA, loopback not set
  Keepalive set (10 sec)
  Full-duplex, 100Mb/s
  input flow-control is off, output flow-control is unsupported
  ARP type: ARPA, ARP Timeout 04:00:00
  Last input never, output 00:00:43, output hang never
  Last clearing of "show interface" counters 6w5d
  Input queue: 0/2000/0/0 (size/max/drops/flushes); Total output
  drops: 0
  Queueing strategy: fifo
  Output queue: 0/40 (size/max)
  1 minute input rate 0 bits/sec, 0 packets/sec
  1 minute output rate 7000 bits/sec, 9 packets/sec
    4182737 packets input, 719363170 bytes, 0 no buffer
    Received 5970 broadcasts (174 multicasts)
    0 runts, 0 giants, 0 throttles
    0 input errors, 0 CRC, 0 frame, 0 overrun, 0 ignored
    0 watchdog, 0 multicast, 0 pause input
    0 input packets with dribble condition detected
    45957071 packets output, 19815895675 bytes, 0 underruns
    0 output errors, 0 collisions, 0 interface resets
    0 babbles, 0 late collision, 0 deferred
    0 lost carrier, 0 no carrier, 0 PAUSE output
    0 output buffer failures, 0 output buffers swapped out

ASW3# show interface counters

Port          InOctets    InUcastPkts    InMcastPkts    InBcastPkts
Fa1/1          6658590         73024             27             95
Fa1/2        719363238       4176768            174           5796
...

ASW3# show interface counters errors

Port   Align-Err   FCS-Err   Xmit-Err    Rcv-Err UnderSize OutDis-
  cards
```

Example 2-1   Continued

Fa1/1	0	309	0	309	0	0
Fa1/2	0	0	0	0	0	0
...						

Duplex mismatch is a common cause of forwarding problems. Half-duplex is unusual in modern networks, so duplex mismatch usually occurs when one port is set to auto and the other to full. Setting everything to auto is the Cisco recommendation.

Note

When speed and duplex are auto, Cisco switches also support auto-MDIX. (The switch adjusts the port to be straight through or crossover as needed.)

```
Interface f0/0
  Mdix auto
```

Troubleshooting Scenario

A user calls to complain that a new lab is not working. Initial tests show that the lab switch (ASW3) is not responding to **ping**, nor is it showing as a CDP neighbor from the distribution switches (DSW1 and 2).

This type of disconnect could be a programming issue, but in this case a quick walk to the new lab shows something interesting. The switch is powered but doesn't show a link light on the uplink port. In this case, a visit to DSW1 demonstrates that the cable hasn't yet been connected.

VLANs

Virtual LANs are logical broadcast domains, administratively assembled from component ports on the switches in the network. Switches are typically interconnected by Ethernet lines that use 802.1q, a shim header inserted in the Ethernet frame.

When troubleshooting VLAN switching issues, concentrate on three types of failure:

- **Wiring issues:** Cabling issues, power outage, or bad switch ports

- **Switch issues:** Software bugs, hardware bugs, loops, and ARP issues

- **Logic issues:** Misconfigured VLANs, VLAN Trunking Protocol, and trunks, and native VLAN mismatch

Troubleshooting VLAN issues often trace the path that traffic takes through the switch. Switches keep several mapping tables that can be used to follow the flow. Table 2-3 shows key mapping tables and IOS commands to examine them.

Table 2-3   Switch Mapping Tables

IOS Command	Table	Notes
show mac address-table	MAC address table	Associates MAC addresses with ports. Use **ipconfig** (Windows) or **ifconfig** (UNIX) to learn a station MAC.
show arp	ARP table	Associate MAC addresses with IP addresses.
show vlan	VLAN database	Lists administratively defined (available) VLANs on this switch.
show vlan, show interface switchport	VLAN assignments	Shows VLAN to port mapping.
show platform tcam table all	TCAM table	Displays TCAM info.
show interface switchport, show interface trunk	Trunk list	Shows trunk ports.

Use **show platform tcam table all** to display the TCAM table.

Start by identifying endpoints and determine their MAC. Remember, if the ultimate endpoint is on a different subnet, the local Layer 2 endpoint is the gateway! After detecting the (intended) source and destination ports, identify any issues that prevent traffic from flowing. Examples include

- Missing VLAN in VLAN database

- Misassigned VLAN

- Trunk or EtherChannel not active

- Broadcast storms

DHCP Troubleshooting Example

A user calls and reports that her PC is down and unable to resolve a DHCP address. Her neighbors' PCs are working fine.

A classic "follow-the-path" approach starts at the user and verifies that she is attached to the switch. Because she doesn't have an IP address, **show**

ARP won't help much, but the MAC can be found from the PC, and **show mac address-table** confirms that the switch has seen traffic from the PC. In this case, the switch doesn't see the PC and **show interfaces** shows the port as *inactive*. The assigned VLAN isn't present in the VLAN database, either through misconfiguration or a VTP error. Because you notice that the gateway address is active, conclude that the port was inappropriately assigned a VLAN.

Spanning Tree Protocol

Redundancy is a common technique to increase availability in computer networks. Most networks are set up with classical Ethernet redundancy: multiple core switches and multiple paths between access switches and the cores. Multiple paths mean loops, and Ethernet lacks a mechanism for dealing with loops.

Spanning Tree is a protocol that detects potential loops and breaks them:

- Each switch advertises Bridge Protocol Data Units (BPDU) that periodically announces name (*bridge ID*), current root, and cost to the root. Each switch starts believing it is the root.

- If a switch receives a BPDU with a different root, it compares roots. If the received BPDU has a lower bridge ID, the switch changes root and recalculates cost to the root. The port that received the superior BPDU is the *root port*—the port that leads to the root. Other ports are *designated ports*—ports leading away from the root.

- Each link has a cost based on its speed, as shown in Table 2-4. Spanning Tree costs have been updated as higher-speed interfaces are introduced, so the default costs vary depending on the IOS version loaded.

Table 2-4   Spanning Tree Link Costs

Link Speed	Cost
Ethernet	100
Fast Ethernet	19
Gigabit Ethernet	4
Ten Gigabit Ethernet	2

- If a switch receives two BPDUs with the same root but different costs, it uses the one with the lower root cost. The port with the higher cost is blocked (it filters all traffic except BPDUs) to prevent a loop. Blocked ports are also called *nondesignated*.

At the end of the process there is one root bridge. Each nonroot switch has one root port.

To see Spanning Tree status, use the **show spanning-tree** [**vlan** *vlan-id*] command, as shown in Example 2-2.

Example 2-2   Spanning Tree

```
ASW1# show spanning-tree vlan 1
VLAN0001
  Spanning tree enabled protocol rstp
  Root ID    Priority    8192
             Address     001d.4664.7d01
             Cost        4
             Port        641 (GigabitEthernet6/1)
             Hello Time  2 sec  Max Age 20 sec  Forward Delay 15 sec

  Bridge ID  Priority    32768
             Address     001d.46c8.ac01
             Hello Time  2 sec  Max Age 20 sec  Forward Delay 15 sec
             Aging Time 300


Interface        Role Sts Cost       Prio.Nbr Type
---------------- ---- --- ---------  -------- --------------------
Fa1/2            Desg FWD 19         128.2    Edge P2p
Fa1/3            Desg FWD 19         128.3    Edge P2p
Fa1/4            Desg FWD 19         128.4    Edge P2p
Fa1/5            Desg FWD 19         128.5    Edge P2p
Fa1/7            Desg FWD 19         128.7    Edge P2p
Fa1/9            Desg FWD 19         128.9    Edge P2p
Fa1/10           Desg FWD 19         128.10   Edge P2p
Fa1/11           Desg FWD 19         128.11   Edge P2p
Fa1/12           Desg FWD 19         128.12   Edge P2p
...
```

To see the details of received BPDUs use **show spanning-tree vlan** [*vlan-id*] **detail**, as illustrated in Example 2-3. This command shows root status, cost, and timers.

Part III: TSHOOT

Example 2-3   Spanning Tree Detail

```
ASW1# show spanning-tree vlan 1 detail

VLAN0001 is executing the rstp compatible Spanning Tree protocol
 Bridge Identifier has priority 32768, address 001d.4664.cc01
 Configured hello time 2, max age 20, forward delay 15, transmit
  hold-count 6
 Current root has priority 8192, address 001d.4632.6c01
 Root port is 641 (GigabitEthernet6/1), cost of root path is 4
 Topology change flag not set, detected flag not set
 Number of topology changes 119 last change occurred 25w6d ago
         from GigabitEthernet6/1
 Times:  hold 1, topology change 35, notification 2
         hello 2, max age 20, forward delay 15
 Timers: hello 0, topology change 0, notification 0, aging 300

 Port 2 (FastEthernet1/2) of VLAN0001 is designated forwarding
   Port path cost 19, Port priority 128, Port Identifier 128.2.
   Designated root has priority 8192, address 001d.4664.ec01
   Designated bridge has priority 32768, address 001d.4664.cc01
   Designated port id is 128.2, designated path cost 4
   Timers: message age 0, forward delay 0, hold 0
   Number of transitions to forwarding state: 1
   The port is in the portfast mode
   Link type is point-to-point by default
   Bpdu guard is enabled
   Root guard is enabled on the port
   BPDU: sent 9120, received 0
   ...
```

Before Spanning Tree, loops meant that traffic cycled continuously. Over a short time traffic accreted in the loop until it consumed all capacity. This is called a *broadcast storm*. Broadcast storms are still a real danger, but Spanning Tree has mitigated this almost entirely. The danger today is that—through protocol failure or administrative misprogramming—when a broadcast storm forms, few administrators have seen it before and know how to deal with it.

A broadcast storm can be diagnosed when the switches become saturated with traffic. All the traffic lights are solid, the switch is slow to respond, and users complain about network speed.

The only fix for a broadcast storm is to break the loop. If the switches are accessible, it might be possible to fix Spanning Tree. Otherwise, the administrator must manually remove redundant links.

As previously stated, the purpose of Spanning Tree is to select one root path and filter all others. When there are multiple links between two switches it seems intuitive that, rather than turn one off, the switches use all the links together. This is possible using EtherChannel.

Cisco has a number of Spanning Tree enhancements, including PortFast, BPDU Guard, and BPDU Filter. These three enhancements are particularly interesting because they can easily affect user connectivity.

PortFast is used on ports where it is assumed there is an end system. It enables a switch port to skip the listening and learning stages of the Spanning Tree startup and start forwarding traffic immediately. It shuts down and goes through the full startup process if it sees a BPDU. Without PortFast, interfaces often start too slowly for DHCP to complete, and users end up without an address.

BPDU Guard causes a port to go into an errDisable state if a BPDU is seen. If BPDU Guard is enabled globally, BPDU Guard is applied to all PortFast ports. BPDU filtering prevents ports from sending out BPDUs and is similarly enabled on all PortFast ports when globally enabled.

EtherChannel logically combines several physical links between switches, and Spanning Tree treats the bundle as a single port. Up to eight physical lines may be combined in this way.

EtherChannel failures cluster into three groups:

- All ports must be identical (speed, duplex, access or trunk, VLAN). If EtherChannel does not form, look for inconsistencies between ports.

- Both switches must either be enabled statically or a link aggregation protocol (LACP or PAgP) must be used. If only one side is configured for EtherChannel, look for EtherChannel ports that are error disabled.

- The channel might form, but traffic might still be traveling predominately over a single link. This is because traffic is statistically multiplexed using a three-bit hash. This means that the traffic is split over eight paths, and an EtherChannel of three links will split the load in a 2:1:1 ratio. Fix this by using 2, 4, or 8 links. Second, the hash uses a user-selectable Ethernet or IP field. If all traffic comes from a single source and the switch is hashing on source MAC, it does not multiplex. Fix this by selecting a different hashing method.

Part III: TSHOOT

BPDU Guard Example

A user calls to report that his port is down. Using the follow-the-path process, the MAC address of the PC is not found on the switch. The **show interface status** command, however, does show a port as errDisabled. BPDU Guard has disabled the port because the user tried to attach an unsanctioned device—a consumer access point—to the network.

SVIs

Routing between VLANs is accomplished on a Layer 3 switch or on a router. Troubleshooting the control plane (the Layer 3 structures) is identical between the two. This means that OSPF runs the same on the two platforms.

The data plane (the structures and hardware that handle frame forwarding) is different between routers and Layer 3 switches. In both cases, using **show ip cef** shows the CEF forwarding table, and **show adjacency** displays the Layer 2 headers used in forwarding.

On Catalyst 3560, 3750, and 4500 switches you can also use **show platform** to see detailed forwarding information.

Get Catalyst 6500 switches to display forwarding details by using **show mls cef** commands.

Another difference between routers and Layer 3 switches, in the context of troubleshooting interVLAN routing, is the concept of a switched virtual interface (SVI).

Routers forward traffic between ports using Layer 3 information.

Layer 3 switches make a port a routed port, like a router, or can have multiple ports in the same Layer 3 subnet and aggregate them together logically. A virtual port that handles the routing (a switched virtual interface or SVI) is used for the configuration.

From a troubleshooting perspective, routed ports and SVIs do not run switching protocols like Spanning Tree or EtherChannel. SVIs are extremely stable. An SVI changes only state to down when all the VLAN ports are down.

Troubleshoot SVIs

To separate the routing function and the VLAN piece, troubleshoot SVI just like a VLAN connection to a router.

- Confirm the VLAN is active by using **show vlan brief**.

- Confirm the VLAN is correctly assigned using **show vlan id 123**.

- Troubleshoot any trunks or EtherChannels along the path.

Examine the routing function. Confirm that the IP information is correct and consistent, and verify that routing information has populated correctly.

Trunking and EtherChannel

Trunking enables uplink ports (ports between switches) to carry traffic in more than one VLAN. EtherChannel permits multiple ports to be grouped into one logical interface. The EtherChannel has a capacity equal to the sum of its component links, load balances across links, and fails gracefully (so a bad member link is simply not used for traffic). Spanning Tree treats the EtherChannel as one line.

For trunking to work correctly, trunking mode, encapsulation, native VLAN, and allowed VLANs must match. Mode can be on (**switchport mode trunk**—local end is always trunking), auto (**switchport mode dynamic auto**—trunk if the other side tries to trunk), or desirable (**switchport mode dynamic desirable**—try to trunk).

Both ends must use the same trunking encapsulation. Inter-Switch Link (ISL) is an older standard that is for the most part deprecated—IEEE 802.1q is almost always used today. Native VLAN is the assumed VLAN of untagged frames. Trunks can support some or all VLANs, but peer ports must support the same list.

Generically, both ends must be set up as in Example 2-4. Verify trunking by using **show switchport trunk**.

Example 2-4   Trunk

```
Switchport mode trunk
Switchport trunk encapsulation dot1q
Switchport trunk native vlan …
Switchport trunk allowed …
```

EtherChannel ports move into an errDisable state for a number of reasons, including if the neighbor isn't configured as an EtherChannel, a unidirectional link detection (UDLD) failure, or for a trunking failure.

EtherChannels are configured by placing interfaces into a channel group and configuring the port-channel interface as shown in Example 2-5. The channel number dictates the port-channel interface number.

Example 2-5   EtherChannel

```
Interface GigabitEthernet0/1
    Switchport mode trunk
    Channel-group 1 mode on
Interface port-channel 1
```

Verify the EtherChannel setup with **show interface port-channel** or **show etherchannel summary**, as shown in Example 2-6.

Example 2-6   Show EtherChannel

```
DSW1# show interface port-channel 1
Port-channel1 is up, line protocol is up
...
 Members in this channel: Gi0/1 Gi0/2

DSW1# show etherchannel 1 summary
Flags:  D - down          P - in port-channel
        I - stand-alone s - suspended
        R - Layer3        S - Layer2
        U - port-channel in use
Group Port-channel  Ports
-----+------------+---------------------------------------------------
1     Po1(SU)      Gi0/1(P)   Gi0/2(P)
```

Port Security

Port security restricts the MAC addresses allowed to connect to a switch port. It can be configured administratively to allow specific addresses, to dynamically limit to the first addresses seen, or both. Unwelcome source MAC addresses are called a *security violation* and the port can react by dropping the traffic, dropping traffic with a SecurityViolation error, or disabling the interface.

Configure port security as shown in Example 2-7. Security violations can be set to protect (drop traffic), restrict (error), or shut down. By default, secure ports are limited to one device but this can be configured. Permitted devices may be either statically assigned or "sticky." Sticky ports dynamically restrict themselves to the first MAC address(es) seen.

Example 2-7   Port Security

```
Interface gigabitethernet1/1
    Switchport port-security
    Switchport port-security violation shutdown
    Switchport port-security maximum 2
    Switchport port-security mac-address sticky
```

Sticky MAC addresses are cleared by shutting down the port and reenabling it, by the **clear port-security dynamic** command, or allowed to reset themselves periodically with the **errdisable recovery cause psecure-violation** command.

Port security does not support EtherChannel ports, SPAN ports, or dynamic trunks. You can review settings as shown in Example 2-8.

Example 2-8   Show Port Security

```
ASW1# show port-security
 Secure Port  MaxSecureAddr  CurrentAddr SecurityViolation  Security
 Action
              (Count)        (Count)       (Count)
--------------------------------------------------------------------
     Fa1/1    1              1             0                Shutdown
     Fa1/2    3              2             0                Restrict
     Fa1/3    2              2             0                Protect
--------------------------------------------------------------------
```

Port security can be a huge commitment of time to support, so it is usually employed only in public areas and when use rarely changes. For instance, companies wouldn't want someone to unplug the guest phone in the lobby and use that port to access the corporate network! The most common troubleshooting problem is that it works as intended, but the user is confused because a port that was "just working" is suddenly dead. The confusion can lead a guilty party to call the IT helpdesk!

Part III: TSHOOT

CHAPTER 3

Troubleshooting IP Networking

IP Address Assignment

This section describes issues regarding IP services and starts with a discussion about IP addressing. Even when Layer 2 connectivity is intact, failures at Layer 3 prevent communication.

IP addresses identify interfaces, not devices. The principal IP parameters are address, subnet mask, and (except on routers) default gateway. Addresses are unique, but a mask and gateway should be common on a subnet. Address information can be either statically assigned or obtained from Dynamic Host Configuration Protocol (DHCP).

When troubleshooting IP connectivity, refer to the following steps:

Step 1. Use **traceroute** to test connectivity or (if broken) the last point working in the path.

Step 2. If the problem is in the local subnet, ensure that the IP address is unique. Non-unique addresses create a log message that looks like "1w2d: %IP-4-DUPADDR: Duplicate address 10.1.1.1 on FastEthernet0/1, sourced by 0002.1234.5678." Also ensure that the subnet mask is the same as the one on the gateway, and that the gateway IP is correct. Many organizations use the first usable address in the subnet for the default gateway to prevent such confusion.

Step 3. If the problem is between the local subnet and the endpoint, verify whether routes exist on the intermediate devices. It is easy to forget to troubleshoot the return path, but make sure you check this as well. If the far end doesn't know how to route back, the symptoms will be identical to an outbound routing problem.

Step 4. Check intermediate devices for logic that would interfere with routing, such as policy-based routing, access lists, and network address translation. If possible, remove these elements for testing.

Addresses can also be assigned through DHCP. DHCP is sometimes used for network devices, particularly on commodity connections to service providers. More commonly, DHCP is used on end systems, and troubleshooting from a network perspective involves understanding how DHCP is supported by the router.

DHCP passes configuration information, including IP configuration, upon request. A client sends a broadcast DHCPDiscover to ask for information and the server responds with DHCPOffer. Because more than one DHCP server could respond, the client responds to the offer it is accepting with DHCPRequest. Most clients accept the first offer received. Routers can either act as DHCP servers or as relays, which forward the broadcasts to remote servers.

A simple DHCP configuration is shown in Example 3-1. It supplies DHCP addresses in the range 10.1.1.0/24 and runs on the interface attached to that subnet. Verify the current assigned addresses using **show ip dhcp binding** or **show ip dhcp pool**. You can also see the action of DHCP by using **debug ip dhcp server packet|event**.

Example 3-1   DHCP

```
Ip dchp pool tshoot
  Network 10.1.1.0 255.255.255.0
  Default-router 10.1.1.1
  Dns-server 10.1.1.3
```

Supporting a remote DHCP server requires forwarding broadcast DHCPDiscover messages to a remote server. For instance, a branch core switch might forward DHCP requests back to a central resource using the helper address, as shown in the following configuration:

```
Interface vlan100
  Ip helper-address 10.1.1.1
```

DHCP events can create a disproportionate amount of drama because of the impact on users. The principal way to recognize a DHCP problem is that PCs have addresses that start 169.254. These are auto-assigned addresses used when no DHCP server is found. DHCP problems break into three large groups.

Start-up problems are issues where network connectivity starts slowly and is not in place until after the DHCP process times out. A perfect example is when spanning-tree startup places a port in blocking. Start-up issues can be recognized because rerunning DHCP works after the port is active (on Windows, this can be tested using **winipcfg/renew**). Spanning-tree startup can be fixed by applying PortFast.

Part III: TSHOOT

Connectivity failures to the server also prevent DHCP from completing as expected. In this second type of problem, PCs also auto-assign an address but will not be fixable by renewing later. Troubleshoot this by following the path back to the DHCP server and verifying whether DHCP traffic can flow. DHCP servers can fail, and a best practice is to run multiple DHCP servers within an enterprise. A failed server is also verified (and worked around) by temporarily placing a DHCP server on the local router.

The third group of DHCP problems is the ignorant or malicious introduction of an unauthorized DHCP server in the network. Surprise! If a consumer device is brought in, such as a wireless access point, it can be recognized by 192.168.1.0/24 addresses being assigned. When a rogue DHCP server is introduced maliciously, detecting it can be difficult. An attacker could do this to assign legitimate addresses with a traffic capture device listed as the gateway. When recognized, the ARP table can be used to track back the switch port of the bogus gateway.

DHCP snooping is a technique to deal with spurious DHCP offers. An administrator identifies a port that has an authorized DHCP server (this works best if the DHCP server is the only device attached through that port). DHCP snooping then drops DHCPOffers coming from untrusted ports. It also drops release messages coming from ports other than the port where a user was assigned a given address. Violations also get logged, such as %DHCP_SNOOPING-5-DHCP_SNOOPING_UNTRUSTED_PORT.

Configure DHCP snooping globally and identify a trusted interface as shown in the following configuration. View DHCP snooping information by using **show ip dhcp snooping**.

```
DSW1(config)# ip dhcp snooping
DSW1(config)# interface f1/1
DSW1(config-if)# ip dhcp snooping trust
```

NTP, Syslog, and SNMP

NTP, Syslog, and SNMP are services that aid in troubleshooting. Each needs to be set up beforehand so that data can be used in the troubleshooting process. Network Time Protocol (NTP) helps establish causality—which event came first—when comparing logs from different devices. Syslog allows log collection in a central location. Simple Network Management Protocol (SNMP) collects network telemetry in a central location. SNMP can gather data points, such as capacity utilization, processor and memory usage, and error rate. From the SNMP collector, these data points can be graphed to show sudden changes or to analyze trends and suggest proactive next steps.

NTP

Example 3-2 is a standard NTP setup. NTP starts by identifying a time zone. NTP draws time from a time server on the Internet—clock1.unc.edu in this example—and acts as a time server (master) for the network. Two important pieces to this configuration are to protect time records from changes meant to obfuscate an attack (time communication is encrypted to prevent malicious changes to time records) and to communicate time to known devices only.

Example 3-2   NTP Configuration

```
clock timezone EST -5
clock summer-time CDT recurring
clock calendar-valid
ntp update-calendar

ntp master 2          !stratum 2
ntp authenticate
ntp authentication-key 11 md5 tshoot
ntp trusted-key 11

access-list 1 permit clock1.unc.edu
access-list 1 deny any
access-list 2 permit R2
access-list 2 deny any

ntp access-group peer 2
ntp access-group serve-only 1

ntp server clock1.unc.edu
ntp peer R2
```

Verify NTP using **show ntp associations**. In Example 3-3, a public NTP server is specified and synched. If a server does not sync, it is almost always because of a communication issue. Troubleshoot by verifying whether the server is reachable with **ping** and that NTP traffic is not blocked by a firewall or access list.

Example 3-3   NTP Associations

```
R1# show ntp associations
address              ref clock          st      when    poll    reach
  delay     offset   disp
*~152.2.21.1         152.2.21.1         1       29      1024    377
  4.2      -8.59     1.6
* master (synced), # master (unsynced), + selected, - candidate,
  ~ configured
```

Syslog

Logging errors to the system is enabled by default, but it must be enabled to ship the logs to a remote destination. The logging level must be specified as well. Figure 3-1 illustrates levels 0 through 7. Logging at least at level 3 and making sure that the time on the device is accurate are good practices.

Figure 3-1   Logging Levels

7. Debugging
6. Information
5. Notifications
4. Warnings
3. Errors
2. Critical
1. Alerts
0. Emergencies

Logging issues are generally related to routing; however, the local device keeps a copy of its logs in memory and can be referenced if logs are not flowing to the central server. A generic configuration for logging is shown in the following configuration:

```
Service timestamps log datetime
Logging trap 3
```

SNMP

Most of TSHOOT concerns active break/fix situations, but the most common problems are usually the slowly developing, insidious type. A good example is when capacity utilization creeps up. By the time the default network monitoring system (users) recognize there is an issue, it is too late! Ordering and receiving new service takes months, during which time service will be unsatisfactory. Enterprises of any size should have some system to gather SNMP telemetry and analyze it regularly. A number of commercial and open-source packages are quite good.

SNMP is also a way for an attacker to control a network, so it must be used cautiously, kept updated, and secured. A sample SNMP configuration is shown in Example 3-4.

Example 3-4   SNMP Access List

```
Snmp-server community tsh0ot RO
Snmp-server community S3cret RW 10
Snmp-enable traps
Snmp-server host 10.1.1.3
Ip access-list 10 permit host 10.1.1.3
```

Two communities are defined—one is read-only and one allows administrative changes. The read/write string is limited to the defined host.

Gateway Redundancy

Hosts are configured with a default gateway—a router address that passes traffic off the local subnet. The problem is that router failures strand the hosts. The solution is first-hop redundancy protocols, which enable two routers to cooperatively support a single IP, which is then given to hosts as a default gateway.

The three first-hop redundancy protocols are as follow:

- Hot Standby Router Protocol (HSRP) is an older Cisco proprietary protocol. One router is the active and one is the standby. The routers pass keepalives that enable the standby to recognize failure of the primary router.

- Virtual Router Redundancy Protocol (VRRP) is an open standard but is otherwise similar to HSRP. Because HSRP works, many organizations have continued to use it.

- Gateway Load Balancing Protocol (GLBP) is an open standard, but it enables simultaneous load balancing over as many as four gateways.

Because HSRP is the most common, this section focuses on HSRP. The general configuration and troubleshooting strategy applies as well to VRRP and GLBP, however.

Part III: TSHOOT

HSRP is configured under the interface using standby commands. Routers in the same HSRP group share a MAC address and IP address, so **standby** is used to identify the group and virtual IP.

By default, each HSRP speaker has a priority of 100. The speaker with the highest priority is the active router. If a new router starts, however, HSRP does not change the active router until the failure of the active router. To change this so that the higher priority is instantly recognized, use the **preempt** command. Example 3-5 shows an HSRP snippet to illustrate the configuration.

Example 3-5   Example HSRP

```
Interface f0/0
  Ip address 10.1.1.2 255.255.255.0
  Standby 2 ip 10.1.1.1
  Standby 2 priority 120
  Standby 2 preempt
```

Verify the HSRP state of a router using **show standby**, which summarizes this information to a table as shown in Example 3-6. To see detailed information on HSRP, such as timers and virtual MAC, use **show standby** (as shown in this example).

Example 3-6   HSRP

```
R1# show standby
GigabitEthernet0/1 - Group 135
  State is Active
    23 state changes, last state change 25w6d
  Virtual IP address is 135.159.64.1
  Active virtual MAC address is 0000.0c07.ac87
    Local virtual MAC address is 0000.0c07.ac87 (v1 default)
  Hello time 5 sec, hold time 20 sec
    Next hello sent in 0.284 secs
  Preemption enabled
  Active router is local
  Standby router is unknown
  Priority 150 (configured 150)
  Group name is "hsrp-Gi0/1-135" (default)
Richardson-rtr01# show standby interface gi0/1
Global            Config: 0000
Gi0/1 If hw       BCM1125 Internal MAC (27), State 0x210040
Gi0/1 If hw       Config: 0000
Gi0/1 If hw       Flags: 0000
Gi0/1 If sw       Config: 0000
```

```
Gi0/1 If sw      Flags: 0000
Gi0/1 Grp 135    Confg: 0072, IP_PRI, PRIORITY, PREEMPT, TIMERS
Gi0/1 Grp 135    Flags: 0000

HSRP virtual IP Hash Table (global)
103 172.25.96.1    Gi0/1      Grp 135

HSRP MAC Address Table
43 Gi0/1 0000.0c07.ac87
   Gi0/1 Grp 135
```

Just as **show standby brief** provides an HSRP overview, **show vrrp brief** and **show glbp brief** describe the VRRP and GLBP environments, respectively. Similarly, **show standby interface** and **debug standby** have equivalents for the other first-hop redundancy protocols.

A simple configuration for HSRP might look like the following:

```
Interface f0/0
 Ip address 10.1.1.2 255.255.255.0
 Standby 43 ip 10.1.1.1
```

Troubleshoot first-hop redundancy protocols by using the following steps:

Step 1. Make sure that the "real" address of the routers is unique. Two routers in a standby group each have a different permanent address. In the previous simple configuration, the interface is addressed as 10.1.1.2/24.

Step 2. Check that the standby IP and group numbers match. In the previous configuration, the interface is in HSRP group 43 and the shared IP is 10.1.1.1.

Step 3. Verify that the standby IP address is in the local subnet. If the shared address isn't in the local subnet, local devices won't be able to reach it! In the earlier configuration, 10.1.1.1 is in the 10.1.1.0/24 subnet.

Step 4. Verify whether access lists are not filtering standby traffic. Access lists must permit keepalive traffic between the participating routers and allow clients to use both routers as a gateway.

Filtering

Access lists (ACL) are a tool to block traffic as it crosses a router. Standard IP access lists filter traffic based on source address. Extended access lists filter traffic based on source and destination IP address, as well as transport layer details.

Note

Filter traffic based on destination address using a route to null0. To filter traffic going to 192.168.21.0/24, enter a static route: **ip route 192.168.21.0 255.255.255.0 null0**.

Standard IP access lists are numbered 1–99 or named. Extended access lists are numbered 100–199 or named. Using named access lists is strongly encouraged because this aids in understanding the intent of the ACL later. Access lists are applied to interfaces in a direction (in or out, relative to the device), and access lists always end with an implicit deny.

A simple standard access list might be used on the perimeter to block bogus source addresses (known as *bogons*) as illustrated in Example 3-7. Assuming that fastethernet1/1 is the outside interface, the access list needs to be applied inbound (traffic coming into the router from outside would have source addresses that should be blocked).

Example 3-7   Bogon List

```
Interface fastethernet1/1
  Ip access-group bogon_list in
Ip access-list standard bogon_list
  Deny 0.0.0.0 0.255.255.255
  Deny 10.0.0.0 0.255.255.255
  Deny 127.0.0.0 0.255.255.255
  Deny 169.254.0.0 0.0.255.255
  Deny 172.16.0.0 0.15.255.255
  Deny 192.168.0.0 0.0.255.255
  Deny 224.0.0.0 31.255.255.255
  Permit any
```

A slightly more complicated configuration might be used to limit access from a "guest" network as shown in Example 3-8. The idea here is that guests are allowed to attach through fastethernet1/2 (perhaps this is attached to a wireless access point). Guests should be allowed DNS and web access, but nothing else. Note that the access list allows tcp/80 and udp/53—everything else is denied implicitly.

Example 3-8   Guest ACL

```
Interface fastethernet1/2
  Ip access-group guest_access in
Ip access-list extended guest_access
```

```
Permit tcp any any eq 80
Permit udp any any eq 53
```

Focus on four principal areas for access list troubleshooting:

1. Is this an ACL problem? If possible, remove the access list and test.

2. Check the applied interface and direction. The temptation is to review the access list first, but verifying direction is important so that sources and destinations are correctly interpreted. It is also possible that the applied interface is not on the path the traffic is taking!

3. Check the access list entries. Are addresses and port numbers entered correctly?

4. Review the order of operations. Remember that ACLs are processed top-down and the first match (permit or deny) is executed. Could the traffic be matching an earlier statement? Check this by moving the line in question to the top of the list temporarily.

NAT

Network Address Translation (NAT) is the process of translating source or destination IP addresses as traffic traverses a router. Router interfaces are described as outside (the public side) or inside (the private side). Translations are described from points of view—*local* describes the address seen by an inside observer and *global* describes what a public observer sees, as shown in Figure 3-2.

Figure 3-2   NAT Terms

NAT can map addresses to pool or to a single address. Mapping all the inside connections to a single public address is an example of Port Address Translation (PAT) or overloading.

Steps to Troubleshooting NAT

Consider the following steps to troubleshooting NAT. Each step is explored further in the sections that follow.

Step 1. Attempt to rule out NAT. Check connectivity.

Step 2. Understand the objective of NAT.

Step 3. Verify the translation.

Step 4. Verify whether the translation is being used.

Rule Out NAT

From the translating router, source a **ping** from the outside interface as shown in Figure 3-3. This verifies that traffic flows bidirectionally from the router and that neighbors have a return route. If **ping** doesn't work, check the connectivity from the router. If all lines appear stable, then investigate routing, especially the return path.

Figure 3-3 Simple NAT

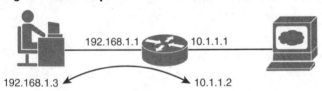

192.168.1.1   10.1.1.1

192.168.1.3   10.1.1.2

As shown in Figure 3-3, use an extended **ping** or **traceroute** to originate traffic from the 10.1.1.1 interface to check connectivity. If possible, examine neighboring devices to determine whether their routing tables include the return route to 10.1.1.0/24.

Understand the Objective of NAT

Review what the NAT configuration is trying to accomplish, and verify that all elements of the configuration appear correct. A generic configuration for NAT identifies inside and outside interfaces and an **ip nat** command as shown in Example 3-9. A common error is to either not identify or to misidentify interfaces.

Example 3-9 Simple NAT 1:1 Configuration

```
Interface f0/0
  Ip add 10.1.1.1 255.255.255.0
  Ip nat outside
Interface f0/1
  Ip address 192.168.1.2 255.255.255.0
  Ip nat inside
Ip nat inside source static 192.168.1.3 10.1.1.2
```

In Example 3-9, which builds on Figure 3-3, the router is being asked to translate traffic from the user to a single outside address. Note that the inside and outside are correctly identified and that the **ip nat** statement has the addresses in the correct order.

Verify the Translation

Make sure that the translation is entered into the translation table on the router correctly. This is accomplished by using **show ip nat translation**. We are translating the inside address, so the following configuration tells us that the inside address, as seen from the Internet, is 10.1.1.2. The inside address, as seen from the private network, is 192.168.1.3.

```
R2# show ip nat translation
Pro Inside global    Inside local     Outside local    Outside global
--- 10.1.1.2         192.168.1.3      ---              ---
```

Verify the Translation Is Being Used

Having checked the configuration and the translation table, the last step is to ensure that the traffic is actually being translated. This is accomplished by using **debug ip nat**. Example 3-10 shows the debug output. Here, the PC is pinging an outside address to create traffic.

Example 3-10   debug NAT

```
R2# debug ip nat
R2# show log
Syslog logging: enabled (0 messages dropped, 0 flushes, 0 overruns)
        Console logging: level debugging, 39 messages logged
        Monitor logging: level debugging, 0 messages logged
        Buffer logging: level debugging, 39 messages logged
        Trap logging: level informational, 33 message lines logged

Log Buffer (4096 bytes):

13:53:33: NAT: s=192.168.1.3->10.1.1.2, d=10.1.1.100[70]
13:53:33: NAT*: s=10.1.1.100, d=10.1.1.2->192.168.1.3 [70]
```

Some less common errors can occur in translation, but examining the system log as shown in the preceding calls out these issues as well.

Authentication

Authentication verifies whether legitimate users are accessing the device. CCNA covers simple authentication, such as the enable password. In enterprise networks, using "box passwords" becomes difficult to manage. Passwords become old and can't easily be changed when administrators leave the company.

Centralized authentication is therefore important as networks grow. Centralized authentication is commonly accomplished through TACACS+ or RADIUS servers (IOS also supports Kerberos). Multiple authentication checks can be specified—these are checked in order, checking subsequent sources only if the preceding method times out.

When you're configuring authentication, specify a method name (in Example 3-11 this is *widgets*). If the method name is the default, then the method is applied to all appropriate interfaces on the router. Example 3-11 creates a widgets method and applies it to telnet sessions. Widgets checks an ACS server using TACACS, and if that times out, widgets refers to the local username and password.

Example 3-11   Authentication

```
Aaa new-model
Aaa authentication login widgets group tacacs+ local
Tacacs-server host 10.1.1.3
Tacacs-server key 5tandardW1dg3t5
Username admin password tshoot
Line vty 0 4
   Login authentication widgets
```

Troubleshooting Authentication, Authorization, and Accounting (AAA) involves three important checks:

1. Verify whether the server is working. Can other devices authenticate using the server?
2. Confirm whether the server is reachable. Can you **ping** the server? Is the shared secret correct?
3. Verify whether the credentials are spelled correctly and are still valid.

CHAPTER 4

Troubleshooting Routing Technologies

Network Layer Connectivity

Routers use three tables to make routing decisions: the routing table, ARP table, and CEF mappings.

The routing table is visible using **show ip route**. Each entry in the routing table has an output interface or next hop. Packets are routed per the routing table, matching the longest prefix match. If two identical routes are available, then routing is determined by IGP metrics.

When a determination of the next hop has been made, the router must turn this information into a destination Layer 2 address. For this purpose, mapping tables are maintained that match Layer 2 and Layer 3 addresses. The ARP table (**show ip arp**) is an example of this.

Cisco Express Forwarding (CEF) is the common switching method found on most Cisco gear. CEF combines information from the routing table and the various mapping tables to optimize routing and the construction of new Layer 2 headers. You can view CEF entries using **show ip cef** and associated commands.

When troubleshooting forwarding, start by verifying whether the next hop address is reachable by pinging. If it's not, make sure that the local IP information (such as subnet mask) is correct. Also, check the address and make sure that Layer 2 mapping is correct. The following are other potential issues:

- Duplicate IP addresses
- Bad or disconnected cable
- Access-list filtering

Routing Protocols

Routing protocols are mechanisms that enable routers to share information about the structure of the network. Regardless of the protocol, troubleshooting routing protocol issues has some basic logic that is true for any routing protocol. Troubleshooting routing issues always starts by looking at the routing table. Use **ping** to test connectivity, **show ip route** to inspect the routing table to see whether the route is present, and **traceroute** to inspect how traffic is forwarding. **Show ip protocols** displays information about the current routing protocols, such as autonomous system and timer values.

Troubleshooting routing issues can be summarized by answering three basic questions:

1. Is the correct route advertised?

2. Is the correct route communicated?

3. Is there a more desirable path (lower administrative distance [AD] or longer prefix length)?

One easy way to test routing is to insert a static route. The static route has a lower administrative distance than the one received from a routing protocol and is preferred while in place. This enables you to separate the forwarding issue from the routing protocol.

Router Performance

Routing protocol performance can be symptomatic of general router problems. Routing protocol problems can be seen if the router CPU is overburdened or memory is fully utilized.

Transient events, such as ARP resolution, SNMP communication, or a heavy traffic load, can temporarily spike the CPU. High CPU utilization is a concern when it becomes ongoing. Signs of CPU oversubscription include dropped packets, increased latency, slow response to telnet and console, and when the router skips routing updates.

Show process cpu is the best way to look at CPU utilization, although the best approach is to track and trend this variable via SNMP. Utilization is reported as a percentage. Keep in mind that the router should not run 100%; it needs some extra power to work around short-term issues and if the CPU is overutilized it cannot handle all processes. A reasonable approach is to start considering upgrading a router that is idling above 50%, with more urgency as that number gets higher. **Show process cpu | sorted** can identify processes that are consuming CPU cycles. The ARP input process consumes more cycles if the router has to generate a large number of ARPs; for instance, in response to malicious traffic. Net Background is used to manage buffer space. IP Background is used whenever an interface changes state; utilization here could indicate a flapping interface.

Heavy utilization that isn't dependent on load is a sign of a runaway process. A runaway process continues to utilize more and more CPU cycles. When you see it, you can resolve it temporarily by a reboot, but the issue reoccurs over time. Work through Cisco to update the operating system if you see this situation. **Show process cpu** is shown in Example 4-1.

Example 4-1   CPU Utilization

```
R1# show processes cpu
    CPU utilization for five seconds: 8%/4%; one minute: 6%; five
      minutes: 5%
    PID Runtime(uS)   Invoked  uSecs   5Sec   1Min  5Min TTY
      Process
    1        384      32289     11   0.00%  0.00%  0.00%
      0 Load Meter
```

Show process cpu history displays the overall utilization as a bar graph, as shown in Example 4-2. This is a smart way to see whether the current load is an aberration or the norm.

Example 4-2   Graphical Display of CPU Utilization

```
R1# show processes cpu history
...

    6665776865756676676666667667677676766666766767767666566667
    6378016198993513709771991443732358689932740858269643922613
100
 90
 80         *   *                  * *     *   * *   *
 70   * *  *****  *   **  ***** ***   ****  ******  *  *******     * *
 60   #***##*##*#***#####*#*###*****#*###*#*#*##*#*##*#*##*****#
 50   ##########################################################
 40   ##########################################################
 30   ##########################################################
 20   ##########################################################
 10   ##########################################################
```

Example 4-2 Continued

```
 0....5....1....1....2....2....3....3....4....4....5....5....
         0    5    0    5    0    5    0    5    0    5

              CPU% per minute (last 60 minutes)
           * = maximum CPU%    # = average CPU%
```

A second general router issue is the router switching mode. The three common modes are

- **Process switching:** Uses the CPU to process each packet. Process switching is CPU intensive and reduces throughput and increases jitter. It is used when CEF and fast switching are not. Disable CEF with the command **no ip cef** and turn off fast switching using **no ip route-cache**.

- **Fast switching:** Uses the CPU to process an initial packet but then caches the result. It is less CPU intensive, but utilization still tracks the traffic load. Turn it on using **ip route-cache**, and review the cache using **show ip cache**.

- **Cisco Express Forwarding (CEF):** The default switching mode. CEF is resilient to traffic load. Turn it on using **ip cef**, and see CEF entries by using **show ip cef** and **show adjacency**. CEF is required for some IOS features, such as Network Based Application Recognition (NBAR), Weighted Random Early Detection (WRED), and AutoQoS.

Show the interface switching mode using the **show ip interface** command.

A third general router issue is router memory utilization. Memory is over-used when no available system memory exists or when the memory is too fragmented to be useful. Memory, like CPU, is a good variable to track and trend via SNMP. Routers can be upgraded or replaced before utilization issues occur.

One easy, but not pleasant, way to see a memory problem is to load a version of IOS that requires more RAM than is present on the router. Memory can also be depleted by a memory leak—a bug that assigns memory to processes but does not clean up when the process is complete. You can recognize memory leaks over time using **show memory allocating-process totals** and **show memory dead** and by researching known bugs within Cisco Connection Online (CCO). If found, the only solution is to move to a sound version of IOS.

Memory leaks sometimes appear on interfaces as buffer leaks. You can see buffer leaks using **show interface**, where the "input queue" shows buffer utilization. **Show buffer** also illustrates a buffer leak, here by looking at the number of free buffers.

Finally, you sometimes see memory leaks in Border Gateway Protocol (BGP), which is a heavy consumer of memory in the best of times, so a memory leak here can quickly bloom into a larger issue. **Show process memory | include bgp** shows the memory utilization of the four BGP processes. Use **show diag** to evaluate memory used on the line cards.

EIGRP

After you determine a routing problem in EIGRP using the routing table or **ping**, answer three basic questions to troubleshooting: Is the correct route advertised? Is the correct route communicated (and used)? Is there a "better" route in the routing table?

EIGRP stores information in three tables that can be interrogated as shown in Table 4-1.

Table 4-1   EIGRP Table Lists

Command	Table	Description
show ip eigrp interface	Interface	Lists EIGRP-enabled interfaces
show ip eigrp neighbors	Neighbor	Lists discovered neighbors
show ip eigrp topology	Topology	Lists received EIGRP routes

Is the Correct Route Advertised?

Verify whether the router attached to the destination subnet is advertising the route. There are several ways to see the advertised subnets; two good methods are either direct interrogation of the running configuration using **show running-config | section eigrp** or by reviewing the protocol settings using **show ip protocol**, as shown in Example 4-3.

Example 4-3   show IP protocol for EIGRP

```
R1# show ip protocol
Routing Protocol is "eigrp 10"
  Outgoing update filter list for all interfaces is not set
  Incoming update filter list for all interfaces is not set
  Default networks flagged in outgoing updates
```

Example 4-3   Continued

```
Default networks accepted from incoming updates
EIGRP metric weight K1=1, K2=0, K3=1, K4=0, K5=0
EIGRP maximum hopcount 100
EIGRP maximum metric variance 1
Redistributing: eigrp 100, bgp 65096
EIGRP NSF-aware route hold timer is 240s
Automatic network summarization is not in effect
Maximum path: 4
Routing for Networks:
   10.0.0.0
Passive Interface(s):
   GigabitEthernet0/1
Routing Information Sources:
   Gateway         Distance      Last Update
   10.1.4.254            90      00:39:11
   10.1.4.253            90      00:38:55
Distance: internal 90 external 170
```

EIGRP advertises only subnets of interfaces that match a network statement. The **show ip protocol** command provides the matching network statements.

Is the Correct Route Communicated?

Enhanced Internet Gateway Routing Protocol (EIGRP) shares routes only with neighbors—devices with which it has exchanged hellos. Verify that connected devices are neighbors using **show ip eigrp neighbors**. **Debug ip eigrp packets** shows hellos and updates if devices are connected, and **debug ip eigrp** reveals details about the contained routing information communicated.

EIGRP can form neighbors only when several conditions are met, including bidirectional communication, authentication, a consistent autonomous system (AS), and that timers are close to the same. EIGRP also sends hellos only over interfaces that match a network statement. If a router hasn't identified a link as an EIGRP link in this way, it does not send hellos and form a neighborship relationship. EIGRP values, such as timers, and a list of EIGRP interfaces, are available through **show ip eigrp interfaces**, as shown in Example 4-4.

Example 4-4   show ip eigrp neighbors

```
R1# show ip eigrp neighbors
IP-EIGRP neighbors for process 100
```

```
H    Address          Interface          Hold Uptime    SRTT   RTO  Q   Seq
                                          (sec)          (ms)        Cnt Num
1    10.1.4.253       Gi0/0              14 2w0d          1    200   0  1797
0    10.1.4.254       Gi0/0              14 2w0d          1    200   0   729
Hickory-rtr01# show ip eigrp interface
IP-EIGRP interfaces for process 100

                 Xmit Queue  Mean   Pacing Time   Multicast  Pending
Interface Peers  Un/Reliable SRTT   Un/Reliable   Flow Timer Routes
Gi0/0       2       0/0        1        0/1            50          0
Lo0         0       0/0        0        0/1             0          0
```

If the devices are neighbors, routes could be blocked using distribution lists or route maps. Distribution lists are enumerated by number in **show ip protocol**.

Is There a More Desirable Path?

Finally, if the route is not in the routing table, use **show ip eigrp topology** to see whether the route is known to EIGRP. It could be that the route is known but a more desirable path exists. **Show ip route** shows only the selected EIGRP route. To see all known EIGRP routes, use **show ip eigrp topology**.

OSPF

You can review three Open Shortest Path First (OSPF) tables when troubleshooting, as shown in Table 4-2. A fourth—the Routing Information Base—is used to store SPF calculations but is largely unavailable to the administrator.

Table 4-2   OSPF Tables

Command	Table	Description
show ip ospf interface	Interface	Lists OSPF-enabled interfaces
show ip ospf neighbors	Neighbor	Lists discovered neighbors
show ip ospf database	Link State Database	LSAs received

Part III: TSHOOT

If a routing problem exists in OSPF, follow the same basic steps as EIGRP for troubleshooting.

Is the Correct Route Advertised?

Verify whether the router attached to the destination subnet is advertising the route. Advertised subnets are visible using either **show running-config | section ospf** or by reviewing **show ip protocol**.

OSPF limits advertisements to the subnets of interfaces that match network statements. **Show ip protocol** provides the matching network statements. **Show ip ospf statistics** also helps by showing how often SPF is running, potentially showing network instability.

Is the Correct Route Communicated?

OSPF shares routes with neighbors. Verify whether connected devices are neighbors using **show ip ospf neighbor**. **Show ip ospf database** displays the link state information. **Debug ip ospf adj** shows issues preventing neighbor relationships.

OSPF neighborship requires six parameters to agree:

- Bidirectional communication.
- Equal timer values.
- Matching AS number.
- Routers must agree on the type of their common area.
- Routers must agree on the prefix of their common subnet.
- Authentication, if used, must agree on type and password.

OSPF sends only hellos over interfaces that match a **network** statement. If a link does not match a **network** entry, no hellos are transmitted and no neighbors are formed over the link. See OSPF protocol values by using **show ip ospf interface**.

If the devices are neighbors, routes could be blocked at boundary routers using distribution lists or route maps. Distribution lists are recorded in **show ip protocol**.

Is There a More Desirable Path?

The possibility exists that OSPF has chosen an unexpected path to a destination. It could also be that routes from other routing protocols are present with a lower administrative distance or that an intermediate system has a static route. Checking routing tables along the expected path is the best way to reveal the situation.

BGP

Border Gateway Protocol (BGP) maintains two tables outside the routing table: one for neighbors and one for BGP routing information, as shown in Table 4-3.

Table 4-3   BGP Tables

Command	Table	Description
show ip bgp neighbors	Neighbor	Lists neighbors
show ip bgp	BGP	Contains all received BGP prefixes and associated attributes, as well as showing the BGP best path

BGP troubleshooting can also follow the three basic steps used with EIGRP and OSPF.

Is the Correct Route Advertised?

Verify whether the router attached to the destination subnet is advertising the route. You can see this from the running configuration (**show running-config | section bgp**) or the BGP table (**show ip bgp**—self-originated routes have a next hop of 0.0.0.0).

BGP advertises only explicitly identified prefixes for which there is a matching route from another source (like a connected route).

Is the Correct Route Communicated?

BGP communicates prefixes with administratively defined neighbors. Verify whether defined neighbors are reachable using **ping** and whether they are neighbors by reviewing **show ip bgp neighbors**. A partial output from this is shown in Example 4-5—**show ip bgp neighbors** includes considerable detail. **Debug ip bgp** updates show hellos and advertisements, and **debug ip bgp s** reveals details about the contained routing information being communicated.

Example 4-5   BGP Neighbors

```
R1# show ip bgp neighbor
BGP neighbor is 10.1.255.5,   remote AS 65001, external link
  BGP version 4, remote router ID 59.43.0.71
  BGP state = Established, up for 2w0d
  Last read 00:00:15, last write 00:00:17, hold time is 90,
   keepalive interval is 30 seconds
  Neighbor capabilities:
    Route refresh: advertised and received(old & new)
    Address family IPv4 Unicast: advertised and received
  Message statistics:
    InQ depth is 0
    OutQ depth is 0
                       Sent        Rcvd
    Opens:              1           1
    Notifications:      0           0
    Updates:            2           1162
    Keepalives:         40808       40817
    Route Refresh:      0           0
    Total:              40811       41980
  Default minimum time between advertisement runs is 30 seconds
  ...
```

BGP neighborship requires bidirectional communication, authentication, and that the AS match the expected AS. BGP values, such as timers and AS, are available through **show ip bgp**.

If the devices are neighbors, routes could be blocked using distribution lists or route maps. Distribution lists are listed in **show ip protocols**.

Is There a More Desirable Path?

If the route is not in the routing table, use **show ip bgp** to see whether the route is known and valid. Routes can be invalidated if the BGP next hop is unreachable; if so, routing to this address must be recursively troubleshoot. Example 4-6 shows several routes that are valid and best, shown by the preceding *>.

Example 4-6   BGP Paths

```
R2# show ip bgp
BGP table version is 17312, local router ID is 10.254.254.12
Status codes: s suppressed, d damped, h history, * valid, > best,
 i - internal, r RIB-failure, S Stale
Origin codes: i - IGP, e - EGP, ? - incomplete

    Network           Next Hop          Metric LocPrf Weight Path
*> 0.0.0.0           182.225.207.13          0 65000 65097 i
*> 10.43.0.0/24      182.225.207.13          0 65000 65086 65042 i
*> 10.43.0.0/22      182.225.207.13          0 65000 65086 65042 i
*> 10.45.128.0/24    182.225.207.13          0 65000 65100 65044 i
*> 10.49.0.0/22      182.225.207.13          0 65000 65086 65300 i
*> 10.61.0.0/16      182.225.207.13          0 65000 65060 i
*> 10.63.0.0/20      182.225.207.13          0 65000 65062 i
*> 10.65.0.0/19      182.225.207.13          0 65000 65064 i
*> 10.71.0.0/16      182.225.207.13          0 65000 65086 65302 i
*> 10.87.0.0/16      182.225.207.13          0 65000 65086 i
...
```

Route Redistribution

Organizations sometimes must support more than one routing protocol.
For instance, a business might use EIGRP within a campus and BGP over
the Multiprotocol Label Switching (MPLS) WAN. Routing information is
passed between the protocols using redistribution. Redistributed routes are
treated as external in the receiving protocol.

Redistribution extracts routes from the routing table, so only routes that
appear in the routing table are exported. If routes are not present, confirm the
routes are present in the routing table at the redistribution point. You must
identify and understand the interaction of all redistribution points. Creating a
routing loop through multiple redistribution points is quite possible.

Because routing protocols use different metrics, redistributed routes lose
routing information. Distance vector routing protocols, including EIGRP,
assume that the metric for imported routes should be infinity unless another
value is specified. When redistributing into EIGRP, a default metric must
be set or no routes will be imported! OSPF imports only classful routes
unless the **redistribute subnets** command is used. Review the redistribution commands on your router in troubleshooting to confirm how this import
happens in your specific case.

Part III: TSHOOT

It's worth noting that redistribution is a pain. It causes routing information to be lost, which can easily lead to suboptimal path selection, nonreciprocal routing, and routing loops. Consider whether redistribution is necessary or if routing could be handled in a more straightforward way.

In addition to protocol-specific commands, **debug ip routing** shows routes as they are added or withdrawn from the routing table.

If **ip route profile** is added to the config, the **show ip route profile** command shows routing table changes over consecutive 5-second intervals. This is particularly helpful for confirming whether routes are flapping—being added and withdrawn continuously.

INDEX

6to4 tunnels, IPv6 over IPv4, 21

A

AAA (authentication, authorization, and accounting), 230, 235
  configuring, 231-234
  RADIUS, 231
  TACACS+, 231
  troubleshooting, 302
access control lists (ACLs). See ACLs (access control lists)
access layer, hierarchical design model, 236
access mode (DTP), 154
access switches, 135
ACK packet (EIGRP), 28
ACLs (access control lists), 108-110, 297
  bogons, 298
  guest, 298-299
  IPv4, configuring, 109-110
  SNMP, 295
  standard, 109
Active Discovery, establishing PPPoE connection, 114
Active mode (LACP), 164
Active state (BGP peering), 95
Active state (HSRP devices), 195
AD (administrative distance), 6
  controlling routing, 75-76
AD (advertised distance), EIGRP routers, 31
address-family command, 64
address flooding (MAC), 219-220
Address Resolution Protocol (ARP), 191

addresses
  IP, troubleshooting assignment, 290-292
  IPv4, 12
  IPv6, 12
    simplifying, 12-13
    special, 13
    structures, 12
  MAC, 135
    frame forwarding, 137-138
    learning, 136-137
  troubleshooting NAT, 299-301
addressing
  IP, 89
  IPv6, 12-13
    host, 14-17
administrative distance (AD). See AD (administrative distance)
advanced configuration, OSPF, 56-61
advanced distance vector protocols, 29
advertised distance (AD), EIGRP routers, 31
advertisements, routes, determining correct, 307-311
alerts, logging to Syslog, 261
algorithms
  Dijkstra, 61
  DUAL (Diffusing Update Algorithm), 31-32
  SPF (Shortest Path First), 45
Align-Err error, 278
alternate ports (RSTP), 179
Application-Specific Integrated Circuits (ASIC), 215
archive config differences command, 263
area default-cost command, 58
area range command, 56-57, 62
areas, OSPF networks, 45-46

J-L

M

DR (designated router), 53-55
LSAs (link-state advertisements), 47-49
metrics, 47
neighbor relationships, 50-51
neighborship, 310
network structure, 45-47
networks, 53
  broadcast, 53
  NBMA (nonbroadcast multi-access), 53-55
  over Layer 2 and Layer 3 MPLS, 55-56
  P2MNB (point-to-multipoint nonbroadcast), 53
  P2MP (point-to-multipoint), 53
  P2P (point-to-point), 53
NSSAs (not-so-stubby areas), 58
packets, 49-50
passive-interface command, 57
RID (router ID), 52
routers, 45
  roles, 47
summarization, 56-57
tables, 309
troubleshooting, 52-53, 309-311
verification, 52-53
virtual links, 58-59
ospf router-id command, 52
OSPFv3, 62
configuration, 63-65
LSAs, 62-63
OTP (Over the Top), EIGRP, 44
outside global host addresses (NAT), 128
outside local host addresses (NAT), 128

P

P2MNB (point-to-multipoint nonbroadcast) networks, OSPF, 53
P2MP (point-to-multipoint) networks, OSPF, 53
P2P (point-to-point) networks, OSPF, 53
packet fragmentation, IP (Internet Protocol), 3
packet sniffing, 265-266

packets
  EIGRP, 28
  forwarding, 8
    CEF (Cisco Express Forwarding), 9
    fast switching, 8
    process switching, 8
  OSPF, 49-50
PACL (port access lists), 222
PAgP (Port Aggregation Protocol), 164
passive-interface command, 25, 33, 57, 73
Passive mode (LACP), 164
password command, 107
passwords, Cisco devices, 107
PAT (Port Address Translation), 127-129
path command, 262
path control, 78
  IOS IP SLA, 81-84
  PBR (policy-based routing), 79-81
  VRF-Lite, 84-86
Path MTU Discovery, 3
path vector protocols, 7-8
paths
  BGP, 312
  control, 78-86
  cost, 171
  selection, 96-98
PBR (policy-based routing), 79-81
peer-to-peer applications, traffic flow patterns, 239
peers (BGP), 90, 95-96
performance, routers
  performance, 305
  troubleshooting, 304-307
  router performance, 305
Per-VLAN Spanning Tree (PVST+), 169
PID (Port ID), 171
ping command, 14, 250, 257-258, 293, 300, 304, 311
planning VLANs, 150-152
point-to-multipoint links, IPv6, 22
point-to-multipoint nonbroadcast (P2MNB) networks, OSPF, 53

Q-R

CISCO™

ciscopress.com: Your Cisco Certification and Networking Learning Resource

Subscribe to the monthly Cisco Press newsletter to be the first to learn about new releases and special promotions.

Visit **ciscopress.com/ newsletters.**

While you are visiting, check out the offerings available at your finger tips.

Podcasts

–Free Podcasts from experts:
- OnNetworking
- OnCertification
- OnSecurity

View them at **ciscopress.com/podcasts.**

–Read the latest author **articles** and **sample chapters** at **ciscopress.com/articles.**

–Bookmark the Certification Reference Guide available through our partner site at **informit.com/ certguide.**

Connect with Cisco Press authors and editors via Facebook and Twitter, visit **informit.com/socialconnect.**